"*Conflict inevitably leads to the need fo*
Gilbert Greenall's story can be read with ~~proft by decision-~~
makers and armchair warriors alike."

The Rt Hon Sir John Major KG CH

"... *endearing anecdote and profound statement combine with
ease in Gilbert Greenall's skilfully written memoir that covers
an important gap in public understanding of the consequences
of war while accurately portraying the story of British Overseas
Aid in its heyday. It's fantastic.*"

Lynda Chalker,
The Rt Hon Baroness Chalker of Wallasey PC,
Minister of State for Africa, 1986 – 1997
Minister of State for Overseas Development, 1989 – 1997

"*Gilbert Greenall is an unsung hero who has given a lifetime of
commitment to others in the face of adversity. Many have been
lauded for far less*".

General the Lord Richards of Herstmonceux GCB CBE DSO,
Chief of the Defence Staff, 2010 – 2013

"... *this soldier-turned-doctor, in the mould of Fitzroy McLean
or a John Buchan hero, dodges death in the most dangerous parts
of the world, not in pursuit of battle but in search of peace and
humanitarian relief. Combat Civilian reads like an adventure story.*"

Matt Ridley,
The Viscount Ridley FRSL,
Author, Environmentalist and Politician

COMBAT CIVILIAN

GILBERT GREENALL

The Book Guild Ltd

First published in Great Britain in 2019 by
The Book Guild Ltd
9 Priory Business Park
Wistow Road, Kibworth
Leicestershire, LE8 0RX
Freephone: 0800 999 2982
www.bookguild.co.uk
Email: info@bookguild.co.uk
Twitter: @bookguild

Typeset in Aldine401 BT

Printed and bound in Great Britain by CPI Group (UK) Ltd, Croydon, CR0 4YY

ISBN 978 1912575 848

British Library Cataloguing in Publication Data.
A catalogue record for this book is available from the British Library.

To my children Edward, Freddie, Alexander and Amelia
For long childhood absences in unknown places.

Contents

List of Abbreviations   ix
List of Maps   xi
Acknowledgements   xiii

1   The End of the Khmer Rouge, Cambodia 1979   1
2   The Third Horseman, Famine in Uganda 1980   10
3   Unwelcome Guests, Kurdish Refugees, Iran 1991   32
4   Hope Unbounded, The First Gulf War, Northern Iraq 1991   40
5   No Humanitarian Solution, Bosnia 1992–1993   52
6   Breaking the Siege, Sarajevo 1992-1993   68
7   Corridors of Peace, Angola 1993   81
8   A Failed State, Somalia 1993   93
9   Colonial Misfortune, Montserrat 1995   102
10 Winning the Peace, Bosnia 1996   111
11 The Fires of Irian Jaya, 1997   123
12 An Unusual Request from China, 1998   132
13 A False Start, Afghanistan Earthquakes 1998   138
14 In a Strange Country, Albania 1999   149
15 Not Much of a Solution, Kosovo 1999   158
16 Paper Tiger, East Timor 1999   167
17 Legal Challenge, West Bank and Gaza 2000   178
18 Brinkmanship, Macedonia 2001   186
19 Support and Influence, Afghanistan 2001   198
20 The Sunni Uprising, Fallujah, Iraq 2004–2005   217
21 South of the Litani River, Israel's War with Lebanon 2006   232
22 Hope Fades, Afghanistan 2006   241
23 A Collective Loss of Common Sense, Afghanistan 2010   246
24 The World on the Move, Libya 2011   259
25 Crucible of Chaos, Iraq 2016   267
    Epilogue   280
    Index   282

List of Abbreviations

AICF	Action Internationale Contre la Faim
ASF	Aviation Sans Frontières
CENTCOM	United States Central Command
CHLT	Coalition Humanitarian Liaison Team
DFID	Department for International Development
ECMM	European Community Monitoring Mission
ECTF	European Community Task Force
EPI	Expanded Programme of Immunisation
FALINTIL	Armed Forces for the National Liberation of East Timor
FCO	Foreign and Commonwealth Office
FRETILIN	Revolutionary Front for an Independent East Timor
FYROM	Former Yugoslavia Republic of Macedonia
GDP	Gross Domestic Product
HF	High Frequency
ICRC	International Committee of the Red Cross
IDF	Israeli Defence Force
IDP	Internally Displaced People
IED	Improvised Explosive Device
IFOR	Implementation Force
IFRCS	International Federation of Red Cross and Red Crescent Societies
INTERFET	International Force East Timor
IOM	International Organization for Migration
IRA	Irish Republican Army
ISAF	International Security Assistance Force
JNA	Yugoslav People's Army
MAF	Mission Aviation Fellowship

NATO	North Atlantic Treaty Organization
NGO	Non-Governmental Organisation
ODA	Overseas Development Administration
OECD	Organisation for Economic Co-operation and Development
PKK	Kurdistan Workers' Party
POLAD	Political Adviser
PTT	Postal, Telephone and Television
QIP	Quick Impact Projects
RPG	Rocket-propelled grenade
SCF	Save the Children Fund
SRSG	Special Representative to the Secretary-General
TIPH	Temporary International Presence in Hebron
UHF	Ultra High Frequency
UN	United Nations
UNAMI	United Nations Assistance Mission for Iraq
UNDAC	United Nations Disaster Assessment and Coordination
UNDP	United Nations Development Programme
UNHCR	United Nations High Commission for Refugees
UNICEF	United Nations Children's Fund
UNICEF	United Nations International Children's Emergency Fund
UNIFIL	United Nations Interim Force in Lebanon
UNITA	National Union for the Total Independence of Angola
UNMIK	United Nations Interim Administration Mission in Kosovo
UNOCHA	United Nations Office for the Coordination of Humanitarian Affairs
UNPROFOR	United Nations Protection Force
UNSCO	United Nations Special Coordinator for the Middle East Peace Process
UNRWA	United Nations Relief and Works Agency for Palestine Refugees
USAID	United States Agency for International Development
UXO	Unexploded Ordnance
VHF	Very High Frequency
WFP	World Food Programme
WHO	World Health Organization

List of Maps

Thailand and Cambodia   3
Uganda   11
Iran   34
Iraq   41
Balkans   54
Angola   83
Somalia   94
Montserrat   103
Irian Jaya   124
China   134
Afghanistan   139
East Timor   168
Israel   179
Tunisia   260

Acknowledgements

Travelling to the far corners of the earth, at times, on the strangest of missions, has been almost inexplicable to even my closest family and friends, hence finally the need for a little explanation. This book in part tells what took place during those long absences from my wife Sarah, and my four children Edward, Freddie, Alexander and Amelia, who deserve thanks for their forbearance. It also has been in part cathartic, for although many of the events I describe are uplifting it deals with war and human catastrophe.

I may appear unfeeling in my dealings with human misery but a degree of detachment was central to getting things done – reason had to override emotion and in any case a necessity when working in this field for four decades. Outside civil society, the rule of law and during conflict, a certain robustness is a necessity, a self-preservation mechanism. Caring is shown by action not handwringing and I hope my readers will forgive the apparent understatement or the way I move swiftly on from some hugely disagreeable situation to enjoy my breakfast or similar.

This story is only a selection from over forty humanitarian missions abroad and I hope gives a glimpse of the immediate post-cold war world when humanitarianism was centre stage and where some events have had long-lasting consequences – the creation of the autonomous Kurdish region of Iraq, the secession of Kosovo. It was a huge privilege to be there and readers may be surprised at the arbitrary and chaotic way decisions were made.

Over the decades I have had the privilege to work with extraordinary non-combatants in no less than seventeen conflicts who showed physical courage at its most impressive. In the cause of humanitarianism these unarmed people put their lives at risk to help those in need and a special mention goes to my interpreter in Bosnia, Vesna, whose courage was remarkable.

I was lucky to work with some inspirational military commanders, Andy Keeling, Rob Fry, Nick Pounds, Mike Jackson, John Kiszely, Freddie Viggers, David Richards, Barney White-Spunner and James Bucknall without whom many of the events in this book would not have happened. I would never have reached Kabul in 2010 without the help of Richard King and Wendy Rothery.

I am grateful to Robert Ashe for getting my career started on the Cambodian border. To Francesco Strippoli, Head of WFP Uganda, Grace Natollo my office manager in Kampala who was instrumental in the success of Oxfam's Karamoja programme, and to Mary McLoughlin for assisting me with the pivotal report on Kurdish refugees, which set in motion the first steps in creating the autonomous region of Northern Iraq.

I would also like to thank Brian Sparrow in Zagreb, Dickie Potter in Skopje, Stephen Evans in Kabul and Edward Chaplin in Baghdad for putting up with my unorthodox presence in their embassies.

At the United Nations in Geneva I would like to add Ross Mountain, Jesper Holmer Lund, for their support, Juliette de Rivero for her kindness not only to me but all the UNDAC members and the late Guillaume de Montravel for the humour and optimism he brought to our mission in Kosovo. I was supported by a large number of UNDAC colleagues at the United Nations and especially Ted Pearn whose consummate diplomacy was a joy to watch.

Over the decades journalists have been consistently kind to my programmes but Sam Kiley formerly with the London Times and later Sky News deserves special mention as he took great risks to cover the work I was doing and bring it to a wider audience.

Without David Nabarro's vision and Andy Bearpark's unusual approach I would never have worked for the British Government. I am particularly grateful to Andy for giving me, a non-career civil servant, such a prominent role at ODA and above all for the support of ODA Minister Lynda Chalker.

Sudden absences for prolonged periods would have been difficult without the help of my personal assistant, Michelle Vanner, who for nearly twenty years has run my office in Gloucestershire and for this, I am greatly indebted.

I would never have attempted to write had it not been for the influence of Michael Kidson, the celebrated Eton schoolmaster, whose vocabulary was so enjoyable and who taught me to love the English language. And it was Mark Lee, whom I first met in Kampala and remains a close friend, who inspired me to write this book and who flew over specially from New York to edit my first draft.

Without the advice of Harry Bucknall and my editor, Mary Sandys, the book would have looked quite different and I am also grateful to the Book Guild for their professional contribution.

Lastly and most importantly, this book would not have been written without the constant support and research provided by my partner Melissa, who over the last five years has almost lived through the events that unfold on these pages.

Gilbert Greenall
Bromesberrow Place
February 2019

The meaning of things lies not in the things themselves,
but in our attitude towards them.

Antoine de Saint-Exupery

1

The End of the Khmer Rouge, Cambodia 1979

"Watch out for landmines!" I was warned. Along the track ahead of us the bodies of refugees lay scattered, dressed in the black pyjama suits of the Khmer Rouge. Many had been dead for some time, and the foul stench from their bloated corpses made me retch until I felt my whole body was being turned inside out. Further down the track lay more bodies, some still alive but in malarial comas. At my feet lay two young women who must have been in their early twenties, their mouths foam-flecked, their breathing fitful.

I heard the sound of small arms fire a couple of kilometres away, a stark reminder that the Khmer Rouge were still fighting the Vietnamese, much closer than I thought. Our pace now quickening, we turned onto a different track, which brought us into a vast clearing. There we saw a sea of humanity stretching out into the distance, ten – perhaps even twenty – thousand people, all dressed in the now familiar black. Most peculiar was the silence; tormented, exhausted and anxious faces told their story. The vast majority were women and more were arriving all the time. I glanced down as I walked towards them and saw I was plastered in human faeces from the knees down.

Hundreds of thousands were fleeing Cambodia for sanctuary in Thailand. With so many in desperate need of urgent medical assistance, it was difficult to see what the two of us alone could do. Now we had located the refugees we had to return to Aranyaprathet in Thailand to summon help.

★★★

Between 1975 and 1979, Cambodia and her people endured four years of terror. Following the takeover by Pol Pot's Khmer Rouge in 1975, the capital Phnom Penh was emptied of its population; even hospital patients were wheeled down the roads on hospital trolleys. The population of the city, swollen by refugees from the war, was 2.5 million and the forced evacuation alone claimed at least 20,000 lives. With the announcement of Year Zero, Cambodia became a closed country, the banning of money and commercial activity followed the forced abandonment of towns and any disobedience to the new authority was punished by beatings and summary execution. For four years the entire country was enslaved and starved, and between one and two million people, of a total population of eight million, were murdered. Then in January 1979, the Vietnamese invaded Cambodia, Phnom Penh fell and the regime collapsed. The Khmer Rouge fled back into the jungle, but their leader Pol Pot was still alive and hiding somewhere in these killing fields.

★★★

The idea of travelling to Thailand came about three months earlier, in May 1979. I had just finished an MBA course at INSEAD business school in Fontainebleau, near Paris. I had completed a short service commission in the British Army in 1976 and might easily have stayed in the army. But it was assumed my future would lie in the family company. However, even during my year at INSEAD my enthusiasm for a business career had waned. One day, I watched a refresher course group scurrying across the car park in the rain as piles of leaves blew about in the autumnal gusts. I noticed something extraordinarily dull about them, and realised that in a decade, I too could be back at INSEAD for a refresher course, a competent middle manager with prospects for the main board. At that moment, I knew their world was not for me.

Added to which, my father viewed business schools as places that inspired arrogance and filled the head with nonsense – he may have been right about the arrogance – and decided I could try out my new ideas somewhere other than the family brewery in Warrington, where we had been brewing and distilling since the eighteenth century. This meant that the job I assumed I would do since childhood was no longer on offer.

At INSEAD, my interest had drifted from the core subjects of accounting and marketing towards more exciting ones like economic and political analysis, developing countries and natural resource policymaking. Nicolas Jequier of the Organisation for Economic Co-operation and Development (OECD) gave fabulous lectures on the promise of appropriate technology in the developing world. This was an entirely new approach to development and really caught my interest.

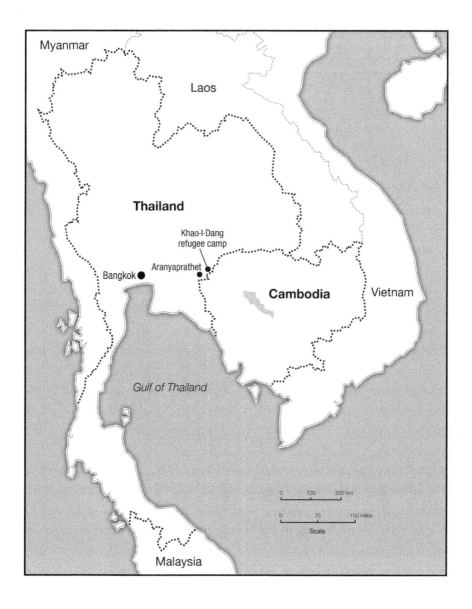

It was a time of numerous exciting publications. The Brandt Report gave prominence to international development for the first time; *The Limits to Growth* explored the interaction of exponential growth with finite resources. And the British economist EF Schumacher had recently published *Small is Beautiful: A Study of Economics as if People Mattered*, which became a best seller overnight. I was twenty-five years old, and a business career in my home town of Warrington did not seem half as exciting as some of these new ideas and the chance of foreign travel.

In many ways, I missed my military life but the sense of adventure that should have gone with it had been absent. Being a Cold War warrior in north Germany was unexciting, and waiting for an enemy that fortunately never came was an underwhelming experience. During my four years in the army, my troop had only fired seventeen shots in anger before the canvas belt in the Browning machine gun jammed. It happened at a vehicle checkpoint at Aughnacloy in Northern Ireland when we had come under fire from the IRA, but that was the sum of it.

Most of my fellow students had already secured highly paid jobs in multinational companies. However, with only a month to go I was still looking for something I wanted to do. I found out that a former INSEAD student was running an appropriate technology project in Thailand, and decided to combine a holiday with – as a bonus – a visit to the project.

There was still enough of the soldier in me to find events in South East Asia compelling. The whole region, which had been in the news for two decades, had been rocked by the fall of Phnom Penh and Saigon in 1975, and reports from Cambodia had been very dark.

Bangkok, in 1979, was a city of badly constructed two-storey buildings. Yet despite the endless breezeblock and concrete, the old city still had great charm. Even then, it was famous for its gridlocked traffic. The locals joked that only the Bangkok traffic could halt a Vietnamese invasion, humour that failed to disguise an anxiety about the fate of their neighbour.

My INSEAD alumnus was tall, stolid, serious, every inch a businessman dressed in grey flannel trousers and wearing a tie in his impressive air-conditioned office, an imposing place near Bangkok's Grand Palace. He welcomed my enthusiasm but proceeded to pour cold water on my rosy visions of appropriate technology. He told me that any development project without a sound commercial foundation was unlikely to prosper, words that have stayed with me ever since. My youthful idealism had a brush with cold reality and I realised my vision was a non-starter. There was clearly a huge gap between my youthful idealism and commercial reality. I was still no nearer to finding myself a career.

On my rather crestfallen return to the bar at the Oriental Hotel, I met a Swiss doctor living in Thailand. Over a drink, he told me that thousands of Cambodian refugees had been seen near the Thai border in a terrible state. He planned to travel that weekend to the border town of Aranyaprathet to join a group of desperately-needed volunteers. I did not take much persuading to go with him. The next morning we were on our way to the Cambodian border 251 kilometres east of Bangkok.

We jostled along narrow roads passing paddy fields, villages and children riding water buffaloes. The air was scented and the birds wonderful in their brilliant plumage, Europe suddenly felt very distant. After nearly a whole day, we reached Aranyaprathet, then only a small town. I was dropped off, as it turned out, at the only hotel. My Swiss acquaintance hurried on, eager to get to a prearranged meeting. His parting words were, "Robert Ashe is the person you need to find."

I glanced up at the front of the hotel. Lumps of cement render had fallen away from its unloved façade, revealing the corroded reinforcement bars of its concrete frame. Inside was all faded paint and dirty walls. It was quite a contrast to the luxury of the Oriental Hotel I had left only hours before. The receptionist, with the usual Thai charm, informed me that the hotel was full; her charm disguising a hidden malevolence and my heart sank. Just at that moment, Neil Davis, the well-known Australian combat cameraman, turned up. He had overbooked rooms for another television crew and, as they were not needed, I was given one. The hotel clearly doubled as a brothel. The toothless crone who took me upstairs assumed that was why I had taken a room, and she took some persuading with the most basic sign language that that was not quite what I wanted.

Aranyaprathet was a small town and I soon found Robert Ashe's house, arriving there in time for his evening meeting. He ran a small NGO called Christian Outreach, coordinating the few volunteers working on the border. He was slightly built, softly spoken and his smile, when I introduced myself, was engaging. I was surprised to find he was my age. He welcomed me into the house as if he had known me for years. Robert's large family, his parents and siblings, were all either ordained or in the medical profession. Several of them even worked with him on the border.

The humanitarian agencies in Bangkok claimed that everything was under control on the border but, as I was to discover, things were far from well and volunteers were needed for even the most basic tasks. I was astonished at the scale of the refugee problem, which was growing every day. Robert said that he could see no reason why a volunteer like me should not make a valuable contribution and asked me to join him on an assignment the next morning. We had to locate sizeable groups of refugees so that humanitarian assistance could be directed towards them on the Thai side of the border.

Soon after dawn, we were dropped off a few kilometres from the town and set off into the bush. It was completely still. We trekked along in silence; the only sound came from our shoes on the baked earth. We had not gone far, perhaps a few kilometres, before we came across two young women lying next to the track, their bundles of personal possessions scattered beside them. As they were still conscious, the emotional instinct to help them was overpowering. Yet, the greater good was better served by getting back to Aranyaprathet and sending help. Utilitarian arguments like these are easily overturned.

This was a turning point in my life, but I did not know it at the time. I knelt beside one of them. She looked frightened, but when I smiled and spoke to her in English, she grew calmer. Robert and I gathered them both up in our arms and returned along the track. The sun was now up and it was stiflingly hot. Although I was twenty-five and fit and the young woman I was carrying weighed less than forty kilos, it was more arduous than I anticipated. A human being is awkward to carry at the best of times and we had to walk a few more kilometres. We crossed and re-crossed the same small wooden rickety bridges and there were moments when I wondered if we were going to make it. It was a wonderful feeling when we finally reached the road, where there was transport to the hospital.

For the next few days, searching the tracks and clearings for new refugees became routine. Then, returning with a small band of volunteers, we picked up those too sick to walk. Robert and I even found a handcart, which we used to carry the children, pushing it together along the narrow tracks towards Thailand. Whatever we achieved seemed insignificant compared to the steady stream of humanity appearing at the border each day.

One of the tracks we used on the first day had become impassable; there were so many decomposing bodies that the paths just became too disagreeable. In one clearing alone, I counted over thirty dead. The Thai farmers over whose land we passed to reach the road became aggressive if they thought that anyone might die on their land. There was a large heap of bodies on the edge of their farmland.

The survival rate was so poor for those in malarial comas that, at a coordination meeting one night, a doctor suggested it would be wiser to leave them. Although that was almost certainly the correct thing to do, it caused outrage among those whose feelings ran ahead of their reason. For us all, the problem was that these were mostly young people and it seemed inconceivable that nothing could be done to save them.

On one occasion, I was carrying a young woman, but after a couple of kilometres, it became clear she had died. I was exhausted and she slipped from my grasp, hitting the ground with quite a thump. Although reason dictated I had done her no harm, I felt uncomfortable, as though in dropping her I had violated some unwritten code of conduct that applies to the dead.

One morning Robert and I heard Huey helicopters belonging to the Thai Army patrolling the border. These iconic helicopters with the distinctive chord of their twin blades could be heard for miles. They had come to represent a war that had engulfed three countries and now threatened a fourth. As we plodded along the baked earth of a narrow track we saw a clearing ahead. To our amazement, there was a large American pickup truck. Neither of us had realised a vehicle could reach this place. Robert signalled to me to crouch down and keep quiet. Through the bush, we watched five men with American accents unload large wooden crates. There was definitely something secret going on and we were glad they had not spotted us; whatever was going on was not for us to see. We very quietly returned the way we came.

Outside the hospital in Aranyaprathet, green military tents were erected to house the large number of sick. Many of them were given the combination antimalarial drug Fansidar. In view of the absence of interpreters, they had "F" written on their foreheads in chinagraph pencil, to save them from being given a second, toxic dose.

One afternoon, on the Cambodian side of the border, I came across something completely different. Instead of the usual emaciated sickly refugees, I found myself amongst fit young men. The sound of small arms fire nearby made me realise this must be the rear position of a Khmer Rouge

Military Headquarters. A teenage Khmer Rouge signalled me aggressively to follow him, pointing his assault rifle in the direction we were to proceed. I felt I did not have much option, since I had compromised his position and he was carrying an AK47.

The soldier led me into a bamboo and thatch hut where a middle-aged man sat behind a trestle table dressed like the others in black. A narrow intelligent face stared at me from behind a pair of rimless glasses. Speaking softly in flawless French, he offered me some tea. As we drank it, he gently interrogated me about the humanitarian assistance and the reception his people were getting in Thailand. In my nervousness, I struggled to respond fluently in French. Yet, after a while, I was allowed to leave. I walked confidently back to the track and as soon as I was out of sight started to run, not stopping until I was well away. I paused by a ditch of foul-smelling water and I realised how lucky I had been. I later heard he was in Pol Pot's inner circle. This was not a time to contemplate what Hannah Arendt called 'the banality of evil'.

Every day presented a new problem. One of the young women I had carried into the hospital tent was particularly emaciated. She had cerebral malaria and was thrashing about continuously. A nurse asked me to stay with her for a while, to stop her pulling out her drip. It was towards the end of the first week and I had been carrying people long distances in the tropical heat for days, neglecting to eat or drink properly myself, and I was exhausted, glad to be sitting quietly. It was dark, and a few lamps glowed gently at intervals along the long tent, where about a hundred Cambodians lay on the ground. An American journalist volunteer was handing out drinking water, and the only sound was the trickle of the water pouring into the enamel cups and the occasional clink as they hit the side of the bucket. Then the patter of tropical rain on the tent roof broke the silence, and I could smell the damp earth. I must have dozed off; waking with a start I realised I had been asleep for at least an hour. The young girl had pulled out the drip; her elbow lay in a pool of blood, and her open eyes stared at the canvas above us. She was dead. I was full of remorse. I had been given such a small task, and had failed to do it. Forty years later, I can still see her face.

In the bright sunlight the next day, the gloom of the previous evening dissipated. I was sent to the new refugee camp at Khao-I-Dang being constructed by UNHCR. As I was leaving, I heard the Thai national anthem that was played over the loud speakers each morning to the town. On arrival, I met Mark Malloch-Brown who was supervising the construction, signalling to a bulldozer working to clear the bush. There was hardly a tree left standing. Mark was in despair that the camp was going to be left without shade. This was not a trivial matter as within days he was expecting 100,000 refugees and he had been given only four days to prepare the camp. As it turned out, on the first day the camp opened, 4,800 people arrived; by 31 December, there were 84,800. Between November 1979 and the end of January 1980 an average of 1,600 refugees arrived in the camp each day.

A cloud of dust engulfed us as five Thai military trucks rumbled past full of feeding bowls. In a few days, I had learnt something about the management of humanitarian emergencies. Even humble feeding bowls were needed by the ton. One needed to think big, one hundred thousand at a time.

That day at Khao-I-Dang was the first time I had seen anyone actually in charge of anything. The UN agencies were essentially bureaucracies, and had no management structure. Over the years, I discovered it was not so much that managers were not attracted to humanitarian work; it was the lack of overall authority and structures that made the problem so intractable. Something that would persist over the next forty years.

Wearily, I returned to the hotel and went out for supper with Neil Davis, who told me gripping stories of his years covering the Vietnam War that I felt privileged to hear first-hand. However, during dinner, I felt ill and thought it might be a good idea to return to Bangkok for a few days. By the time I reached the city, I felt a lot worse. Being only twenty-five, I did not give feeling ill much thought, but twenty-four hours later, I realised that I was in trouble. I had pneumonia. A doctor, some antibiotics, and a return flight to the UK followed in quick succession.

In one intense month, I had been both shocked and inspired. I had found my career.

2

The Third Horseman, Famine in Uganda 1980

Finding a job in humanitarian work proved more difficult than I expected. I wrote to at least thirty humanitarian organisations and got twenty-nine rejections. So I was surprised when Oxfam invited me to an interview. Oxfam has Quaker origins and pacifist roots, and over the decades has developed a left-of-centre political stance. I later discovered that any one of its heads of department could have held, or had held, important jobs in any field they wished to work in. But they were happy to work at Oxfam for modest salaries. These were principled, intelligent and kind people, I thought after leaving the interview.

Within a couple of days Oxfam said they wanted me to cover for Roger Naumann, their Field Director, who had recently returned to the UK with his pregnant wife Anuk. Famine was unfolding in Karamoja, Uganda. With no experience, my role was to 'assess and advise' what humanitarian aid was needed. Idi Amin, Uganda's notoriously brutal third President, had fallen only nine months earlier, and the country was now gripped by civil unrest and civil war.

I flew to Entebbe, in Central Uganda, in an ancient Boeing 707 freighter with just ten rows of seats at the back of the cargo hold, operated by Uganda Airlines. At the terminal, people were checking in such items as bicycles and washing machines, and one passenger had so much luggage it almost required a forklift truck. But different rules apply when flying in the cargo hold of a Boeing 707. We flew first to Rome, where what appeared to be machine guns packed in wooden crates were loaded aboard.

We approached Entebbe Airport over Lake Victoria, a mass of water the size of Wales, set in a lush green landscape but strangely empty of boats or human activity. At the airport, we saw another Uganda Airlines Boeing 707. It had clearly been parked up for some time – a trail of bullet holes ran from its nose to the tail, and a banana tree was growing out of the pilot's window. Just as unsettling was the state of the terminal building. Its enormous windowed façade contained very little glass, giving the building a strangely dead look.

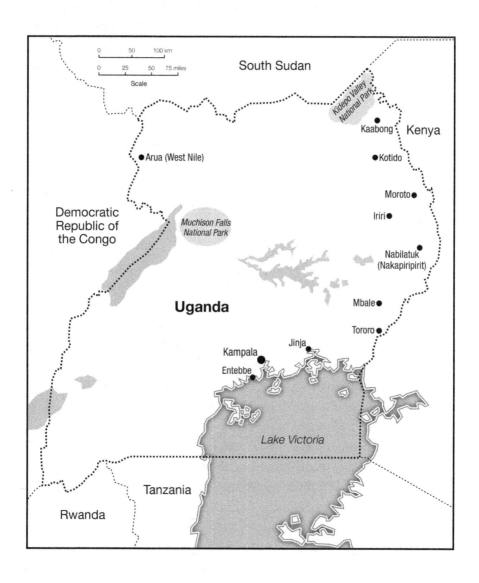

Unusually for an international airport, there was an atmosphere of tranquillity, perhaps because ours was the only inbound flight of the week. At first sight the capital Kampala, with its seven hills, was impressive but became less so as we drew closer along the potholed highway. Like the airport terminal, it looked very strange without any glass in the windows. Half an hour after landing, I had booked into the Speke Hotel.

After Idi Amin's downfall the entire country had been looted. When civil order collapses, looting starts. The public sector is seen as having belonged to the fallen tyrant, now to be rightfully reclaimed by the people. In a second phase, looting develops into an irrational frenzy; everybody wants something – anything – even if they don't need it, and they seize everything from urinals to window latches. A third malign phase follows, when the big fish start to pillage by the truckload. Violence is inevitable. The impact of all this was so profound that it affected everything I was to do for the next fifteen months.

Yet, although Kampala looked sad after this unhappy experience, the people seemed cheerful and friendly. The high level of education and use of English, not Swahili, as the lingua franca were striking. Uganda had been a British Protectorate and attitudes were quite different from those in neighbouring Tanzania and Kenya. In 1980, the population of the entire country was only 12 million, not the estimated 41 million of today, and Kampala felt like a modest market town rather than a city. During the day, it was a bustling, superficially happy place. However, when the sun went down everything changed, as I discovered on my first night. The army had imposed a curfew from 6 pm, after which the shooting began. All night long, small arms fire could be heard all over the city; occasionally mortars or RPG7s added to the din, and great arcs of tracer could be seen. It was the unpredictability of these nocturnal battles that was so alarming. The false comfort of thinking it was on the far side of the city was shattered by a burst of gunfire within 100 metres, or spent rounds striking nearby houses. These battles, often a matter of rivalry between the police and the army, were only extinguished by violent early morning thunderstorms, a regular feature of life on the equator. Whatever the reason, the results were deadly. Months later Mark Lee, a journalist friend working in Uganda, told me that every morning he had seen dumper trucks driving past his hotel, full of dead bodies.

On my first day, I took a taxi out to the edge of the city where the Verona Fathers ran the Catholic Mission, a sanctuary from the general chaos of life in this battered city. They welcomed me into a well-ordered kitchen dominated by a crucifix. Their Italian accents still strong even after half a century in Africa; the Fathers briefed me on the situation in Karamoja. This arid area bordering Kenya is home to the Karamojong warriors, semi-nomadic cattle herders with a fierce reputation, who practice a form of pastoral transhumance. For three to four months a year, the men and boys live in makeshift camps, moving their cattle to richer pastures in search of water. Meanwhile, the women and girls stay in the manyatta, their temporary settlement, to grow crops, grind sorghum and tend to the younger children.

The Karamojong believed their God, Akuj, gave them all the cattle in their known world, which logically included the cattle of neighbouring tribes. The problem was that the neighbouring tribes held the same belief, which resulted in ongoing cattle raids on each other's territories. During the fall of Idi Amin, the Karamojong warriors looted the military armoury, and used the guns to raid cattle from other Karamojong clans. Drought, cattle raiding and civil unrest throughout the country had caused famine, and the fighting had been so violent that no trader was prepared to bring food into Karamoja. Now 100,000 people were facing starvation. The Verona Fathers took me out to look at the Land Rover Oxfam had organised for me. It had definitely seen better days, but I was delighted; I could now visit those organisations in Kampala already involved in bringing humanitarian assistance to Karamoja.

My first visit was to meet Francesco Strippoli, Head of the World Food Programme (WFP), a small, energetic and engaging Italian who seemed to understand exactly what was required. My next port of call was UNICEF's offices in Bat Valley, where I could see and hear huge colonies of fruit bats hanging upside down bothering each other in the palm trees beside the road. The Head of UNICEF, Cole Dodge, was an urbane and smartly dressed American who, unlike Francesco, spoke slowly, his American accent lending him added gravitas. His well-ordered office gave me confidence that here was a rock of reliability in a sea of chaos.

It was quite a different matter at the office of the United Nations Development Programme (UNDP). Their basement car park was full of UN vehicles, many propped on piles of bricks with wheels missing or bonnets up, showing where batteries and other engine parts had been taken from. During the fifteen months I was in Uganda, looters continued to strip these vehicles, under the not-so-watchful eyes of the UNDP, until only the chassis remained. I had a polite and perfunctory meeting with UNDP's Resident Representative. Here I sensed a lack of engagement and, unlike at my three previous meetings, a reluctance to do anything at all. A career diplomat in her fifties, the Representative was tall and rather imperious; a twenty-five-year-old working for Oxfam was clearly not worthy of her busy schedule. She was dressed in a suit, which on the fifth floor of a half-looted tower block seemed rather curious. I noticed the taps on the basin outside her office did not work. If she couldn't organise the water supply to a basin ten metres from her office, here in Kampala, I thought, how on earth could she organise programmes ten hours' drive away in northern Uganda?

The next day I started my humanitarian assessment. This involved a ten-hour drive to another Catholic mission in Karamoja. I had never done a humanitarian assessment before, but reasoned that I needed to be sure of the causes of the famine, to assess the number and location of the people affected, and to find out what they needed and gain some idea of how they could be reached. Equipped with enough fuel to get there and back and two spare tyres, I set off alone. My first stop was Jinja, a market town at the source of the Nile. The tarmac road was in reasonable condition, though there were major potholes. Then I drove eastwards along Lake Victoria, through high canopy rainforest, to the town of Tororo, an area notorious for robbery and casual murder. Checkpoints were frequent, often manned by Tanzanian troops who had come to Uganda to help overthrow President Idi Amin and had outstayed their welcome, supporting themselves by robbing people as they passed through. Getting through the checkpoints was always unpleasant, but the troops were cautious with foreigners. They lacked the Ugandan sense of humour that made Ugandan army checkpoints easier to manage.

Arriving at Tororo I headed north to Soroti District, passing the majestic Mount Elgon, an extinct volcano rising 14,000 feet behind the town. Although on the equator, 4,000 feet above sea level, Uganda didn't feel oppressively hot. The rust-coloured dust billowed like a cloud, stuck to my face, arms and clothes and coated everything inside the Land Rover. I never saw another vehicle for almost four hours and hardly another person. Bands of soldiers, often drunk, had looted anything they could find, which made the rural population cautious of vehicles on the road. The lush smallholdings of plantain bananas and maize gave way to savannah grassland and, as it was the dry season, I crossed many dry riverbeds. These were always a challenge as the sand was soft and it was easy to become stuck, and I was alone and without a winch. But I plunged down the banks, demanding of my Land Rover all it had, my heart in my mouth every time.

Two bumpy hours later, near the abandoned settlement of Iriri, I saw the first body at the roadside. The dead woman was emaciated, practically decomposed, no more than a bundle of rags. There seemed something rather callous about driving past a dead human being. I paused for a moment, yet I knew there was nothing I could usefully do.

I had now been on the road for twelve hours. The sun was setting and I could see Mount Moroto ahead. I was welcomed into the Verona Fathers' mission compound, another reassuring haven of tranquillity and order with citrus trees growing in the quadrangle. I was shown to a room with a polished concrete floor, furnished with an iron bed and a washstand. A crucifix hung on the lime-washed wall. The Fathers had a jug of cold water ready for me when I returned to the kitchen, and a bottle of beer. The beer was precious and I was given firm instructions to drink the water first. The Fathers described their lives at the Mission and the country's descent into chaos. Most were now elderly and had been in Uganda since early adulthood. I had never encountered missionaries before, and had held quite a few prejudices about them. But I was to learn quickly that the Verona Fathers' commitment to the people and what they were trying to achieve was profound. They spoke the language of the Karamojong and, over fifty years, had earned their respect.

Life was hard for the missions due to the breakdown of law and order. All supplies came from Kampala, but after months with very little fuel, these supplies were scarce. The mission had received maize and cooking oil from the WFP to distribute, but the situation was desperate. An estimated 100,000 were now affected by famine, and nearly 3,000 people had come to this one mission alone in search of food. Cattle raiding had escalated after a stockpile of AK47s was stolen from the military armoury in Moroto. The mission hospital at Matani was treating increasing numbers of gunshot wounds.

I woke the next morning to find several thousand people gathered at the mission gates hoping for food. I walked through rows of women dressed in traditional animal hide skirts, squatting or sitting with legs astride, their palms upturned in gestures of supplication. Many suffered from scabies and cradled emaciated babies, and all looked twenty years older than their true age. Their only possessions appeared to be empty aluminium cooking pots and plastic water containers. I learnt later that these were the survivors; the most vulnerable had already died. Life expectancy in Uganda was under fifty and, even in the good times, people here were painfully thin. The missions were now the only hope for the remaining population, and the Verona Fathers desperately needed help to distribute the food aid.

I left the mission the next day, driving further north, to continue my assessment, visiting the towns of Kotido and Kaabong not far from the Kidepo Valley National Park between Uganda's borders with Sudan and Kenya. I was now 400 kilometres from Kampala. In Kotido, I met Jim Rowland, an impressive Anglican priest dressed in khaki shorts and sandals; he had an unshakable optimism that was at odds with the world around him. Despite every misfortune, and having had his vehicles looted, Jim continued to teach dryland farming techniques to the local people. His love for them and his enthusiasm for his work seemed boundless.

As we drove around in the Land Rover, my jerry cans in the back began to rattle, a gentle reminder of my biggest concern, fuel management. The nearest fuel was ten hours' drive away. Other concerns were never far from my thoughts. Even in the dry season there was a danger of becoming stuck, but rolling vehicles was a greater hazard. One would begin a journey driving carefully at 40 mph, but after six hours on the road this inevitably rose. Hitting a rut at higher speed was enough to turn a vehicle over.

My return journey was safe, but no journey across Africa is uneventful. As I passed the former flying school at Soroti, curiosity got the better of me and I stopped. There, in the middle of a looted, roofless and windowless building, stood a telex machine on a pedestal. I sat down on a box and switched it on. To my astonishment, the machine clattered to life. I spent the next hour sending my situation report to Oxfam in Oxford.

Back in Kampala, Francesco came up with a simple plan to relieve the famine. He would organise the food supplies, the UN Refugee Agency (UNHCR) would provide the transport, and the non-governmental organisations (NGOs) would distribute it. Oxfam would provide humanitarian assistance in Moroto and Nabilatuk, in the southern part of Karamoja. Action Internationale Contre la Faim (AICF) would do the same in the north of the region. Save the Children Fund (SCF) would also cover the north, working out of Kaabong. Although I thought it was normal practice for the UN to use NGOs to implement their programmes, this might in fact have been one of the first examples of a practice, which has now become standard.

I immediately started planning for Oxfam's two food distribution centres. Each would need two vehicles, fuel, radios and equipment to sustain two staff in the bush, with the Oxfam office in Nairobi acting as quartermaster. To my amazement, within ten days most of the equipment had arrived in Uganda. In Kampala, I hired two likeable Australian backpackers, Trent and Xave, to work at a food distribution centre in Nabilatuk, eight hours away. They had left Australia six months earlier on a one-way ticket to Africa, dressed, I am sure, in the same T-shirts, shorts and flip-flops. Trent, tall, dark and square-jawed, was a natural leader. Xave, smaller and fair-haired, was quieter and frequently affirmed the views of his more robust companion. The fact that they managed to start almost immediately and with minimal equipment was a tribute to their resourcefulness. They even built traditional African mud houses for themselves.

Within a month, I was running six food distribution camps in the bush. However, the roads were becoming increasingly dangerous. The first attack was on a UNHCR convoy, six hours from Kampala. The drivers told of their terror when bullets hit the windscreen of one truck, wounding the driver. Soon after that, driving alone, I was caught up in an alarming firefight near Iriri. I had to dive out of the vehicle and take cover in a roadside ditch until the fighters had moved away. Another incident involved drunken Ugandan soldiers on the road near Jinja. One afternoon, as I was leaving Entebbe, I came upon a crowd of people clubbing suspected thieves to death in the middle of the road. I had to inch the vehicle through the crowd to get away. The frenzy of those wielding the clubs was terrifying, and to be caught up in such a medieval scene frightening beyond measure.

Five years earlier, in 1975, I had learnt to fly. However, I was not a natural pilot and found flying lessons challenging, so after getting my licence I had flown less than thirty hours a year. A few weeks after my arrival in Uganda, Aviation Sans Frontières (ASF) arrived in Entebbe. Surprisingly, this NGO had obtained permission to fly a single light aircraft in the country. ASF gave me the idea that I too could use a plane to do my job. As one of the food distribution centres was fourteen hours by road from Kampala, flying would make it easier to manage the programme, especially as Uganda was dotted with airfields built during the colonial period. Knowing the use of light aircraft was commonplace in Kenya I discussed the matter with Oxfam. Unsurprisingly, I failed to mention my meagre 110 flying hours and that I had a worthless private licence, not a commercial one. To my amazement, they agreed.

Through the Oxfam office in Nairobi, I bought an ancient 1960s model Cessna 182. At Nairobi's Wilson Airport, I flew one rather ragged circuit with an instructor, my first experience of flying a Cessna 182, and landed safely, whereupon the instructor deemed me competent to fly back to Uganda on my own the next day. He had remained silent throughout the flight, and his lack of comment mirrored my own self-doubt. That night back at my hotel, gnawing anxiety about my first solo flight across Africa – 500 miles in a light aircraft without navigational aids, into a country on the brink of civil war – kept me awake until dawn. Rain began drumming on the tin roof. I now faced flying in bad weather and, in my heart, I knew I was woefully unprepared for this adventure. When I took off, the rain had cleared and I could see for miles. I was hugely relieved. I headed west over the Great Rift Valley and, not surprisingly, after an hour had absolutely no idea where I was. Once past the extinct volcanoes on the edge of the Rift Valley there were very few features to help me navigate. I scanned my map for clues, an East Africa road map favoured by Kenyan pilots, not an aeronautical chart. By keeping a westerly heading, I knew I would eventually reach Lake Victoria, and then if I tracked the north shore of the lake I would eventually find Entebbe. After three hours, the lake came into view. It was more of a sea than a lake, with water stretching to the horizon. And there was the hideous thought of being eaten by crocodiles if the engine failed. I checked the engine instruments nervously, and hugged the shoreline. An hour later, I had no difficulty spotting the enormous runway at Entebbe Airport. I was in such a state of anxiety I managed to land on the wrong runway, later mentioned with mirth rather than censure by the control tower, but this was hardly a problem as there were so few aircraft movements anyway. Within weeks, I was flying fifty hours a month between Karamoja and the old police airstrip in the centre of Kampala, a ten-minute walk from the house I rented.

A Ugandan, Grace Natollo, ran the new Oxfam office in Kampala. Calm and organised, she provided not only seamless administration but also vital local knowledge. Grace knew about both the political and the security situations. She found local staff and helped with vital in-country procurement. Nevertheless, even with her political contacts, it was becoming more and more difficult to know what was going on.

Milton Obote was now once again the country's President, but it was clear the security situation was deteriorating. Soon after I moved to a house in the Kololo area of Kampala I learnt how dangerous the situation had become. A visiting TV correspondent needed to return to a hotel not far away. It was seven minutes to six and almost dark; I thought I could drive him there and get back before the military curfew at 6 pm. Within minutes, I had dropped him off and started my journey home. It was only a few minutes after six and I was one hundred yards from the house. All of a sudden, a child soldier jumped into the road twelve feet ahead of me, and without warning fired the whole of his AK47's magazine at me. The machine gun got the better of him and the bullets sprayed over the top of the vehicle. Some hit the Land Rover behind me. Luckily, nobody was injured. The boy disappeared quickly and I drove home, my pulse racing. Indoors, I poured myself a drink – too much excitement for one evening. That same week one of our new Land Rovers was attacked. Three bullets from an AK47 hit the driver's door, exiting via the passenger door. However, again everyone escaped uninjured. Flying was definitely the safer option, I thought.

… Or was it? Mark Lee had flown up to Kidepo Park to cover the work of the distinguished naturalist Iain Douglas-Hamilton, who was in charge of rehabilitating the National Parks. They were three days overdue to return to Kampala. I tried to reach them by radio without success. Finally, one evening just before dusk, the plane appeared over the city. It was high and turning languidly onto finals at the abandoned police airstrip. This was very unlike Iain, whose usual style was an impossibly low pass over the banana trees and a steep turn with little regard for the fact that we were using an airstrip in the middle of a capital city. I ran down to the airstrip a few minutes away. Iain made an easy landing and taxied towards me, but something was clearly wrong. Neither he nor Mark got out when the engine stopped. I opened the doors. They both looked terrible, unwashed and exhausted. Fuel was pouring onto the tarmac from bullet holes that had punctured the wing tank. Another bullet had hit the radio stack between them, showering the cockpit with plastic shards, and a third had just missed the main spar. They had seen poachers in the National Park and flown down to get a better look, and this had been the result. Added to which Mark was suffering from malaria; a couple of days' stubble and dehydration gave his face a haunted look. The plane remained on the airstrip in Kampala for some time.

To help with the six food distribution camps in the bush, I now had fourteen international staff and eighty local staff. Food for the teams was unavailable in Karamoja and they survived on an unhealthy diet of British Army compo rations supplemented by fresh vegetables that I delivered each week, buying them from the local market in Kampala before I left. I flew to the dirt airstrips, no more than tracks in the bush, near each camp every Thursday and back again on Sunday, combining management and resupply. Perhaps it was cupboard love, but the baskets of vegetables always made me popular.

I was always nervous of overloading the plane. I once had a very near miss over some trees at Nabilatuk, which gave me a huge fright. I had only a few inches to spare and would certainly have died. At over 30°C and 4,000 feet above mean sea level it was my first brush with density altitude – air is less dense at both altitude and higher temperature, and so the wings provide less lift and the engines less power – a topic that had not featured at my flying school, or to which, if it did, I had not paid much attention. It is the major killer of bush pilots in East Africa.

There were only around three hundred foreigners working in Uganda at that time. Around a third of them were working in Karamoja and all relied on UNHCR for the delivery of food aid. UNHCR – set up to run refugee camps, not trucking fleets – were struggling with their food convoys, using two-wheel-drive Fiat 110 trucks that were robust enough for local deliveries in Europe but ill-suited to off-road work in Africa. The trucks were new, but after only a month they began to break down continually and there were neither enough spares nor a workshop to maintain them. Failure to deliver the food made the teams in the bush anxious. They had thousands of starving people outside their compounds, and if expectations were not met their own lives were in danger.

Meanwhile, back in Oxford, Oxfam were under the impression that the famine had been caused by desertification and overgrazing. I now knew the real cause was cattle raiding. Two clans of Karamojong warriors armed with automatic weapons had raided all the cattle from their neighbours, and the resulting insecurity had deterred traders from bringing supplies into the area. Absolutely nothing could be done about the security, which was not just a problem in Karamoja. I now envisaged a one-year emergency programme to break the famine, followed by another one-year development programme to improve food security. I had asked Oxfam to place orders for seed and tools, but seed was not available in any volume. In addition, slight differences in climate, seasonal patterns and altitude made imported seed unreliable. The answer, I thought, would be to recruit somebody who knew everything there was to know about dryland farming. Oxfam knew exactly who to approach. Brian Hartley was seventy-six, he had lived in Africa and Yemen most of his life and his knowledge was legendary. As a young man, he had worked in the Sudan Colonial Service where he had learnt Swahili and several East African languages. When he arrived from Kenya, I had all the advice I needed.

It was essential that the clans who had lost their cattle were now able to grow more sorghum and maize. Brian thought that growing enough seed in Karamoja was the only way to break the famine, as most families had eaten everything including their seeds. He advised me to find a farmer to manage a seed bulking project to produce enough seed for the following planting season. It was a bold move and Oxfam recruited John Whitechurch, a Devon farmer. Surprisingly, given the insecurity, he arrived within days with his wife and young children. John was a large man with a commanding presence, used to being good at whatever he did, who beamed with self-confidence. He had been a successful opera singer, was now a farmer, and though only in his early thirties was now a serial entrepreneur.

John immediately set up a seed bulking scheme in Iriri, on an abandoned former agricultural research station. The colonial buildings were just about habitable and it was a perfect location. The land was fertile volcanic soil and, by chance, there was an airstrip unused since colonial days. John planned to grow 300 tons of seed, and to do this he needed six tractors. Oxfam was stubbornly against tractors, adamant that they only favoured the better-off. I suspected political ideology behind this. At that time, research papers were being written on the use of tractors in rural Africa and their limited success in the role of development. However, I was faced with a dilemma when asked what we would do with the tractors at the end of the project.

I told Oxfam we would remove them once we had achieved our goal; they were won over, and the tractors arrived.

Now I had the team in place, food distribution was beginning to make a real change. Gone were the listless crowds ever-present at the food distribution points. We ordered agricultural tools and, with the seed project underway, there was a real chance we could provide food security for the year ahead. In retrospect, it was unusual to have such a clear plan. A one-year emergency famine relief programme followed by a one-year development project to strengthen food security could not have been easier.

Once the acute stage of the emergency had passed and food began to reach those in need, the differences in approach – sometimes incompatible – of the various organisations began to show. In Nabilatuk, the Oxfam team worked alongside an Irish team from the charity Concern. Our team believed that food for work was appropriate. Concern did not. The roads were in a desperate condition, and wrecked the trucks bringing the food. To us, repairing the roads in return for food seemed a sensible way ahead. I employed a young civil engineer and in no time he had engaged hundreds of Karamojong to repair the roads and build concrete fords over riverbeds in return for food. Concern was running a free food programme in the same settlement as our food-for-work programme; they thought what we were doing was exploitation, and relationships became difficult.

Relationships with UNHCR were not always wonderful either, but unfairly so. UNHCR, as the UN refugee agency, were showing goodwill in running logistics for WFP. WFP did not have the expertise to manage a trucking fleet which, given the conditions in Uganda at the time, was not surprising. One of the problems they faced was the official exchange rate, which for the UN was seven Ugandan shillings to the UK pound. The black market, or real, rate was seven hundred Ugandan shillings to the pound, making the price of spare parts with import taxes on top ruinously expensive. UNDP, who might have been helpful, failed to engage with the Ugandan government. Neither were they supportive of the work all the humanitarian agencies were doing. I do not recall a single visit to Karamoja by the UNDP Resident Representative. It was also surprising that we had so little contact with the British Embassy, given that eventually more than fifty UK nationals were working in Karamoja in difficult and dangerous conditions.

Security was always a worry, and after an attack on a food convoy UNHCR banned travel on the road south to Mbale. It was surprisingly difficult to get the road open again, and months passed before it was. Once roads were deemed dangerous, there was no mechanism for reviewing the security risk.

As the months passed, the nagging uncertainty of daily life had a cumulative effect on us all. One evening I was sitting outside a former colonial bungalow in Moroto with the Oxfam team when fighting broke out between the police and the army. We found it quite a spectacle until suddenly I heard spent ammunition hitting the roof. Falling bullets can kill, even at extreme range, so I rallied everyone inside, keeping the house in darkness.

I was about to leave Moroto for Kampala one day when one of the Fathers from the mission arrived at the Oxfam house, flustered and out of breath. There had been a cattle raid just north of the town, and he needed us and our Land Rover to help bring the wounded back to the mission hospital. We could see smoke rising in the distance, and when we reached the village sadly little remained of it; every hut had been burnt to the ground. We searched for any signs of life, but the people had fled. Propped up against an acacia tree was a warrior staring straight ahead, his face expressionless; a discarded AK47 lay nearby. Whether a survivor or one of the raiders, it was impossible to know. He remained immobile as I approached. The remains of his shattered leg lay at right angles to his body. A bullet had removed at least three inches of bone from the tibia and fibula mid-shaft. A pool of blood soaked the red earth and only arterial spasm prevented him from bleeding to death. He looked as though he had accepted his fate, but arrangements were made to get him to the mission hospital. As I flew back to Kampala thoughts crowded my head distracting me from flying the plane. The counterpoint between compassion and the bestial cruelty I had witnessed was difficult to accommodate. The reality of what modern assault rifles could do to the human body is always shocking. It leaves lifelong images that are impossible to eradicate.

Our convoy leaders were two young women who escorted the vehicles all the way from Kampala. It was their responsibility to see that the food did not disappear in transit. Their personal bravery, as they travelled throughout the country alone, impressed me hugely. Equally impressive was an Irish doctor from Save the Children Fund, who came to supervise the supplementary feeding programme and help at Moroto hospital. He transformed the place and inspired me to enrol at medical school when I returned to the UK eighteen months later. What was so appealing was the idea of focusing on one patient at a time, and the satisfaction of seeing them get better, compared to the enormous numbers we looked after during a humanitarian emergency, when most of the time success just meant making things less bad.

Quite unexpectedly, two French Army Puma helicopter pilots arrived in Karamoja, and helped us to distribute maize to the remotest settlements. Even with a modest payload, they achieved in two days what would take us more than a week. And it was not only the presence of the helicopters, but also the military organisation and communications, so different from the amateur logistics of the humanitarian agencies. This was the first time I had seen the military deliver humanitarian assistance, and it made a deep impression on me.

Towards the end of the dry season, the strain on all the international staff began to show. Nobody had taken any leave. Now that the food stores were full and the population was in reasonable health I had to deal with illness and tensions in the team. Two members of the team suffered scorpion bites and the neurotoxin in the venom caused an extreme reaction in both.

Xave, in Nabilatuk, had been unwell for days. However, feeling a little better he decided to cancel his trip back to Kampala to see a doctor. Two days later, I got a call from Trent on the HF radio to say Xave was *in extremis*. They were about fourteen hours' drive from Kampala, the rains had arrived and the airstrip was now unusable. I left Kampala immediately in our Mazda two-wheel-drive pickup. It was a terrible vehicle, its standard road tyres useless on the rain-soaked black cotton soils. It took fourteen hours to reach Nabilatuk; the last four of those I was driving in the dark, ploughing through flooded riverbeds, and occasionally catching the glint of hyenas' eyes in the headlights.

When I arrived at the camp Trent greeted me with a diatribe of complaint. I entered the mud shelter, lit only by the soft light of a paraffin lamp. I seemed to be responsible for Xave's misfortunes, along with those of the entire country. As he ranted, he was eating fried flying ants from an old baked bean tin – watching the wings poking out of his mouth was particularly revolting. He had definitely been in the bush too long. His wild eyes, ferocious invective and the sound of drums beating nearby in the bush made it feel like the end of the world. Xave was in a terrible state, dehydrated, sunken-eyed and lying with his knees bent. I had seen typhoid fever before, and knew the dangers of a perforated bowel and death from peritonitis. We set off at speed in a thunderstorm, the pickup truck sliding about on the sodden earth. Xave moaned for a while in the passenger seat, then became unnaturally quiet. We arrived at the hospital in Kenya as dawn broke, just in time to save his life. I did not do a lot better myself catching dysentery immediately on my return to Kampala. At least there I was able to find the British Embassy doctor and made a swift recovery.

Now the emergency programme was well past its midpoint I needed to send some of the team members on leave. I had been concerned for a while about one of our more intelligent and creative team members who had failed to return to the house where the team stayed in Moroto. He had been seen walking up Moroto Mountain and was now with the Tepeth tribe. This was a shy tribe, who lived on the mountain to keep clear of the warlike Karamojong. With Father Mario Cisternino at the mission, who knew the Tepeth, I went up the mountain to collect my colleague, who was the second team member to return to the UK suffering from stress. Today, both would probably be diagnosed with post-traumatic stress disorder.

Back in Kampala, I was driving through one of the poorer districts late one afternoon. It was oppressively hot, the sky full of towering cumulus clouds, the signs of an impending thunderstorm. As I approached some dukas – primitive African shops – I could see people running. Two hundred metres away an army pickup truck full of soldiers wearing bright red berets was bouncing up the road. Red berets were always a sign of danger; they were the favoured headwear of soldiers, who were spoilt and given special privileges. Some shots rang out and everyone began to run. I pulled into the side of the road, quietly jumped out of the car and stepped under the concrete colonnade of a more substantial shop as soldiers came running up the street armed with assault rifles. Suddenly I saw a young soldier, no more than a teenager, five yards in front of me. His eyes were wild and frightened, and he looked drunk. He raised his rifle, his finger coiled round the trigger, and I froze, not daring to move or show any expression fearing that anything at all might encourage him to kill me. Two more shots rang out. At this critical moment, several red beret soldiers ran past; he turned and ran off with them. I never found out what this was all about, but it certainly changed my view of the risk of living in this chaotic country.

No journey in Africa is uneventful and unwanted drama is never far away. Returning from Entebbe, on the outskirts of Kampala, I crossed an old railway line near a tunnel. A large crowd had gathered and a young boy ran towards me, signalling me to stop, imploring me to follow him. I followed him to the mouth of a railway tunnel. A young man was lying by the track; blood was running down his face and he was babbling in Luganda. He had been riding on top of a train, and his head had smashed into the roof of the tunnel, which had removed a third of his skull. His friends bundled him into the passenger seat of my pickup and I set off at speed to Makerere hospital. He soon fell silent, and his body slumped over onto me as I drove. His blood ran down my shoulder, congealing in a pool in the footwell. It was getting dark as I arrived at the hospital. A single 40-watt bulb lit the dirty, blood-stained entrance flanked with broken windows. I found some souls inside who returned with an ancient canvas stretcher. Without a hint of emotion, they laid his inert body on it and disappeared into the cavernous interior. This massive building, a monument to the prestige of a different era, could now hardly provide clean drinking water. I drove home slowly, drained of feeling and inwardly exhausted.

As the famine was finally broken, I had time for other projects. Oxfam wanted to support the orthopaedic workshop at Makerere Hospital in Kampala, an important project given the number of amputees in Uganda at the time. The workshop needed some refurbishment and I needed to find someone to do it. Somebody recommended an engineer called Lawrence Ascot. He was a UK national living and working in Kampala, who had a reputation for kindness and great wit. Yet, for some inexplicable reason, nothing in his life ever quite went to plan. Lawrence had left a job as an engineer at Hammersmith Hospital, London in the 1960s to repair the autoclave at Makerere Hospital and had never gone back. He was now in his fifties, balding and unhealthily overweight. His warehouse in Kampala, where his employees repaired everything from cars to washing machines, was a chaotic unruly place, and to visit him was always entertaining. Lawrence amused visitors with a repertoire of ludicrous stories. His favourite theme was the fall from the Garden of Eden. Uganda, he declared, had been one of the most beautiful countries in the world; now it was in a state of chaos. When he worked on hospital projects, medical staff objected to his Alsatian trotting behind him. "My dog's the cleanest thing in this hospital," he would say. And perhaps he was right. The Verona Fathers heard that Lawrence had been a hospital engineer and asked if he could repair the autoclave at Arua Hospital in West Nile Province. Lawrence drove alone to this remote region, a long and dangerous journey, and returned with alarming stories. Some local soldiers had tied him to a hospital trolley and threatened to kill him. But he made them laugh so much that in the end they let him go. As with all Lawrence's stories, I never knew how much to believe, but humour like his was certainly a lifesaver in Africa.

The Fathers also wanted me to visit the mission hospital in Arua, which was running short of medical supplies. It was too risky to attempt to fly, as I had no idea of the security situation on the ground or the state of the airfield. I had also been warned about the dangers of travelling near the Congo border. So I drove up there.

My brother Johnny and his girlfriend Gabrielle had been on holiday in East Africa and were coming to Uganda to spend a week with me. They agreed to come with me to Arua. Mark Lee, now a correspondent for the *Daily Telegraph*, was coming too. It would take us two days by Land Rover to reach West Nile Province. We planned to reach the Murchison Falls National Park on the first night. The first part of our journey was easy enough; most of the roads were relatively pothole-free. We drove for hours across the fertile central plains, but never saw another vehicle or human being. Even when we entered the National Park there was not an animal in sight; the soldiers had eaten most of them during the fighting after the fall of Idi Amin. At Chobe Safari Lodge, where we planned to stay, a shell had demolished a large section of the hotel and it looked hardly habitable. That evening the Lodge was expecting several members of the Ugandan government, so some food was available. The staff were surprised and rather disconcerted to have other guests, and we got the impression that the food was not really for us.

We spent the next day driving through herds of African buffalo, praying we did not get a puncture. None of us wanted to be the one to change a tyre amongst these dangerous beasts. The map was almost useless and I began to worry about fuel. We had a 200-litre fuel drum in the back of the Land Rover, which made the journey fairly unpleasant for those in the back. Especially so when I hit a huge pothole and it toppled on top of them. We had punctured two tyres since leaving Kampala and now had no more spares. Our second day passed without sight of another human being – on the one hand alarming if we broke down, but also fortuitous, as meeting soldiers here was dangerous. We passed close to the River Nile and saw a stone plaque that said *Camp of Emin Pasha, Capital of Equatoria 1885*. Emin

Pasha, the ill-fated Governor of the Egyptian province of Equatoria, was rescued here by Henry Morton Stanley in 1888. It was a desolate place now, completely reclaimed by the bush, with no evidence of the former settlement.

As we approached the Catholic Mission at Arua, we could hear small arms fire not far away. It was unclear who was fighting whom, but this had been Idi Amin's home town and the inhabitants were unlikely to be favoured by the new President's Acholi people to the south, who made up most of the army.

The Fathers looked exhausted. They had seen eighteen months of turmoil and faced huge personal danger in this remote place. Gabrielle, to her surprise, was led away by the sisters who ran the mission hospital to spend the night in a nearby convent. Over dinner, we heard a harrowing account of the situation. The fighting was now in its second month and it had not been safe to leave the mission for several weeks. Most of the town's inhabitants had fled over the Congo border to avoid summary execution. Bodies lay unburied where they had been slaughtered.

The next day we visited the mission hospital, where the war-wounded lay silent, their eyes imploring for help, their wounds covered with flies. The smell was appalling. The injuries caused by modern assault rifles were horrific, and despite the heroic efforts of the Verona Fathers, few would survive. I thought I had become inured to such sights, but each time I went on a field trip it was moments like this that spurred me to action. I quietly went through a list of drugs and surgical supplies with one of the doctors. I knew if I flew here, to Arua, I could deliver these medical supplies within a few days. Later we found that the nearby airfield was in reasonable condition. With my goal accomplished, I was hoping to leave for Kampala at first light the following day. On our way back to the town we came across an earth satellite station built by the Amin regime, now in ruins having been looted by soldiers. What they had not taken they had smashed, and circuit boards lay scattered over hundreds of metres around the station. A wrecked helicopter, brought down during the fighting, sat on its side nearby. Rather unwisely, we drove towards the border with the Congo where we stopped at a scaffolding pole resting on an oil drum. My brother got out to raise the pole so we could drive through. Only we all failed to see the small sign warning *Méfiez-vous des abeilles*! A swarm of bees emerged from the end of the pole and he only just jumped back into the safety of the Land Rover in time. During the commotion, I had failed to notice a group of armed men emerging from the bush surrounding the vehicle. Given they were carrying French weapons, I quickly identified them as Congolese bandits. I spoke to them in French and it became clear that humorous banter was going to be essential in this situation. One of them was eyeing up the Land Rover, but a Toyota would have been a more attractive prize. I instinctively knew some barter was required and delved into a box of British Army compo rations. Pulling out a tin of jam, that I thought would be just the job, there were immediate smiles on their faces and with lots of thumbs up and slaps on the back, they went on their way.

I flew up to Arua a couple of times with medical supplies. It was a long flight of nearly three hours, so I kept jerry cans of 100 octane aviation fuel behind the front seats. This was not a very safe practice, but it allowed me to refuel immediately on arrival. On my second visit to Arua, although I had talked to the soldiers at the airfield the week before, that did not stop them firing wildly at the plane from the ground. I was on finals to land and lucky not to be hit, considering I was a relatively easy target. When I chatted to them later, their grievance seemed to be mainly that the plane flew at all. They had a firm view that this was unnatural and that it should not. This incident was not unusual. Ground fire was something I encountered from time to time from soldiers with AK47s. It was disconcerting, and evasive action beyond increasing speed was not really possible.

We had now distributed the agricultural tools and the seed. The supplementary feeding had ceased several months earlier. Now the upper-arm circumference of a child, a measure of nutrition, was back in the normal range. Our presence had also had a calming effect in Karamoja, which was now quieter than the rest of the country. The emergency programme was to close at Christmas, though a small core team would remain for a follow-up development programme. I flew back to the UK for a holiday.

I returned to Uganda for twelve weeks in 1982, to ensure a smooth handover to Roger Naumann, who was now back, and to David Campbell who was to take over the project. I was now in demand to fly NGOs and UN staff around the country. I was not there to be a pilot, but when I could, I did. Once, in Kidepo, I met the pilot of the National Park's Cessna 182. He had just collected the plane from Kenya and had not flown at all during the last eighteen months. As I took off downhill on the rather rough runway I saw him taxi to the other end. He took off uphill, but into wind. Although technically correct, with the slope and density altitude, it was wiser to take off downhill and downwind. I held my breath. I saw him later in the day but thought myself ill-equipped to give advice; every pilot had more experience than I did. Disaster struck two days later, when he stalled the plane soon after take-off and both he and the hotel manager were killed on impact.

With my limited experience, flying for me was always challenging. The first time I flew to Moroto, I was unsure of the location of the airfield. I circled the plane over where it was marked on the map. Only when I saw the faint numbers indicating the runways in the long grass did I know I was in the right place. I taxied over to the roofless remains of the hangar and turned off the engine. A gazelle grazing nearby trotted off, and a group of waterbuck looked on attentively. Far away I saw someone running and after a few minutes the airfield supervisor arrived, breathless, holding an enormous wheel chock in each hand and an aircraft movements log book in his mouth ready for me to sign. The last entry in it was the month before Independence, in 1960.

Returning from the UK after Christmas, I found my attitude to risk strangely altered. In none of the incidents over the last year had I felt remotely in danger. Now things were different, and I felt in danger almost every hour of the day. Perhaps I was more aware of the dangers, or perhaps the strain of living in this unpredictable place was getting the better of me. But I certainly saw the dangers of expatriate life in these ungoverned places. George Orwell intimated that it is not the Almighty that keeps us in order; it is our neighbours. There were no neighbours here. Equatorial Africa had a habit of finding weakness in the most robust of characters. It was time for me to go home. I had been in Africa for fifteen months, although chronological time did not seem to have much relevance. My brief deployments to Northern Ireland, Cambodia and now Uganda seemed already a lifetime.

As I gradually readjusted to home life, I reflected on what I had learnt from my first posting. Uganda is a small beautiful country, and had then a tiny population. Analysis of why there was a famine had been correct from the start. Despite the bickering between international staff, the distribution of food aid followed by the provision of seeds and tools had been well-managed. Also, the emergency programme appeared to have had a clear end-point. However, I suspected this was a very Western view. I have no idea how many died – without question a very large proportion of the population of Karamoja. I wondered if the follow-on development programme had made a difference. Did those who lost their cattle ever restock? When I left, I had seeds of doubt. Cattle raiding with spears was self-limiting and social structures here could cope. Cattle raiding with automatic weapons was another matter. Sometimes the advent of new technology can damage societies in ways that cannot be easily mended.

But the humanitarian agencies were all very pleased with what had been achieved and that we had saved many lives. However, for the most part I had been struck by the power of social conservatism. Change is generational, not something that happens in a few months or even a few years, and I had my reservations about how successful it had all really been.

I had been hugely impressed by the efficiency of the two French Army helicopters during the rains at the beginning of the year. The use of military assets in humanitarian disasters was going to be very useful. Yet it would become a highly controversial subject over the next twenty years, and I was to play a central role in this.

3

Unwelcome Guests, Kurdish Refugees, Iran 1991

After returning from Uganda in 1982, I had no involvement in humanitarian work for nearly ten years. Instead, I qualified in medicine at Bristol University, beginning with a first-year university course in physics, chemistry and zoology (I had never studied science at school), before going on to join the other medical students for six more years of study. I really enjoyed medicine, and the challenge I had set myself to become a doctor. Also during this time, I got married and became the father of a young family.

Then, just after Christmas 1990, I attended a dinner hosted by the Old Etonian Medical Society. The Gulf War had dominated the previous months, and the entire Kurdish population of Northern Iraq, 1.2 million people, had fled in terror from the forces of Saddam Hussein. Inevitably, we discussed the unfolding situation and the plight of the Kurdish refugees now on the Iranian and Turkish borders.

After dinner in College Hall, Doctor Ricky Richardson, a consultant at Great Ormond Street Hospital, stood up below the vast stained-glass window and spoke passionately about the atrocities committed by Saddam's troops on the columns of fleeing Kurds, between five hundred and a thousand of whom died each day in the mountains. We all leant forward on the ancient benches of the medieval hall, straining to hear every word, and were horrified by his description of the cars, buses and trucks being attacked from the air, that now lay abandoned along with their slaughtered occupants. Ricky Richardson ended with an appeal to our humanity: as doctors, were we prepared to go to Iran and assist the Kurds?

Now I was a qualified doctor this talk of Kurdistan had a persuasive pull. I was lucky – my next job in the Accident and Emergency Department at Cheltenham General Hospital did not start until August, so I had the time and now the opportunity. The next day I rang the British Red Cross and within ten days found myself en route to north-west Iran to carry out a humanitarian assessment of the situation on the Iraq border.

Encouraged by what they had taken as positive signals of support from the Coalition fighting against Saddam Hussein in southern Iraq, the Kurds had taken up arms. But the uprising had been brutally suppressed by Saddam's troops, and now more than 500,000 displaced Kurds were concentrated on the Turkish border near Zakhu. The rest had set off through the mountains hoping to find safety in Iran. It was March and night-time temperatures dropped below freezing. Attacked by helicopters, many had jumped into their cars, fleeing with only what they had with them, some even without shoes or warm clothes. They drove up into the mountains until the roads became boulder-strewn tracks and the tracks became no more than footpaths. Eventually, when the roads or the petrol ran out, they abandoned their vehicles and continued on foot. Terrified, exhausted, with children clinging to their mothers or riding on their fathers' shoulders, they reached the Iranian border. However, this proved no sanctuary. Without water, food and shelter thousands died; those still alive had only days to live. The Kurdish people, 7 million in total, had straddled the borders of Iran, the Soviet Union and Turkey and, harbouring ideas of an independent Kurdistan, were seen as a menace by their respective governments. But the Iranians opened their border and let them in. They were directed to camps run by the Iranian Red Crescent Society and incarcerated in military-style establishments surrounded by barbed wire.

Mary McLoughlin, a highly-respected doctor with Save the Children Fund, was on the flight with me to Urmia, the largest city in Iranian Azerbaijan, near the Turkish-Iraqi border. Mary was delightfully Irish, with Gaelic looks, a soft accent and a charming idiom. "They wouldn't have a bull's notion," she said quietly, describing our colleagues on the flight, a comment that soon proved to be only too true. I liked Mary's sharp intellect; also, having worked in many humanitarian emergencies, she was very experienced. We had the same objectives and, given how little medicine I knew, I was keen to work with her, something she quickly agreed to. This was rather unusual, in view of the traditional rivalry between NGOs.

We were some of the first Westerners to arrive in Iran since the revolution. Throughout the whole process of going through immigration and collecting our bags, men in black clerical dress watched us silently, their body language expressing visceral hostility. From the moment we left the airport, our movements were closely monitored.

I was surprised by the size of Urmia, a modern sophisticated city with a population of over one million. The contrast to neighbouring countries was striking. The hotel was a functional concrete cube on a busy street with clean modern rooms. On the ground floor, where one would normally find a bar in the West, was a room for drinking tea. Over the next few weeks we drank many gallons of green tea while we endured endless delays and prevarications, until we began to suffer tea-induced diuresis.

I found a sharp contrast between the friendliness of the people and the suspicion and outright hostility of officialdom. All the foreign humanitarian agencies were guests of the Iranian Red Crescent, and it

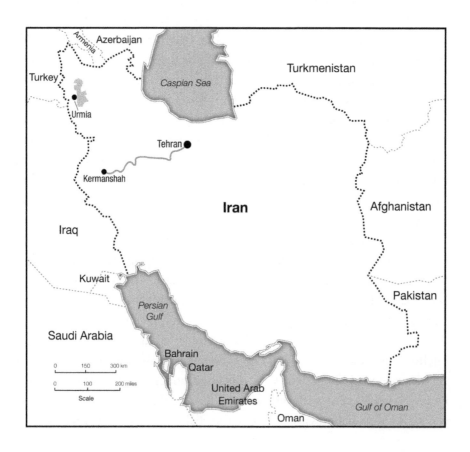

was clear from the start they were not going to make life easy for us. As soon as any humanitarian aid arrived from the UK it was taken directly from the aircraft and driven away in military trucks, never to be seen again. Since permits were required for everything, my immediate priority was to visit the Provincial Governor's office. There I found several NGO representatives complaining bitterly about their missing aid supplies – Oxfam were particularly irritated by losing water pipes. It was clear that the Iranians considered these supplies as assistance to the Islamic Republic of Iran, to use as they saw fit. They had no need of us nor did they want us in their country; once they had the charities' supplies, they would frustrate us in any way they could. However, their courtesy was impressive. "You're here to see the Governor? He will come, but you must wait... The Governor has been delayed, but he will be here this afternoon... He's been called to an urgent meeting in Tehran, but will be here tomorrow... Can we give you something to eat? Some tea perhaps?" At the time I was reading Tolstoy's novel *Resurrection*, not realising that Tolstoy is highly regarded in Iran. This proved a good move. I read quietly for nearly three days outside the Provincial Governor's office, while a long queue of foreigners shouted at the Iranians. I got the permits I needed; on the whole the others did not.

Rather surprisingly, Mary and I were instructed to set up a health clinic at a refugee camp near the Iranian border about an hour's drive from Urmia. The next day we were provided with transport by the Iranian Red Crescent and after several delays arrived in a small settlement visibly poorer than Urmia. We were taken to a sinister-looking camp, which I suspected had been used for prisoners during the Iran-Iraq war three years earlier. Inside the barbed wire was a dusty hut, which was to become our health clinic for the next two weeks. Mary and I were delighted with our task. It would not only be useful from a medical point of view, it would also give us a fairly accurate sample of the health problems of the Kurdish refugees.

On our second day there, a great commotion erupted outside the hut. The door burst open and a large number of people crowded in, carrying a middle-aged man on a door. There was a sense of panic and much shouting. Mary and I did what we could, but within minutes it was clear the patient was dead. When we communicated this to what appeared to be the immediate family, the women started to pull out their hair and tear their clothes. This biblical moment of grief was frightening in its intensity.

We stayed at a small hotel near the centre of the town, an ugly bleak building with coloured panels on its concrete façade. The hotel sign tilted forlornly, and several letters were missing. The rooms mirrored the exterior; a layer of grime coated everything and the lavatory in my adjoining bathroom leaked disagreeably. The water was intermittent; the foul smell was not.

Mary McLoughlin's husband had been killed in a car accident two years earlier. She still wore her wedding ring and dressed appropriately in an abaya and headscarf. However, despite every attempt to comply with Iranian propriety I was sensitive to the fact that a foreign man and a woman, unrelated but working together, was unlikely to meet the approval of the authorities. It didn't take long. That evening Mary and I had just sat down to supper at the hotel when suddenly a large man with a pockmarked face loomed up. Stabbing his finger at me, he said in English with a heavy Iranian accent, "You come with me – now!" I was led into an empty back room, over-lit by fluorescent tubes, with just two chairs on the concrete floor. An accomplice joined us, similarly dressed, his jeans rather too tight. He asked for my passport, which I handed over. He wanted something else, but his poor English made it unclear exactly what, so his frustration made him increasingly aggressive. I remembered the letter from the Governor and produced it with a flourish. They both examined it for several minutes and eventually I was let go. It seemed moments, but I had been gone over half an hour. I returned to my cold kebab, thoroughly relieved; so was Mary, who was as surprised as I was that I had managed to extricate myself.

It was soon obvious that the Kurds were not going to prosper in Iran. They were kept behind barbed wire in refugee camps that were little more than prisons with brutally sparse facilities. If any of them wanted to return to Iraq, they had to hand back all their humanitarian relief items; tent, blanket, water container, even food. I had doubts about what could be achieved in Iran, or even if we should be working here at all. Surely it would be better to deliver humanitarian assistance in Iraq, where these people actually lived. All that had been achieved so far was an airlift of limited quantities of humanitarian relief, obstructed in every possible way by the Iranian government. This hardly touched the problem. Mary and I prepared an assessment report along these lines, arguing for a well-managed delivery of humanitarian assistance inside Northern Iraq, and decided to return promptly to the UK to persuade our respective organisations that this was the direction to take.

We travelled to Tehran, but while Mary flew home I was given an additional task. The British Red Cross had received reports of large numbers of Kurdish refugees on the Iran-Iraq border near Bakhtaran, and I was asked to assess the situation before returning to London. Bakhtaran was 500 kilometres away, a day's journey by taxi across country, and I went to the market to find someone prepared to drive me there. This was far easier than I had imagined, as there was no shortage of taxis, and after a brief negotiation, I was off.

Much of the journey passed through a vast, hot desert. My driver stopped just once for something to eat and kept up a vigorous pace, which at times was alarming. The car had a big V8 engine and we never seemed to travel at less than 80 mph. It was very hot and at one point, I dozed off, but not for long. The driver in front of us suddenly lost control; his car spun three times along the road in front of us then rolled three times before plunging down into a steep river valley. We stopped immediately amongst the debris from the car. It was lying at the bottom of the ravine a hundred feet below us, and appeared to be completely flattened. As we scrambled down, I braced myself for what I would see. We found the car on its roof, the wheels still spinning. On one side, however, there was a slight gap between the rocks the car was wedged into and, to my amazement, a head appeared. Within a few seconds, no fewer than three young men had extracted themselves unharmed. Our journey continued.

As we climbed through some mountains, the air became cooler and pine trees grew beside the road. In the town of Bakhtaran I easily found the UN office and arrived in time for the daily UN coordination meeting. The UN coordinator was an impressive man in his fifties who had recently arrived from Geneva. This was much more professional than anything I had experienced in Uganda. I heard expressed the same frustrations, exasperation and misgivings that we had felt at the camp further north.

I was invited to join the UN on a visit to refugees in a river valley nearby. As we travelled down the valley, I could see the river was being used as a latrine as well as a source of drinking water. At a camp on the border, I talked to the refugees. Their stories were very similar to those I had heard in Iranian Azerbaijan. I was offered a cup of tea, but after what I had just seen in the river, and knowing cholera and typhoid were endemic, I declined, making a mental note not to be killed by politeness. After the near miss on the road, this was the second attempt on my life in one day.

Back in Tehran the next day, after another marathon journey across the desert, I booked a flight back to the UK. With so few foreigners in the country, it was not surprising that at Tehran airport the Islamic religious police took a special interest in us. I was travelling with Save the Children's Logistics Coordinator. He was a rugged former soldier, not yet fifty, but he looked older; his face was worn by a life in harsh environments. He wore tattoos on both forearms, and his eyes had a coldness to them. At customs, he was asked to open his suitcase. On top of his clothes were several music cassettes, which were immediately removed by the bearded cleric. To my absolute amazement, my colleague grabbed the man by his beard and said quietly, "Put… them… back…" I saw myself being chained to a radiator for the next decade. But the cleric, happier admonishing women for their lack of modesty, with a look of astonishment and terror, gingerly replaced the cassettes. With great courtesy, we moved on.

While I was in Iran, David Nabarro, a senior civil servant at the Oversees Development Administration (ODA) in London, had reached the same conclusion as I had about supporting the Kurds from inside Iraq. He had recently returned from a brief trip to Northern Iraq where the Royal Marines 3 Commando Brigade had been deployed. International outrage at Saddam Hussein's treatment of the Kurds in Northern Iraq had led to Coalition troops being deployed at short notice to establish a Safe Haven across the mountains of Northern Iraq. David wanted the humanitarian agencies to provide support for the Kurds inside Iraq. This was at first widely mocked by the humanitarian agencies, who did not want to work with the military and were highly sceptical of the intentions of the British government. Also, since the war had only just ended, the situation in Iraq was unstable and civilian deployment was high-risk. David had no option but to recruit a hundred civilians to work with the Royal Marines and provide the humanitarian programme so desperately needed. It was a bold plan. David was known for his imaginative, iconoclastic and unusual solutions to problems; even so, his idea of hiring a hundred British nationals to go to a conflict zone would definitely raise eyebrows in Whitehall. He needed reliable independent external support for the idea. Mary's and my report had been sent by the British Red Cross to the Foreign Office at just the right moment. It was exactly what David needed.

In London, I was told by the British Red Cross that the Foreign Office wanted to see me. David Nabarro met me on the second floor of the ODA office, bounding towards me with an energy and intensity that I almost found alarming, and immediately bombarded me with an avalanche of questions. From time to time a new person would come in, until the room was quite full. When I had finished, David told me of his own recent trip to Iraq and his plan to put together a humanitarian programme for the Kurds. I suddenly realised I was being interviewed. David said, "Would you like to take a hundred civilians to Northern Iraq? Next Saturday?" I agreed without hesitation, and set off home to announce to my family that after my month in Iran I was now off to Iraq, a country still at war, for an unspecified length of time.

★★★

Five days later, I arrived at the Harlequin Hotel at Stansted Airport. My only instruction had been to get there at 2.30 pm. I was told, "Everyone is in the conference room." With no idea what "everyone" meant, I went in and found Guy Mustard, an ODA civil servant, giving admin instructions to about a hundred people. These were the thirty doctors and nurses, thirty engineers and fitters, and thirty firefighters who were to travel with me to Iraq. "Ah," Guy said, "Gilbert Greenall has come to brief you." I had no idea I was to do this and was quite unprepared, so it was not my best moment. I didn't think many of them had ever seen a humanitarian emergency so I talked about the situation on the Iranian border, and the Kurds in general, and hoped I wasn't making a fool of myself. I found out later that there was no unanimous view at ODA about who was to lead this mission. I suspected that I had been deliberately wrong-footed to try to strengthen the argument for another candidate.

4

Hope Unbounded, The First Gulf War, Northern Iraq 1991

The flight the next morning to Turkey was a Dan-Air charter flight. This was a budget airline, and the rather ancient Boeing 727 with its tired interior was an indication that the company was financially stressed – little did we know the airline would be sold that year for £1. Yet the flight attendants were cheerful and wished us well. My fellow passengers were quiet and reflective – perhaps we were all wondering what we had got ourselves into. Four hours later, we were at Incirlik air base and being bussed to a vast tented city beside the airfield. I was astounded at the scale of it, but remembered that hundreds of thousands of servicemen and women had been deployed to the Gulf, many of them through Incirlik. Two of the huge tents were allocated to us and, after a bossy briefing from a sergeant, we were dispatched to a canteen. Trying to identify our particular tent from the thousand others in the dark proved quite a challenge, as some later found out.

The next day we set off to Iraq in two coaches, a bizarre experience. The journey – a hundred or so kilometres along the Syrian border – was long, hot and tedious until finally we crossed unescorted into Iraq near Zakhu. It was now dark. I sat at the front near the driver, following our progress on my map. We came to a fork in the road and the driver continued straight ahead. I was alarmed and rechecked our position – we were on the main road to Dohūk, which was still held by Iraqi forces. I tapped the driver on the shoulder and, after much reversing, we managed to avoid an embarrassing and possibly fatal error. It was the middle of the night when we arrived at Brigade Headquarters at Sersink, an airfield in Northern Iraq recently abandoned by Iraqi troops that had been built next to one of Saddam's palaces. Both the airfield buildings and the palace had been in the middle of construction when the war started. Our accommodation was in the unfinished terminal building, where I was met by Annabel Ross, daughter of the Lieutenant-General commanding all British troops in Northern Iraq. Annabel was in her twenties, energetic and bursting with enthusiasm. She was to act as my PA while I was with the brigade.

3 Commando Brigade had been deployed to Northern Iraq from Turkey in late April 1991. After crossing into Iraq, they had met almost no resistance although three Iraqi soldiers had reportedly been killed in one

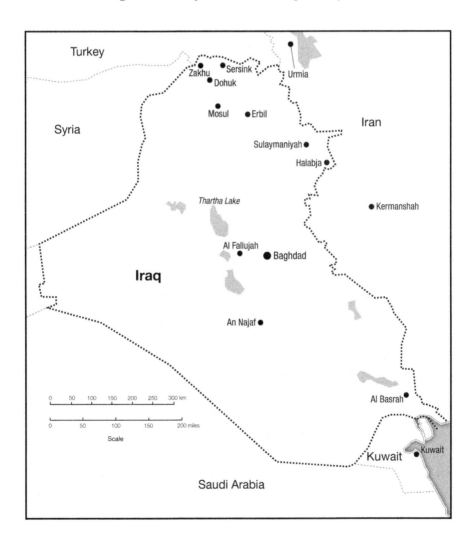

firefight. The brigade was now fully deployed across the mountains north of Dohūk. A few miles from us, half a million displaced people were in the mountains without water, sanitation, shelter, food or medical support. The task I faced made my work in Uganda look very modest.

I was to join the Brigade Commander the following morning at 8 am for the 'bird table' brief – the Commander's daily briefing from his staff officers. I woke at 6 am, pulled myself out of my sleeping bag and found I was in a valley with astonishing views despite it being an inhospitable place of barren scrub dotted with exposed rocks. The headquarters was on the northern side of the valley and looked down on the airfield. The runway had only recently been constructed and bulldozers and other machinery littered the site as if they had been used the day before. It was an ideal location for the headquarters. The buildings also provided some welcome shade in these barren hills, where within weeks the daytime temperature would soar to over 50°C. Beyond the airfield were the Mountains of Kurdistan, which ended abruptly only twenty kilometres away where they met the great plains of the Tigris and Euphrates rivers. Baghdad and Saddam were 500 kilometres further to the south.

I had never been near a Brigade or Division Headquarters before and was not quite sure what to expect of the 'bird table' brief. I had left the army as a subaltern and was only used to regimental life. To my surprise, I was shown to a seat next to the Brigadier, who had yet to arrive. At precisely 8 am, Andy Keeling, the Brigade Commander, and Rob Fry, Chief of Staff, appeared and all eighty of us stood as they took their seats. Various staff officers gave reports on the activities of each component of the brigade and the latest refugee situation a few miles away on the Turkish border. Afterwards the Brigadier introduced me to his staff officers, finishing with, "Dr Greenall is here to advise me what we should do next." I had absolutely no idea what to do next.

"So what would you like to do?" I was asked. Looking as confident as I could, I asked for a helicopter reconnaissance. I certainly needed to look at the problem from the air. And I needed time to think.

From the Gazelle helicopter, I could see thousands and thousands of Kurds scattered across the mountains, huddled in groups against the bitter cold, their cars abandoned where the roads had become mud tracks. We needed to get them off the mountains, to somewhere where we could help them. Importantly, before they would move, they needed reassurance that they would be safe. David Nabarro had mentioned 'way stations', stopping points along their journey where they could get fuel for their vehicles, drinking water and food. I certainly couldn't think of any better way to encourage them to move.

The key question was where they were going to move to. The Kurds had previously lived in Northern Iraq along the Syrian, Turkish, and Iranian borders. But Saddam Hussein had forcibly moved them to cities further south, destroying their villages. There was no possibility they could return to those cities as they were still under Saddam's control. In any case, the Safe Haven controlled by the Coalition did not extend beyond the mountains of Kurdistan.

We had been in the air for an hour and a half, the helicopter would soon be landing back at Sersink, and I needed a plan. Remembering what I had learnt from the Cambodia mission, I knew I needed to think on a big scale. Suddenly, the answer came to me, and it was remarkably simple. If we could get enough tents – thousands of them – the Kurds could return to their original villages in the mountains. My anxiety had gone. I had a plan.

I needed to persuade the Brigadier that David Nabarro's 'way stations' concept was not just the best, but the only solution. As a former soldier, I had some credibility at headquarters, but it was nearly a decade since my experience in Cambodia and Uganda, and those working for the UN or NGOs were in any case viewed with caution by the Armed Forces. The Royal Marines considered them to be yoghurt-knitting do-gooders, a view they were not shy of expressing. Fortunately the Brigade Commander and Chief of Staff were enthusiastic about the idea. Within hours, plans were being made.

Getting the refugees to leave the mountains was easy enough, but shelter now became the critical issue. I asked for 50,000 tents and within twenty-four hours, C-130 Hercules were landing at the airfield loaded with family tents. The Royal Marines distributed all 50,000 in ten days.

Many of the refugees wanted to return to Dohūk, a few kilometres outside the Safe Haven, which was now held by the Peshmerga, Kurdish irregular troops. Typhoid was endemic amongst the refugee population, so there would certainly be some cases in the coming days. It was important that Dohūk had a functioning hospital. Travelling around the Safe Haven was a problem, as initially we were obliged to use military transport. It was considered safer for vehicles to travel in pairs, so there was a two-vehicle rule, which was complicated to organise and a burden on the Royal Marines. So I asked Neil Coffee, the ODA fixer who ran our finances, to sort out some local transport. Neil was a master of improvisation, and soon had a fleet of twenty-five local taxis parked outside the headquarters. I felt that the risk was low and allowed our team to travel in the taxis unescorted.

Dohūk's hospital, like the town, had been completely abandoned. It needed a major clean-up and I gave the firefighters this task. Once this was done, I considered Dohūk safe enough to leave a team of nurses there overnight. As Dohūk was outside the brigade's area of responsibility we were now on our own and could not expect automatic support if things went wrong. My assessment was clearly wrong; on the second day fighting broke out in the town.

I asked the firefighters to accompany me to Dohūk to collect the nurses. To my astonishment I was met with folded arms and a refusal. I was dumbfounded. I gave them five minutes to be in the cars or be on the next plane home to the UK. We drove to Dohūk in stony silence. When we arrived there seemed to have been a fairly minor skirmish with Iraqi troops south of the town. Morale was high amongst the nurses, who did not feel that they had been in any immediate danger, quite a contrast to the reluctance of the firefighters. In Cambodia and Uganda I had seen astonishing bravery from all the civilians involved. These firefighters, however, were not humanitarians and the acceptable level of risk for them was clearly different.

David Nabarro's deployment of a hundred civilians was a response to a difficult problem. It would have been impossible for the humanitarian agencies to deploy quickly enough to deal with a problem of this magnitude during the war. Yet the NGOs had ridiculed the use of troops to do what they considered was their job. Without them, the only answer was for Overseas Development Administration to become operational. The firefighters were recruited because they were thought to be practical people and the Home Office could organise it relatively easily. The engineers and fitters were meant to deal with water and sanitation, but for much of their time in Northern Iraq they lacked the necessary equipment. Yet they were very resourceful and managed to get damaged infrastructure to work, which was almost more valuable. The doctors and nurses were obviously vital to run the clinics across the Safe Haven now the Iraqi government facilities had been abandoned. Managing this group was challenging, especially the doctors, who were more accustomed to issuing instructions than receiving them.

Once the tents had been distributed, the refugee population dispersed rapidly back to the villages they had been expelled from by force some years earlier, and where not a house was left standing. Ugly heaps of concrete with protruding reinforcing bars were all that remained, but the Kurds were happy to be back. Small groups of white tents began to appear across the mountains of Kurdistan, and in every settlement, there were radiant smiles. Now it was safe for the inhabitants of Dohūk to return, 170,000 Kurds made the journey from the border in a single weekend.

We now had the task of feeding the dispersed population. CARE International had opened a warehouse in the town of Zakhu and I flew there. The idea of military personnel being involved in humanitarian work was viewed with suspicion, but CARE's director was prepared to let us have the food. Distribution, organised by the brigade, was not going to be difficult. Half a million Kurds were dispersed throughout the Safe Haven and the danger of waterborne disease was no longer critical. Kurdistan has bountiful spring water, so at least one of the four basic needs was easily met. By the end of the second week, food was being distributed to all parts of the Safe Haven and mobile medical clinics were visiting the newly-tented settlements. Morale was high now the Kurds were safe from military attack and back in their home villages.

With the humanitarian situation now stabilised, the political issues became increasingly obvious. Both Iran and Turkey were suspicious of the encouragement the Safe Haven gave to Kurds living in their countries, who nursed a long-term political ambition to have their own state. Millions of Kurds were living in Turkey, Iran and Iraq, and there was potential for trouble now this part of Northern Iraq was no longer under the control of Baghdad. All the government's Arab employees had fled when the Coalition forces had entered Northern Iraq. Without them, I needed help from the Kurds in the Safe Haven to provide some form of administration. It was inconceivable that Kurdistan would ever again be governed from Baghdad. Initially, I encouraged a fledgling administration to help with water and sanitation, health and infrastructure repair. To achieve this, ODA provided funds and some vehicles that were received enthusiastically. Things moved quickly, and the Brigade Commander's Political Adviser, a senior diplomat, hinted that things might be moving a little *too* quickly. Given the political sensitivity, I got the impression from the Foreign Office that I might be exceeding my brief. But whatever they thought in London, it was too late; the semi-autonomous Kurdish region of Iraq had been born.

I was given a room next to the Commander's accommodation in an unfinished airport building. I had supper every evening with him and Rob Fry, Chief of Staff. The views across the mountains were fabulous and the conversation was always lively. It was the first time that they had done anything like this and they were excited by the challenges. Unlike many servicemen I met over the next few years, who saw humanitarian work as 'blunting their swords', Andy and Rob were very prescient and saw it as the future now that the Cold War was over.

After three weeks, the Kurds asked for food and relief items for villages east of the Safe Haven. They were able to deliver these supplies in their own trucks, they said. I had no objection in principle, but thought it prudent to make an assessment. I set off the next day in a couple of battered Toyotas with Peshmerga bodyguards who loved posing with their AK47s and artistically draped machine gun belts. We were stopped by a band of Kurds whose body language and gesticulations were anything but friendly. Exchanges became heated until one of them cocked his weapon. It was time to intervene. I stood between the antagonists, calling through my interpreter for calm, and was eventually able to get to the bottom of the dispute. They were Kurds, but from a different clan, and they claimed some were getting a greater share of humanitarian assistance than others. This was an argument I had heard many times before, but it was fascinating to see that even with the Iraqi Army only twenty kilometres to the south, local disputes were never far from the surface.

A month had now passed and it was horribly hot, with temperatures soaring to 50°C by midday. We were at an elevation of 4,000 feet, making it mandatory for everyone to drink a litre of water at lunchtime. Back at Brigade Headquarters, I organised the food convoy, but when I told the US servicemen in charge of Sersink airfield that the Peshmerga would be coming in their own trucks to collect it, they were deeply unhappy. I carefully explained the situation to the Colonel, who looked confused and asked, "Are they the goddam Shiites?" Kurds are Sunnis and the Shiites were a thousand kilometres south of us. We were clearly not in Kansas anymore.

The Turks had been unhappy since the creation of the Safe Haven, but at least the Kurds on the Turkish side of the border had all returned to Iraq.

The NGOs working there were going home, and one of them gifted us several tons of medical supplies. I sent a Chinook to collect them, but as soon as the aircraft landed the crew were thrown into jail by the Turks for failing to observe customs regulations. My satellite telephone was glowing as I spoke to Stephen Evans, Head of the Political Section at the British Embassy in Ankara, who had to unscramble a most delicate situation and deal with the diplomatic fallout.

Now that the brigade objectives had been met, political pressure was building for the brigade to withdraw, and the headquarters was making complicated drawdown plans. My plan for the civilians was a slightly more sophisticated version of "Everybody on the bus on Friday night", but this was upgraded to flying out by Chinook helicopter. With the ramp down everybody was able to get sensational photographs of the mountains of what now was the semi-autonomous Kurdish region of Iraq. We had been there only months, but given what had been achieved it felt like a year.

★★★

So soon after the end of the Cold War, and being such a departure from the fighting the troops had spent their careers training for, the operation was much discussed in military circles. Soon after returning to the UK, I was asked to join the Royal Marines for a presentation at the British Army's Staff College in Camberley. The progressives saw huge merit in what had been achieved, but the dinosaurs maundered on about 'blunting their swords'. The humanitarian agencies were not convinced. They were concerned about the concept of neutrality, an argument that would dominate the next ten years. Humanitarian work had expanded hugely in just a decade, and it was now possible to forge a career in it. Military involvement suddenly looked very threatening. In Uganda, I had seen what the French Army had achieved with two helicopters in a single week. The military had the airlift, radios, vehicles, fuel and organisation. UK taxpayers' money was being used for something which was without doubt extremely valuable now the Cold War was over. From my own point of view, I had learnt how the headquarters worked, and could implement a humanitarian programme using every component of a brigade or division. It was extraordinary what could be achieved in such a short space of time.

Back in the UK, the situation in Iraq still dominated the news. Deploying 3 Commando Brigade into Northern Iraq was one thing; withdrawing the force was another, and politically complicated now expectations amongst the Kurds were so high. In London, David Nabarro was working on a face-saving plan that would involve a return to Iraq, on a joint UN-EU mission to find ways of supporting the Kurds while British troops withdrew from the Safe Haven. I was asked to join him.

This time we flew on a UN charter flight to a military airfield outside Baghdad. Everyone was tense as, officially, the war had only ended weeks before and we were not certain how we would be received. At least I was travelling on a UN passport, not a British one, but even the UN had not remained untouched by the conflict, having been involved with unsuccessful attempts to resolve the dispute over Kuwait before the war. Unsurprisingly, we found the airfield severely damaged. Wrecked aircraft lay everywhere, but it was the hardened shelters that caught my attention; each one had been hit by a bomb that had penetrated the roof, striking the jet fighter stored inside dead centre. All that remained was the nose cone and the tail, with nothing between them. As we drove to the hotel in Baghdad, it was a similar story – the majority of buildings remained untouched, yet every now and then one had been destroyed. I had heard of smart bombs, but this was the first time I had seen the astonishing precision of these air strikes.

It was difficult to believe the country had just lost a war. Baghdad was full of traffic and I was impressed by the friendliness of the Iraqis at the hotel. Our team was a strange mix. We were led by a Norwegian working for UNHCR, charming, experienced and relaxed, all qualities he was going to need on this mission. There were two French diplomats, she unfriendly, he taciturn; they were deeply unconvincing as diplomats and the finger of suspicion pointed to other interests. Besides David and myself, there was an Italian official from the EU, clever and pugnaciously anti-British. It did not seem an ideal combination and they were not comfortable travelling companions in immediately post-war Iraq. Our group really needed a sense of humour – whatever we started out with was soon exhausted.

The mission was to travel north to Halabja, Sulaymaniyah, Said Sadiq and Kirkuk, to carry out an assessment of humanitarian needs along the Iranian border and the mountains east of the Safe Haven. Our two UN Toyotas were shadowed by Iraqi secret police, which caused anxiety to everyone except the French, who remained impassive. I was not concerned, as I felt the Iraqis did not seem to have much appetite for more trouble and needed the UN now the war had been lost.

As we drove north through the flat desert of the Euphrates and Tigris plain, we passed a division of Iraqi troops deployed in the desert, their guns pointing forlornly towards the British positions to the north. We arrived in Said Sadiq and Halabja. The Halabja chemical attack took place in 1988, killing thousands of Kurdish civilians and injuring many thousands more. It was a key event in turning world opinion against Saddam Hussein.

At a border crossing point into Iran we witnessed a brisk trade in looted Iraqi government equipment. Bulldozers, graders, government trucks and a mass of other improbable items were parked in the mountain passes waiting for customers in Iran. The large number of Kurds who were now returning from Iran to Kurdistan surprised me.

Each night we discussed what measures the UN and EU could put in place to support the displaced Kurds. The military Coalition was looking for a generous package of measures to help them and to mitigate what might otherwise appear as betrayal once the troops started to withdraw from the Safe Haven. It was to be a UN programme funded by the EU, and our job was to make recommendations as to what these measures should be. The Kurds' expectations of what might be achieved were running high. The humanitarian needs we saw along the border were not complicated; what was needed to support the Kurds was straightforward, yet our discussions each evening were anything but straightforward. From the beginning, it was difficult to get a consensus from our group on very much. Congeniality was turning to exasperation.

What the mission highlighted was the animosity and competition between the EU and the UN. Even relations between the French and the British at diplomatic level appeared to be strained. The EU official's view of the British did not help. He had a visceral dislike of the British and of landowners in particular; they, he claimed, would be the last to resist the European project. This was unhelpful, given the political pressure to formulate a plan that could be announced as the last troops left the Safe Haven.

It was fortunate that we had a Scandinavian as our team leader. Fifteen years older than the rest of us and with a gentle nature, he applied balm to the aggressive egos of this disparate group. Every evening, after exhausting travel, we struggled to find common ground. This was not helped by the French response to almost everything, which was *"Non"* – no further qualification was forthcoming or even thought necessary. Political pressure was building back in Europe and eventually a horrible compromise was cobbled together, which David and I could see was not going to meet the needs of our political masters. David decided that to sort this out he would have to return to Europe as quickly as possible with the others after we had met Jalal Talabani, a leading Kurdish politician, later that day. I would continue the assessment through Kurdistan to the Safe Haven to report on progress made since ODA withdrew six weeks earlier.

The following day we arrived at Talabani's house. Tall, with a commanding presence, he made a big impression and, as is usual with warlords, he was surrounded by a large entourage. His house was bustling with activity. Our meeting was surprisingly brief by Middle East standards, but it was clear that unity even amongst the Kurds was quite fragile.

After the meeting, I set off to the west of the country alone. There were very few British troops left in the Safe Haven, and NGOs had gradually been moving in as the troops withdrew. By dusk I reached Sulaymaniyah, a fabulous and ancient town perched on top of a rock where some of the original hundred ODA civilians had stayed on to complete their work. In all the settlements I passed through I heard misgivings about the imminent departure of the last British troops.

The next day I reached the most easterly position held by the Royal Marines. It really was a last outpost and in ten days they too would be gone. They had been tasked to get me out of Iraq and provided me with a grid reference for my helicopter pickup. I arrived at the spot; checking and double-checking the grid reference, I sat on some rocks waiting anxiously. It was now uncomfortably hot; the barren mountains were completely silent, with not a soul in sight.

My anxiety was misplaced. At exactly 2 pm the Lynx landed, and with the rotors still turning I jumped on board and was soon on my way to Diyarbakir. During the three-hour flight I realised they were going to drop me on the military side of the airfield. I had no entry stamp into Turkey in my passport, which might take some explaining to the immigration officials when I wanted to leave.

As soon as we landed, I was taken to the civilian terminal by military Land Rover. Instinctively I could feel something was not right. There had been an attack somewhere in the town by the Kurdistan Workers' Party (PKK). They were considered a terrorist organisation and police cars were dashing about at high speed. Inside the terminal the last flight to Ankara was about to close. I had only ten minutes and it took me nine of those to buy a ticket and check in. I spotted a public telephone and with a couple of coins managed to get through to the British Embassy and give my flight number before I was cut off. The embassy car was at Ankara to meet me and a room was booked at the Hilton. I was told that Stephen Evans, Deputy Head of Mission from the embassy, was expecting me for dinner. What a contrast it was to the last three weeks.

It felt even stranger to be back in London the next day, but not before an anxious moment in passport control at Ankara. The airport official, a grim-looking individual with a hare lip, thumbed the pages of my passport aggressively back and forth, looking for the elusive entry stamp, but lost interest when interrupted by a colleague. The stamp went down on an empty page. I was on my way home.

5

No Humanitarian Solution, Bosnia 1992-1993

Although my work in Uganda was engaging, fascinating and challenging, I did not view it as a career. During the ten years since 1981 I had got married, qualified as a doctor and had four young children, and I was now thirty-seven. But after working in Northern Iraq, my earlier view that working in humanitarian relief was not a career was beginning to change.

Cambodia and Uganda had been run in an amateurish way, but once the Cold War was over the military had become interested and the scale of intervention was huge by comparison with a decade earlier. After Operation Safe Haven in Northern Iraq, it was inevitable that future humanitarian emergencies would involve direct government intervention.

I had been recruited by the British government for Iraq because, quite fortuitously, I had the right skills – I had been in the Armed Forces yet knew about humanitarian relief, something unusual at the time. The armed services were traditionally prejudiced against 'yoghurt knitters', but they considered me, as a former soldier, one of their own. Now that I was being paid, I saw there might be a humanitarian career for me after all.

★★★

It was obvious, in retrospect, that after the end of the Cold War in 1989 the Balkans was going to be the flash point. The area had been a diplomatic headache in the 19th century and a political problem held in aspic since World War II by the firm hand of Marshal Tito, then President of Yugoslavia.

That firm grip had been relinquished on his death in 1980 and now, twelve years later, local animosities resurfaced.

If the EU had promised Yugoslavia economic support in 1989, as the Soviet empire collapsed, things might have been different. The economic collapse was bad enough; the political one was worse. The EU reacted to events in the Balkans as they unfolded, yet with so much historical dirty laundry it was difficult to see how the EU could have been proactive. The Croats, being fellow Roman Catholics, had been favoured by the Austrians during the Austro-Hungarian Empire and had managed their agricultural estate in the Balkans in the 19th century. Britain and the Serbs had once been allies. The Ustasha Croat fascists had supported the Nazis, and the Greeks did not recognise Macedonia as a separate country. It was an unpropitious start.

Religious animosity dominated everything. The Serbs were Orthodox Christians, the Croats Roman Catholics. All were southern Slavs, but some had retained their land in exchange for converting to Islam under the Ottoman Empire and thus were hated by the others. The mixture of Serb, Croat, and Muslim populations varied in each country that made up the former Yugoslavia. The first outbreak of violence began between the Croats and Serbs in 1991, in what was to be the Croatian War of Independence. The EU's response was to send in an unarmed European Community Monitoring Mission (ECMM), consisting of a mere seventy-five field individuals with headquarters in Zagreb. To reinforce the concept of neutrality they were given white uniforms, which unfortunately invited ridicule. By 1992, the Yugoslav People's Army (JNA) had ceased combat operations in Croatia and the war moved to Bosnia. Its capital, Sarajevo, was surrounded by the JNA and 1.5 million civilians were cut off behind the front lines.

Since returning from Iraq a year earlier I had been working in the Accident and Emergency Department at Cheltenham General Hospital. Each night on television, I watched events unfolding in Bosnia. I wondered if anything we had learnt in Northern Iraq about protecting civilian populations during conflict might be applicable there. David Nabarro clearly thought so, and I was soon called to a meeting at ODA in London to meet Andy Bearpark, the new Head of the Information and Emergency Aid Departments.

As I arrived, the receptionist was having an animated conversation with someone else. I was going to be late for my meeting, so I bypassed her and found my own way to Andy's office. "How the hell did you get up here?" was his first comment, followed by, "Well, I suppose if you can't get round the security in this building there's not much point sending you to the Balkans."

Only a few years older than me, Andy was everything I did not expect of a civil servant. Within minutes, it was obvious he was a stranger to convention. He was distinctly overweight and wore an earring, and his tie was loosened. Yet he had a striking intellect and a presence that dominated the room. I could detect subversion and not-so-restrained rebellion. Andy had been picked by Margaret Thatcher to be her Private Secretary. He, like her, was a chemist. Brilliant, practical and mischievous, he did not care a fig for protocol, standard operating procedures or rules in general, except one

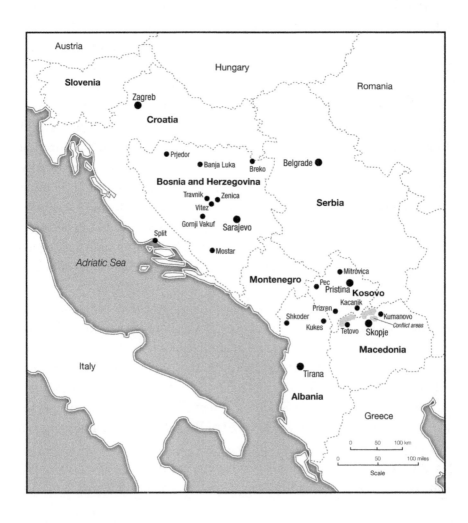

– he drew up precise and meticulous terms of reference and they had to be followed to the letter. I had found the perfect boss and Andy had exactly the right person to implement his programmes.

I was to leave for Croatia, again with David Nabarro and I had to find the best way for the British government to support the large numbers of Internally Displaced People (IDPs) in Bosnia. Ethnic cleansing created increasing numbers each week, as could be seen nightly on television, and Lynda Chalker, the Minister for Overseas Development, was under pressure to do something. We had an interminable day of meetings at the British Embassy in Zagreb. Bryan Sparrow, the British Ambassador in Croatia, was a considerate man with a huge knowledge of the Balkans; I liked him immediately. He had worked in Belgrade before, and spoke Serbo-Croat. The British Embassy was one of our 'broom cupboard' budget embassies introduced in 1989 to cope with the large number of 'new' countries that suddenly needed representation after the collapse of the Soviet Union.

After our meetings, David and I flew to Sarajevo in neighbouring Bosnia in a C-130 Hercules that was already delivering humanitarian assistance across the border. We flew south-west from Zagreb following the Croatian coastline to the city of Split to avoid overflying large parts of Bosnia under Serb control. From Split the plane headed into Bosnia. For the last fifteen minutes of our descent into Sarajevo we were asked to put on our borrowed body armour.

As the rear ramp lowered the scene at the airport was lively. The Serbs in the mountains were firing on the city from the east side, the Soviet 152mm shells alarmingly loud on impact. Machine gun rounds from somewhere else were hitting the terminal building, and I could hear windows shattering. From inside the aircraft I watched a forklift driver unloading pallets and later heard that he had been hit by a bullet and died instantly. As David and I walked down the ramp, striding towards us came a striking young woman in a blue UN flak jacket with a daffodil tucked into her blue military helmet. "I'm Amra, from the UNHCR office, and you must be Gilbert," she said with a lovely smile. No one paid any attention to the shelling and shooting; it was clearly bad form even to flinch when a shell exploded nearby. The noise and chaos was very disorientating and it was soon an obvious part of daily life in Sarajevo. We set off for the Postal, Telephone and Television (PTT) building in an unarmoured UN Toyota. Amra said, "Better wind down your windows. There'll be a lot of shooting, and if any bullets hit the windows the broken glass might cause us injury." We drove down a deserted and ruined suburban street from the airport to Sarajevo city centre; this was the infamous Sniper Alley where during the Bosnian War travellers were fired on by snipers from the high-rise buildings that lined it.

The houses were badly damaged by the fighting and abandoned; there was not a person in sight. Burnt-out cars and rubble lay in the road. It was a short and frightening journey, but one I was going to have to make every week for the next six months. As we came to a junction on the dual carriageway, a sniper started shooting in our direction. Again, no one else in the vehicle seemed remotely frightened. I admired their composure and robust attitude but wondered if I had what it took to work in this terrifying city.

Ten minutes later, we arrived at the PTT building, a concrete lump with commanding views over the city. It was the headquarters of the French troops and housed the UN office. Inside it certainly seemed a lot safer, not from the shelling, but at least from small arms fire, and it was a comfort that the UN staff were cheerful and friendly. Their operations room was bustling with activity and the attitude of everyone working there seemed at odds with the calamitous situation around us. An HF radio sat on a central trestle table, receiving reports from field officers out in the city. The concrete floor was scattered with foldable chairs and cardboard boxes full of equipment. Body armour and helmets lay where they had been discarded.

We were in for a tour of the city, something for which I felt a distinct lack of enthusiasm – I had seen enough of it for one day. But the French troops were waiting for us downstairs with an armoured vehicle. It was impossible to see where we were going; the only daylight came from the machine gunner's turret above us. I listened to the changing engine note and heavy tyres on the hot tarmac. My Samsonite briefcase bounced along the metal floor, just the product, I thought, for this type of mission. After about twenty minutes, we stopped and it was a relief to climb out into the bright sunshine. We were in the attractive old town on slightly higher ground at the north-east end of the city. The pantile roofs and kiosks in this charming district were still intact, but I could see the damage, sometimes severe, in the streets below us. Artillery shells landed somewhere in the city every few minutes.

The UNHCR Field Officer bombarded us with a multitude of facts, which boiled down to 1.5 million people being cut off by fighting, a shortage of food and everything else, and though the August sun was beating down a hard winter was only six weeks away. The big concern was the power supplies for heating and cooking, now under the control of the Serb forces. My previous experience had been in developing or mid-income countries. This was a developed country in Europe, yet the problems were the same: no access to water, sanitation, food, shelter or medical services. The response was going to be very different, as was the scale. In Cambodia and Uganda there were only a few hundred thousand beneficiaries. In Iraq, there had been 1.2 million, but my immediate concern had been only 500,000. In central Bosnia alone there were 1.5 million people. Urban populations are especially vulnerable; even a city of 250,000 requires a minimum of 500 tons of life support every day. The humanitarian organisations had simply never been exposed to such an emergency, and the scale and the cost of running programmes in Europe would surprise everyone.

Sarajevo was a city of over 400,000 people, of which nearly 14,000 would die during the siege. The Serbs controlled the road access and electricity supplies, so the future looked bleak. Cut off road access and a major problem will emerge within twenty-four hours. Cut the electricity and the water pumps will stop and no one will be able to cook or keep warm.

David and I flew back to Zagreb. That evening in the bar at the Hotel Intercontinental, the scenes we had witnessed in Sarajevo seemed a long way away. Yet the fighting was only fifty kilometres from where we were sitting. I was to stay at this hotel for six months. It was built in the 1970s as one of Zagreb's leading hotels. The war had been good for trade and occupancy stood at one hundred per cent. Men dressed in battle fatigues made up a large proportion of the guests. Army boots were wearing out the carpets and there were no plans for their replacement. In the basement restaurant, a band played melancholic Balkan music that captured the tragedy of the moment. Meanwhile in the lifts I had the opportunity to enjoy *Peer Gynt* on loop every single day. My room had the standard international fit-out in brown and beige, a prominent television, a king-size bed and a mattress that had not been replaced since the hotel was built. However, it was very comfortable; this was guilty luxury.

Lying in bed unable to sleep, I stared into the dark, thinking about Sarajevo. The town clock across the street struck three. I realised that in Cambodia, Uganda, Iraq and now Bosnia, despite caring for those I had come to help, I did not do empathy very well. Sent away to boarding school at the age of seven, I was part of the last generation to embrace the stiff upper lip. In my head I could still hear the platoon sergeant screaming at us in the Guards Depot, after someone had been foolish enough to say he 'felt' about something, "You what! You *felt*? Get feelings out of your head and replace them with something better. Get a grip of yourself!" In Cambodia, I had observed that one of the problems with humanitarian work was that people's actions were based on feelings rather than reason. Yet, the problem here was very different. Only months earlier these people had been living normal European lives, chatting amicably to the neighbours who now wished to kill them. In South East Asia, Africa and Iraq we had been almost observers. Now we, the humanitarians, were part of the conflict, wrapped up in it emotionally as well, and this would influence the course of the war.

David returned to London, but I flew south to Split where the humanitarian agencies delivering aid to Bosnia were based. Split was a charming Mediterranean port, with Diocletian's palace in the Old Town. The view from the airport, though, was blighted by hideous tower blocks constructed in the 1970s. This was the day I realised the humanitarian response used in developing countries was not going to work here in Bosnia. I had been used to the absence of telephones, and towns so small you could find the aid agencies on foot. Split was a busy modern city with a population of 150,000, and trying to find the UN and NGO offices was a challenge. The other difference was cost. Most aid agencies had brought in staff from Africa to run their operations and were shocked to find that hotels, wages and fuel all cost many times what they were used to. The British government had already funded a fleet of delivery trucks and UNHCR was running convoys to Bosnia from Split. But the two-wheel-drive trucks, only built for tarmac roads, were inadequate for 14-hour journeys on appalling roads through the mountains to avoid the front lines.

Back in Zagreb, and Bryan Sparrow started the long and complicated process of teaching me about Balkan politics. He was deeply pessimistic about the direction of the war. I needed a vehicle, and within days a brand-new Land Rover Discovery was sent to me by ODA. I now needed an interpreter and, through a recommendation, I met Vesna. She was twenty-six, had studied as a chemical engineer, and was interested in philosophy. This was just as well, as many of our journeys lasted more than ten hours and a philosophical approach to everything was a bonus. With a car and an interpreter, I was ready for my first assessment mission. My destination was the UN office in Vitez, Central Bosnia.

Climbing away from Split, with the Mediterranean glittering behind us, the extensive limestone mountains looked fabulous. Bosnia was equally beautiful, but the forests had a brooding sinister feel. All the checkpoints were similar: a scaffolding pole, an oil drum and a string of anti-tank mines strewn across the road, which were rather surprisingly kicked aside once one was allowed to pass. With a UN pass, there was never any question of not being allowed through a checkpoint, although on occasion there was quite a delay, especially if there was shelling ahead. Frequently, the soldiers at road blocks were drunk on slivovitz, and sometimes there were female soldiers at the checkpoints outside Sarajevo, where I sensed vindictive cruelty. It was always unpleasant. The tell-tale signs of trouble were burnt-out vehicles and a sentry crouching in a foxhole near the road. At one checkpoint, Vesna spoke to a very animated soldier. I asked her what was happening. She said, "It's OK if we're quick." Several burnt-out cars marked the passing of those who had not been quick enough. Giving the Discovery some encouragement we bounded forward and, on cue, someone started shooting, but we safely reached the forest beyond. Vesna remained remarkably relaxed.

I began to pick up ethnic signs as we travelled – women in Turkish trousers, smart suburban streets with newish cars, or solid Tito-era villages. Vesna was a talented linguist and spoke to the soldiers at each checkpoint in their local dialect. The language had become so divided that if there were two words for something, using the wrong word would be enough to get us into trouble. Vesna was a Croat, but I made sure that she had nothing with her that might betray this in Serb territory.

I was one of the very few foreigners travelling in Bosnia at the time and a magnet for intelligence gatherers back in Zagreb. The most expensive restaurant in Zagreb was a fish restaurant. If I was ever invited there, the conversation was predictable. I would say, "Just wait a moment while I go and get some cash," and the reply was always, "You won't need any cash tonight." It was never just dinner, but yet another interrogation.

In Africa, fuel management had been my great concern, and it became so once again. As there were no filling stations in Bosnia, we took jerry cans of diesel to get to Vitez and back. From time to time, the road was blocked by fighting and for several hours we would follow a track across the mountains.

Such detours made even the briefest journey a marathon. With winter approaching, the tracks would eventually become a sea of mud with a liberal coating of snow and ice. Maps were not particularly useful, but Vesna made up for the lack of them; in between discussing Hegel, she got directions from the locals. Evidence of ethnic cleansing was everywhere. Sometimes as we approached villages, we saw soldiers with jerry cans of fuel setting houses on fire. These were dangerous situations to witness. Villages where every house had been burnt were a melancholy sight, as were the families forced to flee, on tractors and trailers piled high with their possessions, to an uncertain future. It was also becoming clear that the ECMM was increasingly futile and that the ethnic cleansing would only be stopped by robust military force.

Towards the evening, we entered Zenica on the Bosna River. We had reached it without mishap, quite an achievement considering the minimal preparation and planning involved. Local knowledge had been our strong point and Vesna had been responsible for getting me there. I did wonder what her parents thought about her new job.

Zenica, an appallingly ugly Eastern Bloc city, was Bosnia's fourth-largest city and 40,000 people had been employed here in the steel industry before the war. Now the steelworks were silent. We stayed in a hotel Vesna knew in the city centre, which was a triumph of Soviet-style architecture, all concrete outside and grim dark brown panelling inside. The receptionist was, not surprisingly curious and brusque, but at least the hotel was open and there was something to eat. There had been high unemployment here since 1989 and Zenica had a reputation for crime, especially recycling cars stolen from EU countries.

The next day, there were no more front lines to cross. Vitez lay in a wide fertile valley that was still being farmed and was, by Bosnian standards, quite an attractive place. At the UN office, they were pleased to see us and we sat down for a long briefing session over Bosnian coffee. Increasing numbers of Muslim IDPs were arriving in the town of Travnik as they were ethnically cleared from the west. The supply of humanitarian assistance from Split was inadequate, electricity supplies were intermittent, and it was now September – winter would soon set in. It was clear that the relief operation, limited to a few flights a day into Sarajevo and a few convoys from Split, needed rethinking.

In Travnik we could hear the sound of shelling beyond the old town. Around 5,000 IDPs, mainly families with small children, were being housed in a former seminary. The sanitation was appalling and I was greeted by the smell several hundred metres before I arrived. Several thousand people were milling about or standing listlessly in small groups, tractors and trailers piled with possessions were everywhere, and mud coated everyone and everything. Through Vesna, the families talked about their experiences and more importantly their needs now they had reached safety – at least for now. Bit by bit I was beginning to understand the task before us; there would be limited opportunity to provide shelter, but the two deliverables were food and medicines. The volume required and the means of delivering them was going to require some thought. I had at least my first ideas for the British government's contribution.

We made our way back down to the coast and as we approached Croatia our mood lightened. She was good company with her sharp wit, chatting about her interest in philosophy and Albert Camus. It was rather apt, as we had recently passed deserted villages recently torched during the ethnic cleansing and driven through checkpoints manned by unwashed unshaven soldiers smelling of slivovitz. Back in Split, I dropped Vesna off and drove to the airport. I left the Discovery in the car park and caught the first flight back to Zagreb.

The Bosnian emergency was coordinated from the UN building in the Croatian capital. The Head of UNHCR, José María Mendiluce, was young and energetic, with good political skills and considerable charm. It was a fairly typical UN office, good at process, but I had my doubts about the vision. This was the first European humanitarian emergency for everyone since World War II. Except the local staff, they had experience only in developing countries, and I didn't think they really appreciated how different this was going to be. An additional problem was that this UN office dealing with Bosnia was actually in Croatia.

The European Commission Monitoring Mission was based at Hotel I in Zagreb, a quirky building near the city centre. After the Vance-Owen Plan ceasefire between Croatia and Serbia was signed on 2 January 1992, the white-suited monitors were deployed along 1,000 kilometres either side of the front line in Croatia. They had observed the ceasefire even though they were unarmed and it was dangerous work. The Mission consisted of soldiers, ex-soldiers and diplomats from EU countries and three other contributing nations. They had a reputation for competence and accurate reporting, which was vital to counter the rumours that generated so much of the violence. But once the war had moved to Bosnia, things were different; Bertram Borei, a monitor working for the Mission, was killed and the Mission was withdrawn. Their reputation had suffered as a result, and they were desperately trying to show they had a useful role now they were back in Croatia.

The United Nations Protection Force (UNPROFOR), the UN 'blue helmet' peacekeeping force in Croatia, deployed troops to Sarajevo in Bosnia. Colonel Mark Cook was sent out to command the British contingent of the UN troops in Croatia. The UK had committed a military ambulance unit and in charge of it was Major Vanessa Lloyd-Davies, the first female medical officer in the Household Cavalry. Mark and Vanessa were based near Zagreb International Airport and were helpful to me the moment I arrived in Croatia. I was staying, like many international staff, at the Intercontinental Hotel in Zagreb. The bar there became a meeting point every evening for those working in Bosnia and for journalists covering the war. From my base at the British Embassy, I did a daily round of meetings with the UN, ECMM and UNPROFOR. Political pressure was building for Britain to do more. So far, there were British trucks, drivers and a C-130 Hercules for the Sarajevo airlift. Only international truck drivers could cross the front lines in Bosnia and most had been recruited in the UK.

UNHCR's new plan for the winter of 1992–1993 was to be presented by Tony Land, their Chief of Operations, at the UN Military Headquarters near Zagreb airport. I joined Air Marshal Sir Kenneth Hayr, Deputy Chief of the Defence Staff, who had flown in for the meeting with Brigadier David Jenkins, the MoD's Director of Military Operations. Major General Philippe Morillon, the French Commander of UNPROFOR, made the opening remarks, then a Canadian staff officer – standing rather incongruously in front of a road map – started in good military fashion with the 'ground'. My confidence evaporated. At this point Major General Morillon walked up to the map and put his large hand on the Brčko corridor, a narrow strip of land along the southern bank of the Sava river north-east of Sarajevo, connecting the eastern and western part of Republika Srpska (the Bosnian Serb entity). This was an important military and civil supply line for western parts of the Republika Srpska during the war. "This is where I would like to deploy the British battalion," he said. There was a look of amazement on the faces of the British delegation and astonishment on mine.

Next, with consummate authority, Tony outlined the circuitous routes currently made by the convoys, and explained that the direct routes from Zagreb and Belgrade would allow the trucks to deliver the required tonnage on good roads. The snag was that the convoys intended to travel through areas of intense fighting, especially the Brčko corridor, and the UK was required to provide a battalion to protect them. For the three of us in the room who had actually been to Bosnia, it made no sense. This misguided UN mandate assumed peace, but there was no peace, which would present huge problems in the coming months. The meeting broke up unhappily, and the Air Marshal and the Brigadier left in haste to fly back to the UK. One American serviceman commented as we left, "Forget the seventy trucks – what you guys need to do is what you're doing, but with 500 trucks." He was right, but it was too late. Nothing we could do would change anything. Soldiers say that you never recover from landing on the wrong beach. Having the wrong mandate was just as bad.

★★★

I was invited to join a military reconnaissance to the Brčko corridor the following week. In the meantime I went back to Bosnia, under pressure from London to come up with a fresh package of measures to assist the civilian population. By now, I had developed a routine. I was collected every Thursday by an RAF Land Rover, which left for the airport as the clock struck 6 am. I flew into Sarajevo on a UK Special Forces C-130 Hercules. There I would pick up my Land Rover Discovery, which was looked after by the French military – I was always surprised to find it there in one piece. From the airport, I had to drive down Sniper Alley; there was no other route out, but despite the odd shot being fired at me I never came to any harm. I would finally return to Split for the Croatian Airlines flight back to Zagreb. The next week I would reverse the process.

At Split airport I saw an old man wearing a Highland Brigade tie, and gave him a hand down the high step from the airport bus. To my great surprise, it was the war hero and diplomat Sir Fitzroy Maclean, on his way to Zagreb to brief the British military reconnaissance team, which I had been invited to join. During World War II, he had been Winston Churchill's special envoy to the Yugoslav leader Tito. At the briefing, he warned us that the truth was often difficult to ascertain in the Balkans. In fact, he used rather stronger language.

At 6.30 am the next morning I was at the UNPROFOR camp near the airport with my sleeping bag, some food, a full tank of fuel and extra jerry cans of diesel. Surprisingly, no one was ready and even at 7 am the military team was still in some disorder. Lt Col Bob Stewart had clearly enjoyed an evening in Zagreb and was having difficulty getting out of his sleeping bag. He finally emerged, still in his suit – not quite what I was expecting. Eventually, we departed for Belgrade. Evidence of recent fighting was noticeable even on the motorway. Whole sections of the central safety barrier had been flattened by tanks. We passed a burnt-out motorway service station, and the countryside was deserted. Half an hour after the turn-off to Banja Luka, we turned south into Bosnia.

We arrived at a checkpoint on a small country road. A Serb soldier strode out cocking his Kalashnikov, and shouted at us. Although still early in the day, he appeared drunk. I had never approached a checkpoint with British soldiers in uniform, and this was dramatically different from my usual experience. Such uncompromising hostility dictated caution. However, I was not in charge and my enthusiastic companions, new to Bosnia, seemed oblivious to the danger. We were told to wait. Time passed. All of a sudden, a truck full of Serbian soldiers came round the corner at high speed; there was more shouting and pointing of Kalashnikovs. Happily, they were soon gone.

We remained at the checkpoint for several hours. Bob Stewart began to tell us what he would do in this situation if he had a couple of Warriors. I shuddered – I had managed to travel all over Bosnia as a civilian for the last month without any problems. A message finally came back from the Serb headquarters: *Ne* – No. We travelled back to Zagreb in rather a sombre mood. But at least we now knew what was not possible. Another reconnaissance on a more sensible route was planned.

The airlift had been increased over the weeks. Eighteen humanitarian flights now flew into Sarajevo every day. One afternoon I heard that a military transport carrier, a G222 belonging to the Italian Air Force, had been shot down near Sarajevo. Tony Land and I set off from Vitez to where we heard the aircraft had come down. By the time we arrived it was getting dark. We followed a column of white UNPROFOR armoured cars up the mountain, following forest tracks. After a few minutes, we saw blankets in the treetops and then a huge slash in the forest where the aircraft had destroyed hundreds of trees.

Armed men appeared in the twilight, some carrying weapons from World War II, none in uniform. They were almost certainly Serbs. They were angry, and one of them shouted aggressively at a UNPROFOR officer. His interpreter looked delicate and fragile among the men; tears ran down her face, and blonde hair spilled from under her helmet. Tony and I realised there was little we could do in the dark. There was virtually nothing left of the aircraft after the crash and no one could possibly have survived the subsequent fire. We walked silently back down the forest track to where we had left our vehicle. The war had taken a new and very dark turn.

★★★

I had known from the start that the humanitarian response to this emergency would be different from my experience in developing countries. I needed to rethink the four basic needs: water and sanitation, food, shelter and medical provision. Food was already being delivered. But this war was about where people lived, and providing shelter was going to be sensitive. Perhaps we could make the houses where people were living more habitable over the winter. The key to this would be the electricity supply and distribution network. Government medical services had almost collapsed. Even those clinics that were still functioning had neither drugs nor serviceable equipment. The drugs, too, were different from what we had been using in developing countries. Most had been supplied from the Soviet Union and often varied in quality. People here suffered from heart disease, diabetes and other chronic diseases like everywhere else in Europe. There was also an obvious need for anaesthetics and surgical supplies.

I came up with the idea of 'humanitarian infrastructure'. If we could repair vital electricity transformers, substations and water pumps, I suggested, we could deliver basic needs more efficiently. This was equally important for the medical sector too, where repairs to X-ray machines, autoclaves and hospital generators, or simply making sure the hospital had electrical power, were an essential part of healthcare delivery.

The World Health Organization (WHO) was responsible for the health sector, but unlike other UN humanitarian agencies, WHO is not operational, it merely advises governments. However, there was no longer a government in Bosnia. I got in touch with Andy Bearpark in London, who saw no difficulty in making WHO operational. To make matters easy for them, ODA would find the staff, vehicles and equipment and pay for them. Sir Donald Acheson, the UK's former Chief Medical Officer, was appointed Head of WHO for Bosnia. For him it was almost a leap too far from an ordered civil service to the disordered and uncivil world where he now was. To provide advice and help with operational matters he had the hugely competent Christopher Besse, Karen Brade and Tim Healing. WHO was now operational and Karen and Tim travelled extensively around Bosnia. They visited hospital directors and NGOs assessing medical needs and planning deliveries from the warehouse in Split. Given the intensity of the fighting, they were remarkably fearless.

The delivery of medical assistance across the front lines was a major challenge. The solution was to prepare boxes of medical equipment small enough to fit in a pickup truck and light enough to be carried by two people, so these were prepared for the most important medical specialities – surgery, general practice, obstetrics, and anaesthetics – others were added over time.

Urban water supplies were a major concern. With the mountains nearby some systems were gravity-fed; others depended on electrical power. Electricity supplies were also linked to the ability for people to heat their homes and cook, something the Red Cross had been concerned about since the beginning of the war.

In Zagreb, I was invited to a meeting where the Red Cross demonstrated an inexpensive and well-designed wood burner, which doubled as a cooker. The cooker appeared quite heavy, and I was reminded of the distribution of agricultural tools in Uganda. There had been tons of tools, yet their distribution was a modest task compared with delivering these stoves, which were never going to be the answer for the whole of Central Bosnia with its population of 1.5 million. It was a solution for a developing country, but Bosnia was a developed European country and electricity was needed for heating and cooking. We needed to be bolder and think about power stations.

I did some research before Andy came out to Zagreb the following week. There was a coal-fired power station at Kakanj and a hydroelectric power plant at Mostar, both producing very little electricity, due to a lack of spare parts and most of the workforce being either absent or away fighting. The nearby coal mine had exactly the same problem. Running power stations and coal mines was not normally the role of humanitarians, but Andy agreed straight away that we should tackle both problems. The Northern Ireland Electricity Board would be given a contract to support the power stations and a Nottingham coal-mining consultant would be employed to increase coal production. The concept of humanitarian infrastructure had come of age.

It was now late autumn and the roads were becoming increasingly dangerous for the ODA convoy drivers; the British drivers were never shy of telling me so, and much else besides. It was said that some of the drivers had been recruited on leaving prison in the UK. I do not know if that was true, but they were reliable and robust in the face of constant danger, and always seemed to meet all events with a great sense of humour. However, with winter approaching there was a bigger problem – it was going to be impossible to deliver enough food to Central Bosnia using the mountain routes. The direct route ran from the coast through Mostar. However, Mostar was under constant bombardment by the Serbs. There had been various incidents on the Mostar road, and the UN had since declared the road closed.

6

Breaking the Siege, Sarajevo 1992-1993

European leaders had invested much capital in the delivery of .
humanitarian assistance, which was being used as a substitute for robust
military action. This pathetic and pusillanimous approach encouraged talk
of a humanitarian solution to the problems of Bosnia. But as the crisis
deepened a solution to the conflict looked further away than ever. Autumn
was approaching, and it was obvious that we had to use the Mostar road to
reach Central Bosnia or the humanitarian intervention would fail. I had
tried diplomacy; now I had to resort to guerrilla warfare. I had an ally in
Tony Land, UNHCR Chief of Operations, who alone agreed with me.
We decided to drive the 179 kilometres down the road from Sarajevo to
the coast. I discussed it with Vesna, as I needed all the local knowledge I
could get. She did not see it being any more dangerous than other routes
we had already taken. Vesna was disappointed when I said she could not
come with us. I felt I could risk my life, but not hers on what was without
doubt a bold endeavour.

We put the UN flag on the Toyota and, with Tony at the wheel, we
set off at speed, considering this might reduce our chances of being hit,
though as humanitarians our biggest chance of being killed was in a road
traffic accident. The UN embargo had made such an issue of the Mostar
road that it held a special menace. Now we had the great sweep of the
abandoned highway completely to ourselves. During the months of disuse,
fallen branches and piles of leaves had accumulated along the route, and
we passed houses and occasionally entire villages that had been torched

during the ethnic cleansing, with burnt-out family cars still parked in front of burnt-out homes. Throughout the first hour we stared straight ahead, the tension sustained, both plagued with doubt about the wisdom of this venture.

Tony was definitely keeping the speed up, and the UN flag flapped frantically behind us. We had been travelling for around an hour and a half, and I calculated that at this rate we were more than halfway there. I did not really expect to be directly targeted by the Serbs, but I was expecting some intimidation. Perhaps this was just wishful thinking. I had to admit to myself that my usual insouciance had deserted me. We were both now silent; Tony was staring ahead at the empty highway and the diesel engine sounded uncomfortably loud. The road passed through a wooded area, where a rockfall from the cliffs was almost blocking the route.

I glanced at the map; we had passed the mid-point and I was secretly counting the kilometres. If we could just prove the road, it would be a triumph. Mostar came into view. What a sight it was! Heavy shelling had knocked the heart out of the city and the hospital on the east side of the town was on fire. On we went, past some dreary blocks of flats, until we were on the home straight and heard that familiar 4x4 hum of tyres on tarmac. We were too close to the mountain to be seen by the Serb artillery above us. Tony began to look relaxed, and it was infectious. I stopped thinking about the explaining I would have to do had this all gone terribly wrong. We could see the border post ahead; and I felt we deserved a chequered flag.

At the coast, we turned north and within an hour were back at the UNHCR office in Split. When Tony rather proudly announced the time we had left to go to Sarajevo, he got a curious look – the route over the mountains took fourteen hours, and we were back in just over three. Our news was greeted with glacial hostility and my heart sank. We had done the assessment, but we heard the next day that the UN in New York had decided that there was to be no change in policy. It was deeply disappointing, as 1.5 million people depended on the Mostar road being open. There had to be another way.

When I got back to Zagreb, Bryan Sparrow told me that Baroness Chalker, Minister for Overseas Development, was coming out to Zagreb and I was to organise a programme for her. I was a little apprehensive, remembering that when I was in the army, the Visits Officer always got the short straw. If anything went wrong, the person organising the programme got the blame. I talked to Andy Bearpark in London, and the brief became clearer. She wanted to see the ODA convoy teams, but essentially she wanted to go to Bosnia. I had exactly what I needed. "What about a little trip down the Mostar road?" I would go on a recce and see what might be possible.

I picked up Vesna in Split. She never showed any surprise at my plans, and in all the months we travelled together she never showed any sign of fear; for her, danger was something to be looked at statistically. We took the road over the mountains and descended towards Mostar from the west. I needed to know the journey time for the Minister's visit and find something for her to see in Mostar. As we approached the Neretva River, we met two young soldiers in sinister black uniforms. I asked Vesna to get directions from them. She did so reluctantly and there was an animated discussion. We were directed to cross the river by the Mostar hydroelectric dam. I noticed that the buildings at each end had been hit repeatedly by heavy machine gun fire, but we crossed without incident and I thought no more about it.

The hospital in Mostar was badly damaged by a mortar bomb and the fire that Tony and I had seen the previous week. Smoke was still rising from one end of the building, and the operating theatre was now in the basement. I asked the hospital's medical director what he needed, expecting his priority to be surgical supplies and reliable electricity. I was surprised when he asked for an ophthalmic laser. He was an ophthalmologist and this was number one on his dream wish list. I found over the years that this type of request was not uncommon. Fear of failure, fear of exhaustion and fear of death for months on end can distort one's priorities. I put together a simple list of drugs and surgical supplies for him. We did not linger; Mostar was being mortared and shelled intermittently all day.

Lynda Chalker was to have one day of political meetings in Zagreb, then I was going to take her on a field trip to Bosnia. Inevitably the rumbles began from the Foreign and Commonwealth Office (FCO) in London, that infamous hotbed of cold feet. Was this sensible? Was I sure? With only days to go, the rumbles became increasingly frequent and did not stop until midnight the day before the trip.

A ministerial visit was a completely new experience for me. But I learnt very quickly how to manage the entourage, journalists, whirlwind meetings and hectic transfers from one place to the next. Lynda Chalker was warm, friendly and approachable. The first people she wanted to see were the British truck drivers who had been driving into Bosnia for several months, and her appreciation for all they had done was genuine and touching. She fully understood the importance of the Mostar road and Andy briefed her again on the risk she was about to take. She was determined to do it, given the political implications of Sarajevo falling to the Serbs.

We took off for Split at half past six the following morning in the C-130 Hercules with our vehicles in the back. On landing, we drove towards Mostar with a Croatian police escort. The two police officers looked unhappy at the thought of going near the Bosnian border, and one of them was sweating despite the cool autumn morning. The journalists followed in a coach and were surprisingly subdued, whether by the early start or the destination it was hard to tell. When we finally started along the road to the Mostar hydro dam the police made their excuses and headed home at high speed. We navigated the oil drums and lumps of concrete of a former checkpoint and then we were on the dam itself. The coach was in trouble; the concrete step onto the dam was too high. For what seemed like several minutes, it rocked backwards and forwards, unable to proceed. Then the shooting began.

It was not that close, but the journalists on the coach were not war correspondents, and they were horribly exposed. After several attempts the coach mounted the concrete step, but still had to cross the dam, which it did with unsurprising haste. We reached the town and stopped at the hospital for twelve minutes, quite long enough in Mostar. We could hear the sound of shells landing in the distance. The war-damaged hospital gave the journalists almost too many photo opportunities and Andy had to use strong language to get them back on the coach. Then we made for the Mostar road. As we turned right to the coast more shots rang out, but it was only a short dash to the Croatian border.

We had done it. A British Minister of State had driven down the Mostar road and it would be difficult now for the UN to keep it closed. The UN also knew full well that the UK was paying the lion's share of the cost of the trucking operation, so they were not in a position to be stubborn. We had a diplomatic dinner to get to in Zagreb, so we hastened back to Split, drove onto the apron, straight up the ramp and into the waiting C-130 Hercules. The crew were still tying the vehicles down as we taxied out. We made it to the dinner, everyone was euphoric, and some of us drank rather more than diplomatic quantities of wine in celebration. During the dinner, I wondered if there were a real possibility that Lynda Chalker could have been killed. How dangerous had it been really? All the locals knew about our trip and I just didn't think it was in the interest of the Serbs to kill a British Minister. I asked Vesna about the soldiers in black uniforms we had seen on our recce and her reluctance to tell me what they had said. She was quiet for a moment. "Ustasha," (Croat Fascists) she replied. "One hundred and three people have lost their lives crossing that hydro dam."

★★★

The outcome of Lynda Chalker's visit could not have been better. Not only was the Mostar road open, the trucking fleet was to be expanded with bigger and better vehicles, and a new maintenance workshop would be established at Metković on the Croatian border. Doug Houston, a senior ODA representative, was sent out as First Secretary to help me now the power projects had started, which Japan and Germany had joined the UK in funding. Doug had worked for ODA in the Caribbean and Andy thought him ideally suited to the challenges in Bosnia. Doug was indeed the perfect choice. His first job was to find a way of getting 100,000 detonators through no less than three front lines to the coal mine at Kakanj. They were delivered without a hitch. He also became the embassy's point of contact with the Cheshire Regiment, now based in Vitez, and became popular with all of them.

It was now winter and the unsalted roads, covered in snow and ice, made driving conditions alarming. Off-road sections, used as detours around front lines, sometimes took hours, as the mountain tracks were steep and muddy. There was a big debate about using armoured Range Rovers instead of unarmoured 'soft-skinned' vehicles. These very expensive vehicles weighed over three tons, which made them a hazard on untreated roads, particularly going downhill. They only managed a few thousand kilometres between services as the brakes quickly wore out. On balance, we were probably safer in the standard vehicles as – surprisingly – road traffic accidents were always the biggest hazard. I was happy not to be given one.

A few weeks later, I dropped in to see Lt Col Bob Stewart in Vitez. The Cheshire Regiment had been deployed for some weeks and it was a

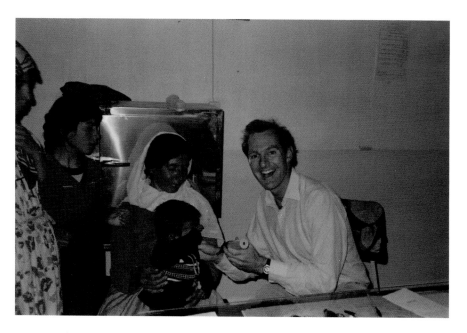

Chapter 3 – With Kurdish refugees at the medical clinic, Iran 1991

Chapter 4 – Kurdish children back in their village, N.Iraq 1991

Chapter 4 – Sartorial elegance, Kurdish Peshmerga, Iraq 1991

Chapter 4 – The Kurds return to their historic villages with the tents,
N.Iraq 1991

Chapter 4 – I set off the next day in a couple of battered Toyotas
with Peshmerga bodyguards, Iraq 1991

Chapter 5 – Following a Danish APC along Snipers Alley, Sarajevo 1992

Chapter 6 – 103 people died trying to cross the notorious Mostar hydro dam,
Bosnia 1992

Chapter 6 – The forbidding Mostar Road, Bosnia 1992

Chapter 6 – We passed burnt houses and occasionally entire villages
that had been torched during the ethnic cleansing, Bosnia 1992

Chapter 8 – My ActionAid Land Rover on the Somali rangelands, 1993

Chapter 9 – Some local residents appear unconcerned
despite the volcanic eruption, Montserrat 1995

Chapter 10 – Flying in a Lynx helicopter to authorise projects, Bosnia 1996

Chapter 10 – Normality indicators, 6 weeks after Dayton,
cut flowers on sale in Croat, Bosnia 1996

Chapter 10 – Wall art in Bosnia, 1996

Chapter 11 – Flying with MAF, the point of no return
was the starting point, Irian Jaya 1997

Chapter 12 – With Terje Skavdal assessing relief needs, Northern China 1998

welcome change having the British base in Central Bosnia. Bob had already visited the town of Maglaj, and was planning to return with a Bedford 4-ton truck full of humanitarian supplies. He invited Doug and me to join him the following day. Maglaj was cut off by Serb forces, but by having the river Bosna on one side they had managed to hold out for months. Because of the fighting, the town could only be reached by a single road that passed through a long tunnel, and then ran for quarter of a mile along the river Bosna, fully visible to the Serbs on the other side. When we arrived at the end of the Maglaj tunnel, the scene was enough to make even the boldest apprehensive. More than half a dozen burnt-out vehicles lined the open road ahead of us. Beyond, we could see Maglaj in the distance.

Without hesitation Bob leant out of his Land Rover window and shouted back to us, "You'll be fine if you keep your speed up!" He was right. We roared out of the tunnel like a cavalry charge, intent on getting across the open ground as quickly as possible. The Land Rovers speeding ahead, the truck doing its best to keep up at the rear. After some very long minutes, we were in Maglaj, where we spent a couple of hours while the truck was unloaded. It was a dangerous place. The Serbs fired mortars sporadically across the river all day every day, part of a deliberate programme of attrition to wear down the occupants until they would finally leave. This was the reality of ethnic cleansing.

I met a woman sitting on the step outside her badly damaged home; her two young children looked at me warily and shyly from inside the door. "You are very welcome here," she said in perfect English. My surprise must have been obvious; she smiled. "And we need you – they will bomb this place until we go." As if to avoid the obvious question about her fluent English, she explained, "I have visited England. And I worked as a teacher in Sarajevo before the war." A mortar landed somewhere in the town, but she remained unmoved. "Every day, every day... this is our life now." I asked about her family. "They are in Sarajevo. I haven't seen my parents for nearly a year. My husband has gone to fight, but he is an engineer – what does he know about fighting?" Another mortar fell, closer this time. She pulled her children protectively towards her. We chatted for another half an hour about the situation in Maglaj, the prospects for her family in Bosnia, her worries for her children, and relations she had not heard from for nearly a year. There had been no running water here for several weeks, and although clearly someone used to high standards, she looked exhausted and unkempt. She shook my hand as I left. It was if she did not want to let me go.

I do not think anyone thought we could do much to help these people, yet the risk of getting into Maglaj had been worth it. The Cheshires had unloaded the supplies and planned to return with more. As we approached the tunnel, a small blue truck overtook us at high speed. Bob took a right fork in the road, which took us on a more circuitous route behind the hill. I said to Doug, "Looks like Bob's lost his bottle since that gallop earlier." I had hardly finished speaking when the Serbs opened fire at the small blue truck. The first mortar landed a mere fifty metres behind it. Thankfully, we were soon safely behind the hill. Bob reminded me thereafter to respect his military judgement.

★★★

The north of Bosnia had yet to receive much, if any, humanitarian assistance. The large Muslim city of Tuzla was particularly vulnerable as the road had been cut off and there was only one route into the city. Before the war, the 120-kilometre journey from Sarajevo would have taken two and a half hours. Now, on tracks through snow-covered mountains, it could take seven. No one knew what the situation was like there; I decided to find out.

When I announced our mystery tour of the week to Vesna, she said, as she always did, "That's fine." Had I announced we were off to South America she might have said the same. It was easy to have an accident on these winter field trips. Soon after heading north from Sarajevo through the mountains we came to a checkpoint of the 'OK if you're quick' variety. I drove too fast across the exposed clearing, and we slid sideways down a steep bank, making two perfect turns around the vehicle's midpoint just missing two trees. Without damage or becoming stuck, I regained the track. Vesna was not impressed. Enemy action was one thing; my driving skills were clearly another.

It took us nearly a day to reach the ugly industrial city of Tuzla. On the way in we passed a hideous plant producing chlorine, allegedly involved in the war effort. Lying in my bed on the seventh floor of the high-rise hotel in the city centre, I could hear shells landing. It was nonsense to worry whether you might be killed on the seventh floor or the ground floor, but the thought descending earthwards still in bed was slightly disturbing.

Conditions in the city were better than I expected. One of the surprising things about the war was the trade that still seemed to go on across front lines. Since road access from the south was the major concern, the following day we went out to have a look at Tuzla's large airfield; this, a few kilometres from the town, would be ideal if road access was impossible. Reassured about access by road and air, we set off back to the Croatian coast, stopping in at the UN Military Headquarters in Kiseljak.

Brigadier Roddy Cordy-Simpson, second in command of the UN forces, was Chief of Staff to Major General Morillon. Chatting to him for half an hour gave me a good idea of what was happening across the country. He was always supportive and liked the ODA's problem-solving approach, which he found refreshing compared with the UN military bureaucracy. Morale at the headquarters was not high; they found the UN Security Council resolution challenging and were well aware that they had the wrong mandate. They were often in danger, drawing fire from all three protagonists, Croat, Serb and Bosniak, but the rules of engagement made it difficult for them to fight back. Their military observers travelled unarmed, in soft-skinned military vehicles, much as we did. Yet being in uniform, they were at much higher risk.

On the way out of Kiseljak, I saw a roadblock ahead. As soon as I stopped, a barrier was erected behind us and a hostile crowd surrounded the car. Although most of them were women, they made way for a large man in a black leather jacket who told us aggressively we were going nowhere until the Serbs released some prisoners. Nothing would persuade them that I had absolutely no influence in the matter. An hour passed before a UN military staff car and two armoured personnel carriers appeared. My spirits rose, but not for long. The rear barrier opened, they drove through and the barrier was reinstated. Although bristling with weapons, they were prisoners. To my amazement Major General Morillon, the UN Military Commander, stepped out of the staff car. The crowd had unknowingly caught the biggest fish of all.

The General was not happy, but there was little he could do. I explained the situation in French and suggested it might take some time to resolve, to which I got a very simple reply – "*Non.*" Suddenly a shot rang out; our captors cocked their weapons and there was a lot of shouting and running about. The situation was on a knife edge until it became clear that one of the UN soldiers had fired accidentally. After a few minutes, things settled down again. We were finally let go eight hours later.

A few weeks later I was invited to dinner at the General's Headquarters in Sarajevo. At least twenty of us sat at a large dining room table decorated with silver, and the mess waiters wore white gloves. In the middle of dinner, a shell landed. Windows blew in somewhere uncomfortably close, dust filled the room, and for a moment the conversation stopped. The General merely looked up and said, "Gentlemen?" The conversation started again, with everyone feeling slightly sheepish.

★★★

Britain now held the Presidency of the European Union and, with growing concern about Bosnia, John Major called a conference in London. There was not much to agree about as no one dared to propose the use of armed force to end the war. The barren idea of a humanitarian solution remained the lowest common denominator. Almost in desperation, to have something positive to announce, it was agreed that a European Community Task Force (ECTF) would be set up to deliver humanitarian assistance. However, a further issue had been dominating the news. The Serbs had set up two prison camps where thousands of Bosniak and Croat prisoners were confined. The press was already referring to them as concentration camps, and photographs of emaciated inmates were on the front pages of the UK newspapers. It was agreed that wounded prisoners would be evacuated for treatment in third-party countries.

The British Ambassador called me in and briefed me on the outcome of the conference. I was to join Thierry Germont, Head of the International Committee of the Red Cross (ICRC) for Europe, to help negotiate the release of what were now referred to as 'medical evacuees'. I was to visit the prison camps as Representative of the EU Presidency and as Observer of the London Conference. I was also asked if I would consider being the first Head of the ECTF, which was to be set up early in the New Year. I could see this would be problematic, and had my reservations.

It took a few days for the arrangements to be made with the Serbs. Barney Mayhew, who had only recently left the British Army and was now working as a ceasefire monitor, would provide me with transport for the mission. In Banja Luka, Thierry Germont handled the negotiations expertly and I was relieved to be with someone who had so much experience. After six hours, as we were getting near the end of the negotiations and I thought it was all agreed, the Serbs suddenly announced they wanted to check before their release that these dying soldiers were not war criminals. Thierry then stood up to sum up the agreement; his voice was almost priest-like. He paused at the end of the first sentence and said, "...and therefore..." In my head this could only be followed as in the 1662 *Book of Common Prayer* with "...angels and archangels and all the company of heaven..." Yet here there were no angels on either side of the long table in this dreary hotel, just war criminals. There was a further delay. Finally, with negotiations done, we set off for the camps at Manjača and Trnopolje.

The picture of an emaciated prisoner had shocked the West and became one of the iconic images of the Bosnian war. I was apprehensive. What should an inspection cover? What sort of reception were we going to get?

The Serbian military had turned a livestock farm at Manjača into a camp with watchtowers, barbed wire, minefields and Alsatian guard dogs. Lt Col Bozidar Popovic, who controlled the camp, immediately took us on a tour. We were led into cattle sheds full of rows of emaciated male Bosniak and Croat prisoners, sitting on the ground in complete silence. It was cold and most of them did not appear to be wearing enough clothes. I asked to see the medical centre, and was shown a cupboard full of antacids for heartburn, a common sign of stress; there was little else. I did get the chance to talk to one prisoner when Barney distracted Popovic and his entourage, but the conversation was too short to be useful. In any case, talking to any of these prisoners could be enough to get them killed. Everything – the cooking facilities, the ablutions block – appeared inadequate for the number of prisoners. Over coffee Popovic gave us a speech about how he really cared for the welfare of the prisoners, and asked us to remember what we had seen as evidence that they were being well looked after.

Trnopolje held both male and female prisoners. This camp had been established in the grounds of a local primary school, so although there were watchtowers and high barbed wire, the camp looked as though it had been put up in a hurry and the atmosphere was not quite so oppressive, though the smell alerted us to the fact that sanitation was poor. Again, the prisoners walked with their heads bowed and, as we left, we were all very quiet; none of us had ever seen human beings quite so cowed. Horrible things were clearly happening here. As we got back in the vehicle, I offered the front seat to the interpreter. Barney had already taken the view that my approach to security was far too relaxed and being responsible for our safety thought vigilance more important than politeness. He installed himself in the front seat and he was not wrong. We had only travelled a few miles when there was a burst of machine gun fire, the rounds passing uncomfortably close to our vehicle.

I later found out that Trnopolje held between 4,000 and 7,000 Bosniak and Bosnian Croat inmates at any one time, and served as a staging area for mass deportations, mainly of women, children and elderly men. Between May and November 1992, an estimated 30,000 inmates passed through it. Mistreatment was widespread, and there were numerous instances of torture, rape, and killing.

One of the outcomes of the London Conference was the decision to have a European Community Task Force for the former Yugoslavia. This was at a time when nothing much was going right and the EU was struggling to find something positive to announce. This idea sounded positive, and it was difficult for anyone to object. However, once the conference chairs had been stacked and the proposal was subjected to cold analysis, questions began to arise. The ECTF was to be a humanitarian task force, but now, six months into the war, the UN were already running an operation reaching 1.5 million beneficiaries. Worryingly, there had already been rivalry between the EU and UN over the lead role. The position of the EU in the Balkans was horribly compromised by 19th- and 20th-century history, making a common position on almost any issue complicated. Brussels was unhappy to fund a humanitarian operation only to see the UN take the credit. To those of us working in the field this rivalry and political manoeuvring was deeply disappointing. As soon as I agreed to be Head of the new ECTF, I became alarmed by the EU's political ambition on one hand and the difficulty of finding an operational role on the other.

Within hours of my taking up the job, Brussels got in touch suggesting I should take over an entire hotel in Zagreb as my headquarters. I discovered rather quickly that it was more important to Brussels that I show *visibilité* than find an operational role. I should have remembered from my days in Northern Iraq that, for Brussels, looking as if you were doing something was more important than achievement. In Kurdistan, where the EU had funded much of the humanitarian assistance, they insisted on issuing several tons of stickers, declaring 'Gift of the European Community'. The Royal Marines, to show their complete contempt, put them on all the lavatory doors and dustbins.

The Head of UNHCR, José María Mendiluce, had always given me good political advice and we got on well. I was now fortunate. He offered me an office on the ground floor of the UN building, not an entire hotel as wanted by Brussels, but this proved vitally important for operational coordination with the UN.

Very slowly, a small team arrived in Zagreb to join me. One of these was James Shepherd-Barron, now a well-known humanitarian adviser, who then had only recently left the British Army Air Corps. Together we had the unenviable task of unscrambling the political and diplomatic muddles caused by my Italian deputy, who found Balkan politics a mystery. Administration from Brussels was non-existent; after six weeks, we still had no petty cash and I had to rely on ODA for office equipment. I needed to find a way of putting the ECTF inside the UN operation, yet provide that all-important *visibilité* for Brussels. Although the Task Force did eventually receive some trucks, it remained a UN operation in Bosnia with some of the convoys branded as ECTF to give Brussels what they really wanted. Over the next few months, the Task Force took over the Croatian food aid programme and the humanitarian infrastructure projects, which were outside the scope of the UN. I had moulded an almost abortive idea into something that would run smoothly and happily with the UN. However, my relationship with Brussels was never easy since the great European project always came before the beneficiaries.

I had been away for too long. Eight months of this miserable war felt like eight years and it was definitely time to go home. The humanitarian operation was now reaching most of those in need; the Northern Ireland Electricity Board had put up sixty kilometres of new electricity cables to reach areas cut off by the front lines; the Kakanj coal mine was back in production, and even the Mostar hydroelectric power plant was functioning again. This was the humanitarian solution favoured as a substitute for proper military and political action by NATO, but it was not a solution. The appalling casualty rate in the first year of the war, when as many as 120,000 may have been killed, was slowing, but the USA was becoming increasingly impatient. My work in Bosnia had changed my views about large-scale humanitarian aid. I realised now that the best humanitarian programme was decisive military and political action, which was yet to come. Indecision and uncertainty were the true drivers of humanitarian emergencies.

Back in Zagreb, Brussels contacted me late one Friday night. The French politician Bernard Kouchner, co-founder of Médecins Sans Frontières (MSF), would be in Sarajevo the next day to hand over a consignment of medicines as a gift from the French government. According to Brussels, the medicines were actually funded by the EU, so I was asked to join the French minister and 'co-give' them. This type of diplomatic skulduggery was commonplace and rather depressing. On the French Air Force flight from Split to Sarajevo, on a Transall C-160, I was introduced to the French minister. Alija Izetbegović, the first Chairman of the Presidency of Bosnia and Herzegovina, was also on the plane, looking tired and old. On arrival, as we made our way to the PTT building, Kouchner stopped for a moment and said, "Gilbert, we need to discuss how we're going to do this." I was immediately suspicious of the sudden informality. He explained that the real reason he was in Sarajevo was for a prisoner exchange. If I waited until this was completed, he would come and collect me for the gifting of the medical supplies. I waited, and at least an hour passed. Suddenly, Kouchner bounded into the room. "My good fellow, I have a terrible confession – I completely forgot about you!" I was not surprised. There had been rumours about the prisoner exchange. It was alleged that the Serbs had rounded up some Muslims, burnt their houses and exchanged them as part of this process. As always in Bosnia, it was almost impossible to separate fact from fiction.

I went to say goodbye to Vesna, and asked what she would do after the war. "I'll go to Canada," she said. "It'll take ten years for this place to settle down and another ten before there'll be any real economic life. I don't want to be forty-five before I start my life. Anyway, there'll only be maniacs and babies left." Sadly, she was right.

A few weeks later, I heard that four young Danes, drivers in an ECTF convoy, had been killed when the Serbs had fired a shell into the mouth of the Maglaj tunnel. The very same one I had passed through only months before.

7

Corridors of Peace, Angola 1993

"At the moment of your greatest strength, you're at the moment of your greatest weakness." These words, spoken by a friend in Luanda, Angola, were to prove prophetic and I should have taken heed. The solution to humanitarian problems in Bosnia had been innovative and imaginative; the management of power stations and coal mines had shown a new approach to humanitarian programmes in mid-income and developed countries. But two unwelcome attributes I had brought home with me were overconfidence and self-regard.

After my return from the Balkans, I worked in the Accident and Emergency Department at Cheltenham General Hospital. I had done my original six months as Senior House Officer there, so it was easy to get locum work between missions abroad. It was a joy to focus on an individual patient rather than think about a hundred thousand people at a time. It was also quite a change to have regular hours and not work for months on end without an hour to myself. I realised that I was never going to achieve as much in medicine as in my work for the British government, work that was increasingly compelling, yet for now the combination of both jobs was attractive, especially as I was only a consultant adviser. I had no job security and I was only as good as my last mission.

One day Andy Bearpark telephoned and asked me to come to London. There was a new mission, this time to Angola.

Angola had gained independence from Portugal in 1975, but was subsequently sucked into a proxy conflict during the Cold War. On one side were the Soviet Union and Cuba backing the Angolan socialist government, and on the other was Jonas Savimbi's UNITA (National Union for the Total Independence of Angola) supported by the USA and South Africa. After seventeen years, Angola had conducted its first democratic elections, supervised by the UN, and there was every expectation that the country might now settle down. Predictably, votes were cast along tribal lines. The outcome being unfavourable to UNITA, Jonas Savimbi rejected it, and between October 1992 and May 1993 the war resumed with brutal intensity. Human Rights Watch estimated 1,000 people were dying every day of disease and starvation as well as in combat. In the 21-month siege of Kuito an estimated 20,000–30,000 people died, mostly women and children. There were now 1.2 million IDPs, and a further 3.3 million were in need of emergency assistance. The country's infrastructure had remained untouched since the Portuguese left in 1975. Access to the main towns was by air alone, as land mines made all the major roads unpassable. An enormous food aid programme had been running for several years and food was being flown to provincial towns by an ageing fleet of Boeing 727s and Russian air freighters.

After a quick briefing, Andy announced we were off for tea and biscuits with the Minister of State for Overseas Development. I was greeted warmly by Lynda Chalker and in less than half an hour was given three British government objectives, some terms of reference and a file for background reading. I was to travel to the Angolan capital, Luanda, assess the suitability of the British government's objectives and return with recommendations in ten days' time.

★★★

Dramatic views of the bay and a cool Atlantic breeze should have been uplifting, but seventeen years of poverty and decay had made Luanda a sad place. It was difficult to believe that during the 1960s it had been one of the most beautiful cities in equatorial Africa. After decades of war, three million people were living in a city built for 500,000, which had broken pavements, raw sewage running along rubble-strewn streets, and children everywhere except at school.

My British Embassy driver weaved from pothole to pothole as I visited every NGO and UN agency in the city. With only ten days, the pressure was on to pull together a consensus view of the situation and return to

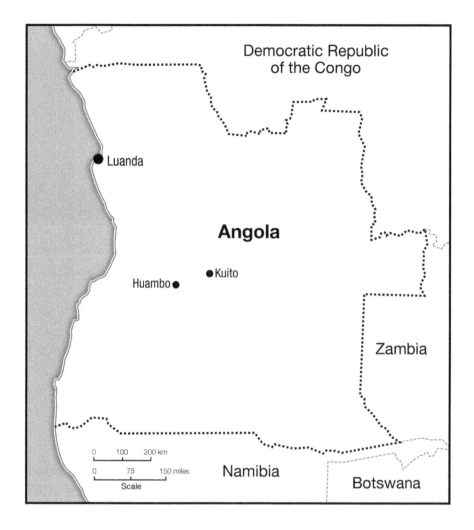

London with some recommendations. In the 1990s, it was traditional for one UN humanitarian agency to take the overall coordination role, and the United Nations Children's Fund (UNICEF) was the lead agency in Angola. UNICEF was underfunded and looking to the UK for support. They made sure I met almost every humanitarian agency in Angola, and they flew me to a provincial capital to see the food distribution operation all the way from port to beneficiary. A recommendation for a major contribution towards food aid and relief items seemed a safe and sensible option. I was soon on a Sabena Airlines flight back to London.

Back at ODA in London I was asked to discuss my recommendations – food aid for WFP, seeds, tools and other relief items for UNICEF – with the department that handled Angola. I was ushered into the presence of the Head of Department and imperiously waved to a seat. There was a long pause while I watched her finish reading the report I had written on the flight back from Angola. She was soberly dressed, hair up, regal, cerebral, every inch a senior civil servant. I could see by the way she held my report that all was not well. Angry comments could be seen in the margin scribbled in red biro, some underlined.

This government bureaucrat found it difficult to criticise my work yet wished to undermine it, which she did with consummate ease. As I was about to leave she asked, "What about the condoms?" I was confused for a moment, but should not have been. The UK had taken the lead in promoting family planning, which was thought rather bold at the time; whatever the project, family planning had to feature in it somewhere. Those seeking funding are always aware of the latest whim of the donors and exploit it ruthlessly. Without this important link, any project would be rejected. In the safety of Andy's office I explained my reception upstairs, repeating the salient points: "The worst report she'd ever seen, the English, my grammar…" He smiled; clearly this was normal.

The skills needed to manage an emergency programme are very different from those for development programmes. Emergency plans inevitably involve quick fixes to save lives, speedy and decisive decision-making, bold and imaginative ideas. They also incur risk.

It was inevitable that different departments handled emergency aid and development. For those in development, we inhabited a different planet, indifferent to the latest development fashions, untouched by concerns for the side effects, which we considered the compromises necessary to save lives. Relationships were difficult, and the development departments had every reason to be annoyed. The handover of country responsibilities was arbitrary and unsatisfactory. We would arrive, ignorant of local politics and much else, and do our work, leaving an eddy of chaos to be sorted out after our departure. The other departments saw those who worked for the Emergency Aid Department as ignorant meddlers unjustly favoured by the Minister of State. I immediately saw the danger of being brought in by the Emergency Aid Department over the heads of those responsible for long-term development programmes in the country.

Andy was Head of the Information Department as well as the Emergency Department, thus responsible for running all British government emergency relief operations, and his idea was for something a little livelier. "What about a team of nurses?" he suggested. It sounded attractive, but I was willing to please for all the wrong reasons. If we went for an Expanded Programme of Immunisation (EPI), it would give Andy the immediate media coverage he wanted or, more precisely, that the government needed.

Three journalists joined the charter flight to Angola carrying humanitarian supplies for UNICEF: John Simpson for the *BBC*, Michael Nicholson for *ITN*, and Steve Back for the *Daily Mail*. Meanwhile, a team of nurses were recruited and I went to brief them at a hotel near Gatwick. The following day we flew to Luanda on a DC8 airliner, stopping to refuel at Kano in Nigeria, where we paid for the fuel – rather surprisingly, or perhaps not – in cash.

In Luanda, I was based at the British Embassy. The Ambassador was not entirely happy, for a number of reasons that were to become clear over the next few days. The Emergency Aid Department had suddenly taken over the ODA programme in Angola with little reference to the country team or the head of their department in London. There had been little discussion with the Ambassador about what I hoped to achieve or even what I was planning to do. I was not a career civil servant and was without natural allies in either Luanda or London. To make matters worse, my team and I worked all hours with little respect for the embassy's rhythm and protocol. As far as the Ambassador was concerned, this put great demand on his limited resources. We did not have enough vehicles, and, given the delicate situation in the embassy, asking for more would fall on deaf ears. However, the British government had provided the UN with a large number of Land Rovers for the recent elections, many of which had fallen into the wrong hands and were now being used as taxis. I spotted one at a petrol station and, after a gentle discussion with the driver, I acquired the keys, and he was invited to come to the British Embassy the next day with the necessary authority to be driving it. I returned in triumph with a brand-new Land Rover. No one ever came to claim it. The Ambassador considered this all very irregular.

With UNICEF, I started to organise the EPI at Kuito and Huambo in the Angolan Highlands. It was a bold plan, but the idea of using healthcare to create 'Corridors of Peace' was a UN initiative at the time, and I had confidence in UNICEF, who knew the country. There was, however, the small matter of how to make it happen. The country was at war and the towns were an hour and a half's flight from Luanda. A ceasefire agreement between the government troops and UNITA was needed, and it would be up to me to achieve it. But I had become overconfident after my experiences in Uganda and Bosnia, and underestimated the risk.

A week passed and the nurses, who were already showing signs of being unhappy with the arrangements I had made for them, were impatient to start work. The Third Secretary at the British Embassy had been asked to help me. He had been a maths teacher before joining the Foreign Office, and nothing had prepared him for life in a country shaken by seventeen years of civil war – or, for that matter, working with me. I noticed that whenever he approached a military checkpoint his timid approach invited trouble. I suggested he wind down the window, give a friendly smile and wave with British passport in hand, keep the car moving ever so slowly, exchange some quick banter with the soldiers and be on his way. At the next checkpoint, he accelerated, shouted at the soldiers, ran over their feet and failed to stop. The fact that the enraged soldiers did not open fire was a miracle. The nurses in the minibus behind were hysterical. As the commotion died down all I could say was, "Not quite like that…" I had just lost another of my nine lives and my credibility had taken a knock.

It took another tumble after a recce to Kuito ended in disorder. The day started well enough. We arrived at 5.30 am at Luanda International Airport in two white Land Rovers, which were loaded with minimal fuss into an ageing Antonov 12. The crew lived on this ancient aircraft, which smelt disagreeably of sweat, vodka and rotting mineral oil from the hydraulics. It was one of thousands stolen by their Soviet crews at the end of the Cold War, flown to Dubai and subsequently contracted by the United Nations. The pilot never stirred; in fact, throughout the flight he slept off the effects of the vodka – a crate of empty bottles was visible next to the flight deck – leaving the co-pilot in charge.

Fighting between the government, who held the town, and UNITA had been going on for several years, and damage to the airport had been so severe that some buildings were only waist height. The crew showed a clear reluctance to leave the aircraft. Through the open door, I saw someone crouching in a defensive position about a hundred metres away behind some rubble, so I waved. He waved back. I took a deep breath and stepped out. He was a UNITA soldier. As I approached with a broad smile, several other soldiers emerged from the broken buildings. Within minutes we had unloaded the Land Rovers and were being escorted to the front line about five kilometres away. As our Antonov climbed away westwards on its way back to Luanda, it felt as though a comfort blanket was being removed.

Crossing the front line was relatively straightforward. After half an hour of talking on satellite telephones we were waved through the last UNITA checkpoint into no man's land, and took the main road into Kuito, through savannah dotted with termite hills. The road was covered with flechettes, little darts released by air-burst artillery shells to maim infantry soldiers. These stuck into the tyres like hedgehog spines, although they did not seem to cause punctures. Often we had to drive around unexploded mortar bombs, their fins just visible poking out of the soft tarmac.

Kuito had been under siege by UNITA since January, a siege that was still ongoing nine months later. Nobody was permitted to enter or leave the city and over 30,000 people had been killed by violence and starvation. It was now down to me to negotiate the ceasefire that would bring this to an end.

The war damage was astonishing. Kuito had been a pretty Portuguese colonial town, but little remained. The perimeter was now no more than 1,500 metres by 500 metres. Soldiers and civilians alike looked listless and emaciated after nine long months of siege. The government troops were close to surrendering and in every house were soldiers with appalling gunshot wounds, who beckoned to us pitifully. I began to wonder if a surgical team would be more use than my intended Expanded Programme of Immunisation.

We arrived at a ruined house, which was the government's military headquarters, where the atmosphere was surprisingly jolly. A soldier in a bright red beret seemed to be in charge, and shouted at other soldiers gratuitously, perhaps a demonstration of authority for my benefit. To my amazement, the idea of both the ceasefire and the EPI programme was greeted with enthusiasm. Given the level of malnutrition, measles was a major killer. Surprisingly, the offer of EPI for children on both sides of the front line was accepted. I felt that after years of conflict they had all had enough and there seemed to be a feeling that our presence might help bring the war to an end. Perhaps 'Corridors of Peace' had some merit after all.

After the negotiations, we wove round the unexploded ordnance and crossed the government lines into no man's land. Suddenly, the sky was full of parachutes. A chartered Boeing 727 was landing to collect us and, unfortunately, the government had decided to use this as a cover to drop supplies to the defenders, who rushed out to collect them. Small arms fire broke out from all directions. I halted our small convoy, and for a moment, we remained stationary in the middle of the battle. Although not a single shot seemed to be aimed at us, it became clear that the sooner we moved on the better. Back at the airport, the Boeing 727, one of a fleet of ancient 727s banned from Europe for being too noisy, had arrived with UNICEF's medical supplies. With their 26-tonne payload and three engines, the 727s were still popular in Africa where they had to cope with both high temperatures and runways at high altitude. Thousands of tons of food aid were being delivered in these ancient machines.

The runway was badly damaged by shellfire and numerous shell holes had been filled in with rubble. The incoming 727 had punctured a tyre on landing at 130 knots, which had then caught fire. As we drove into the airport, it was just approaching the remains of the terminal building, flames from the tyre reaching up towards the fuel tanks in the wing above it. The journalist Sam Kiley had accompanied me on this trip to cover the ceasefire negotiations for *The Times*. He had more than a decade's experience of covering war in Africa, and his inexhaustible good humour made him the ideal travelling companion in a situation like this, as I was now to find out.

We ran over to help the Texan pilot extinguish the fire and remove the damaged tyre. I was surprised to find the aircraft was equipped with an enormously heavy wheel jack, which took all of us to remove from the aircraft. There was also a spare tyre, which took eight of us to get out of the hold. Getting the damaged tyre off was easy enough, and a huge relief as we realised how close we had been to losing the aircraft. There were scorch marks and the metal on the underside of the wing was still too hot to touch. Alarmingly, there were tons of fuel in the wing tank. For the inflated tyre to fit on the hub, the Boeing had to be jacked up higher. Yet the jack simply sank into the soft tarmac. We tried everything we could, even putting sheets of metal under it, without success.

It was beginning to get dark. The fighting had continued since we left the town, but while concentrating on the tyre I had not appreciated how close to us it now was. All of a sudden, the airfield came under bombardment, and mortar shells landed quite near us. With a Maglite torch in my mouth and grease up to my armpit, I was trying to push the bearing onto the hub as everybody else pushed the enormous wheel. It was an activity that could quite easily have removed my hand, and frustratingly it wasn't going to work.

The UNICEF local staff were now clearly terrified. The ancient Boeing 727, with oil weeping from its fuselage, was sitting on only three main wheels, the inner port wheel lying on its side nearby and the damaged tyre still smouldering. It was almost dark and even my inexhaustible optimism was being challenged. "Will it take off on three wheels?" I asked the pilot. We gazed at the empty wheel hub smeared with black grease. "Guess it'll have to," he replied. This was hardly reassuring, but shells were now landing on the airfield and small arms fire was coming from only a few hundred metres beyond the ruined terminal building.

We got on board, and taxied out with only the landing light to show us the way. Flashes of gunfire were all we could see from the cockpit as we lined up at the end of the runway. The pilot pulled down his baseball cap over his eyes and tightened his seat harness, his jaw muscles clenched with concentration. Forward went all three throttles and we bounded into the dark. A hideous rumbling came from the gear as we crossed the potholes. He applied left aileron, taking the weight off the single port wheel. I had my eye on the air speed indicator – 120 knots... 135... 140... The nose came up, some dark shapes flashed beneath us, and we were up and away, soon cruising at 30,000 feet, flying in total darkness but for the light from the instrument panel. Rather alarmingly, creaks and groans came from the enormous cargo door that had been cut into the fuselage when the airliner had been modified at some stage. Even so, Sam and I breathed a large sigh of relief.

As we approached Luanda International Airport, I was concerned about the loose items in the cargo hold. There were wheel chocks for the aircraft weighing fifteen kilos each, and a mass of pallets and tools lay about where everyone was sitting on the floor. If there were a problem on landing the single tyre could burst, sending things flying around the cargo hold with disastrous consequences for us all. All twelve of us crowded into the cockpit and held our breath. The pilot managed a beautifully executed landing on the starboard main gear, only dropping the left wing as the speed decayed. At the apron was a British Embassy car and the Deputy Head of Mission was waiting for me as we lowered the builder's ladder that was the only way down from the cargo door. "Gilbert, the Ambassador would like to see you." Yes, I thought, I'm sure he would.

★★★

Remarkably, our chaotic return from Kuito had not affected the peace agreement I had negotiated. UNICEF were able to communicate with their staff in Kuito and Huambo by HF radio, and they were ready for all ten nurses to deploy to the bush. The UNICEF plan was that each nurse would lead a local team to maximise the number of children vaccinated against measles. However, once in the field it proved too difficult to get them to go out in ten teams as planned. They were unsettled by the security situation and I had to admit they were right. A compromise was reached; they would work in two teams of five.

After their initial deployment, I flew up to Huambo to visit them. The Angolan Highlands were beautiful, and the temperature on the high plateau energising. Huambo had been badly damaged, though not as badly as Kuito, and abandoned after the fighting, but the ruined colonial Portuguese houses still looked charming. Even so, it was difficult to imagine a different life in these abandoned rubble-filled streets. The bush was slowly reclaiming the town.

Back in Luanda, I was having problems getting the media coverage for the trip that Andy wanted. None of us knew that there had been a professional disagreement between *ITN* and the *BBC* over an exclusive interview with Saddam Hussein during the First Gulf War. Although they were scrupulously polite, there was an underlying tension between the two teams. They were happily occupied covering pieces on life in Luanda and the food airlift to the provincial cities, but they wanted to go to Huambo and Kuito. The Angolan government stubbornly refused, and there seemed very little I could do. However, at the very moment I thought it impossible, the British Embassy told me I most probably would get the clearances.

Meanwhile my hapless assistant continued to astonish me. While trying to demonstrate a back flip into the Deputy Head of Mission's swimming pool, he had struck his head and several metres of stitches were required to sew him back together again. He was now sporting a huge bandage. I told him to take the journalists down to a beach bar and give them a drink while I struggled to get the clearances. I arrived later and saw no beer on the table. It was horribly hot and the journalists looked desiccated. "So what did you order?" I asked. Eager to please, he announced, "Two bottles of water!" I groaned inwardly.

Yet, despite these minor trials, all parts of the plan were finally falling into place. John Simpson and Michael Nicholson were now in Kuito, where they encountered some of the most badly wounded soldiers they had ever seen. The government did raise some objections to the media trip to Kuito, but I had reached a compromise – only one cameraman was allowed. Given the strained relationship between the two teams, the visit went surprisingly well, and both correspondents wrote hugely different pieces. While John's described the complicated politics and the mechanics of reaching the beneficiaries, Michael's described what life was like in Angola in these terrible times.

The EPI did not last. The teams never had confidence out in the field and the security situation dominated everything. It was unlike Uganda where, although international staff also worked in very remote places during the conflict, there were plenty of other organisations within a couple of hours' drive. Here there were none, and the team was an hour and a half by air from Luanda. The ability to speak to the soldiers was critical, but only one person in the team spoke Portuguese. Local intelligence was also lacking. At the end of the month they were all back in Luanda, having vaccinated 10,000 children. It wasn't a failure, but I was disappointed. I had to console myself that the EPI was only ten per cent of the ODA programme for the country. The food aid and relief goods for UNICEF had been the lion's share of the programme and had been distributed without a problem. The media coverage could not have been better, not surprising considering I had two of the most experienced and professional teams I could have wished for.

As the Sabena Airlines flight back to London started down the runway, I felt a moment of huge relief; nothing had gone terribly well, but it had not been a complete disaster either. Most importantly, no one had been injured or killed. But that brief moment of relief did not last long. There was a loud bang, and I could see flames engulfing the inner port engine. The brakes were applied vigorously, the fuselage dipped menacingly, our speed dropped away and we bumped along. I could not tell in the dark whether we were even still on the runway. Finally, we came to a halt. There was a long silence followed by an announcement that the 747 had engine failure. Hours of nonsense followed. The airport security and customs staff had all gone home, and no one appeared to have the authority to make a decision. We were told we would have to stay on the plane overnight, but some diplomats made a fuss and, after a further delay, embassy staff were allowed to leave. A car came to collect me, though I had probably caused enough headaches for the embassy without this. I reached London two days later via various African countries including Zimbabwe.

"You realise they've all complained," Andy said laughing, when I reported back to Victoria Street. "And now you'll have to sort it all out. You can stay here as long as it takes and write letters to all these MPs." And he handed me a huge folder. There was not much substance to any of the complaints. There had been shortcomings in the organisation without doubt, but most of the points raised were trivial and were clearly made to justify the decision to end the EPI early. I dutifully wrote what I thought were charming and diplomatic letters explaining things, but I did take the lessons learned from this mission seriously. The days of governments recruiting directly for work like this were over – recruiting individuals was one thing, teams were quite another. The whole process of recruitment, vetting, training and supervision, could not be done by an organisation like ODA. In Iraq, the Ministry of Defence (MOD) had provided the organisation and the quartermaster function, but even then, there had been problems. More important was the need to concentrate on the task and not be distracted by massaging the media image. If the job was well done, the media would give the credit for it. We needed to show the British public how their taxes were being spent, but the image had to come second. We were ahead of ourselves in our attempts at media manipulation – the Blair years were yet to come.

This event in 1993 marked a turning point for me. Many things had gone right on the mission to Angola; the food aid programme was a success, the agricultural tools were a success, but the Expanded Programme of Immunisation was definitely not. Our target had been to immunise 100,000 children, but we probably only achieved 10,000 at considerable cost and an unacceptable level of danger. I knew that amateur handling of emergencies was no longer effective and a more professional approach was now needed.

8

A Failed State, Somalia 1993

"How do you fancy a trip to Somalia?" was Andy's opening bid. "I need someone to represent the UK at the Borama Conference. They're going to elect a new President of Somaliland." Of course I was interested, but why me? If this was a political mission, wasn't there a fully functioning diplomatic service in King Charles Street?

Somalia had been plagued by civil war and famine since the fall of Siad Barre, the former military dictator and President of the Somali Democratic Republic. The capital Mogadishu was already deeply troubled and the timing of the trip was unpropitious. It was now April 1993, and the next few months would turn out to be turbulent. Two US Black Hawk helicopters would be shot down on 3 October during the Battle of Mogadishu, a major humiliation for the Americans, which would contribute to them withdrawing their forces on 3 March the following year.

The situation in the former British Somaliland Protectorate was little better. Italian and British Somaliland had united soon after independence in 1960, but the vision of Greater Somalia had faded, and the former British Somaliland was once more looking for autonomy, if not independence, from its even more troubled neighbour. Various Somali clans were fighting for supremacy, social cohesion had broken down and myriad gangs now controlled the country. Often only teenagers, these gangs drove 'technicals', typically open-backed civilian pickup trucks, mounted with heavy machine guns and rocket launchers. It was easy to see why no one in the FCO had put their hand up for this one.

My terms of reference were interesting. I was to report to the British Ambassador in Ethiopia's capital Addis Ababa for a briefing, as he was also responsible for Somalia. Then I was to be flown by the Red Cross in a Cessna 208 from Djibouti to Borama in north-western Somaliland where I would attend the Borama Conference and then visit Save the Children Fund and ActionAid. The British government was a major donor and both NGOs had UK-funded projects I had been asked to review. I was also asked to look at the International Red Cross project proposals in Berbera.

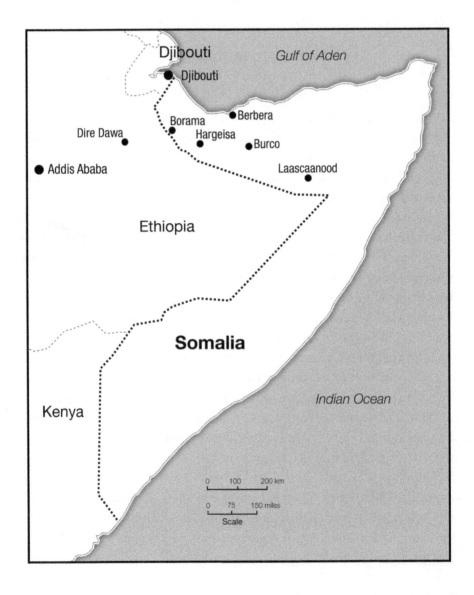

Finding any organisation to work in Somalia was difficult, so ODA was keen to support them. Three weeks later, I would be picked up and flown out of Hargeisa.

During the Ethiopian Airways flight from London to Addis, I asked for a glass of whisky and a quarter of a bottle was slopped into a tumbler. Given the turbulent political situation in Somaliland I was going to need it on this mission. The capital of Ethiopia was horribly poor, and full of refugees. To my surprise, the British Ambassador was unable to see me for two days. I suspected intra-FCO manoeuvring. He had shown no interest in sending anyone to the Borama Conference and, as a result, London had sent me. The potential friction was made worse when he found out that I was a consultant adviser, not a diplomat. I felt I was lucky I only had to wait two days. Our eventual meeting was brief and almost void of content, but protocol was satisfied, and I was off to Djibouti.

The Boeing 727 stopped briefly in Dire Dawa. There were only about twenty passengers on the flight, and when we reboarded the plane nearly every free seat was piled to the ceiling with hessian sacks, and the air was pungent with the smell of khat. Khat is a mildly narcotic plant that contains an amphetamine-like stimulant; when chewed it causes loss of appetite, euphoria and – some say – a fondness for violence. The airfield was nearly 4,000 feet above sea level and the temperature in the high 20s. The hugely overloaded aircraft groaned into the air using every last foot of the runway, and we were lucky to land at Djibouti without bursting a tyre.

Once on the ground there was frenzy amongst the locals to get their hands on the cargo for onward transport throughout East Africa. We, and our suitcases, were quietly ignored. The Consul was coming to pick me up, but two and a half hours later I found myself alone in the terminal. Not a soul was to be seen, nothing stirred, and the heat was intense. Outside stood a particularly decrepit taxi; the driver's leg dangled from the door and he woke with a start as I approached. A wizened old man with no teeth and a deeply untrustworthy demeanour limped over and opened the boot for my bag, the oil-less hinges squeaking. As we puttered along, I noticed that all the interior door panels and roof lining were totally absent, revealing the bare metal. I only had a higher-denomination bank note than I would have liked and hoped against expectation that I might get some change. My driver commented, "*Chez vous, on aime le fric,*" (You people just love money) pocketed my note, and with a rattle of the exhaust he was gone.

I soon found out I was in one of the most venal cities in the world. The combination of the French Foreign Legion, the narcotic trade, the Danakil and the Djibouti-Somalis made this an unusual place.

The city had been built on a saltpan and the heat was now nearing 50°C. I was glad of the Panama hat I had brought as a necessity for Borama. The Sheraton Hotel was on the seashore and the only thing that quickened the pulse in this place, other than the arrival of khat, was the Air France cabin crew on their weekly flight from Paris. Although the country was independent, France seemed to have the unwelcome task of paying for most things that happened in Djibouti. I enquired at the hotel about the Consul who had failed to meet me. "Oh," said the receptionist, "such a charming gentleman – but did you not know…?" She paused and looked perplexed. "He died last year." The British Embassy in Addis, who had made the arrangements, clearly did not care a fig what happened to me, which was comforting as I was just about to leave for the most dangerous country on earth at that time.

I contacted the Red Cross pilot and was at the airport for a dawn take-off. It was an easy flight. The Cessna Caravan was a fourteen-seat version of the Cessna 182 I normally flew, and the Australian pilot let me fly most of the way. As we approached Borama, he said, "Look, mate, two bits of advice – you'll have 90 seconds to get yourself and that bag out of this aircraft when we hit the runway, and don't expect me to shut down either." Seeing my surprise, he added, "And keep your mouth shut – watch what you say or they'll kill you."

We landed on the gravel airstrip, I was out in a flash and the plane was gone. Within a minute, the shooting began, but there was nowhere to take cover. Anyway, I was meant to be representing the British government, and to be found cowering on the ground would not exactly give a very good impression. So I pulled down the brim of my Panama hat and put my hands on my hips in a gesture of defiance. As suddenly as the firing had started, it stopped. Then a mustard-coloured Toyota appeared from nowhere and drove towards me at high speed, stopping uncomfortably close in a cloud of dust. A Somali jumped out, grabbed my bag, opened the passenger door for me, and in perfect English said, "Welcome to Borama." As we bounced down the track to the town, or rather large village, he apologised for the shooting. "It was all about your bag," he explained. "They wanted to charge you for taking it to the town." "Quite," I said.

As we arrived at a building that resembled a school hall, a police band with battered instruments and dishevelled uniforms struck up the British National Anthem. They made a frightful din. Inside were several hundred elders who had come to elect their new President. I was led to the stage and introduced in Somali. I did not understand a word until the man at my side said in English, "Dr Greenall has arrived from the British Foreign Office to address you." There was a roar of approval. I had to draw on every shred of experience I had of public speaking. I began by praising the Somali spirit, their entrepreneurial drive and seafaring skills, their connection to both Cardiff and London Docks, and their love of cattle. I even brought in my own family's passion for cattle breeding in the UK. This was a stroke of luck; I had chosen the right subject, as cattle play a central role in Somali society. I continued with the special friendship of Somaliland and our shared history. It seemed to do the trick, and I definitely represented the UK at the Borama Conference. When the designated President-Elect Mohamed Egal summoned me afterwards, he seemed pleased that the UK had taken the trouble to send someone.

In Hargeisa, I stayed with the UN for a couple of days. The city had been badly damaged by bombing during the final moments of Siad Barre's regime. The international UN staff were cautious, as the violence in Mogadishu had alarmed everybody. I was taken out to meet the Save the Children Fund team who were running mother and child clinics. It was impressive work and, in my role as ODA donor, I was given a tour of their operation with a view to continued funding. I was then off to Las Anod, six hours by car, to visit the NGO ActionAid who were building a rural water project. Again, there was obvious robustness and professionalism, which made my job of encouraging funding proposals easy.

While I was there ActionAid were to entertain a group of elders. I was by now used to eating the local food, but preferred to eat as little as possible on a mission to avoid illness. When the dozen guests arrived, we trooped into a building that was no more than a shed with small windows that let in very little light. A grubby tarpaulin was placed on the cement floor. A man pushed in a wheelbarrow full of cooked rice, and tipped it onto the tarpaulin. Then two men struggled in carrying a whole cooked headless goat by its hooves, and threw it on top of the rice. We all sat down on the ground and a bucket of warm water was passed round accompanied by a tin of Vim to wash our hands. Meanwhile, rivers of molten grease began to run down the heap of rice, pooling on the tarpaulin. I was the last to get the bucket and the water was black.

The pilots who flew me back to Hargeisa from Las Anod on a South African Beechcraft King Air operated by the UN had had enough. The day before, armed Somalis had started to cause trouble on the steps of the aircraft until one shot off his own thumb by accident. They had many more stories to tell, each worse than the last. Travelling by road was equally alarming. ActionAid organised a Land Rover, a Somali driver and a turnboy, or assistant driver, to take me to the town of Burao. For a whole day we crossed the rangelands on narrow marram tracks, passing mile after mile of thorn trees. It was extremely hot and the dust coated everything, almost creating a second skin. We passed checkpoints, which were unlike anything I had experienced before. Numerous 'technicals' were parked at the checkpoints, with militia – some of them only children – wearing red berets and mirrored sunglasses and draped in machine-gun belts, wielding assorted weaponry. It was all very sinister. Unlike in Uganda, there was no possibility of friendly banter. I remembered what the Red Cross pilot had told me, about being careful what I said. It was reinforced by my driver, a man of few words, who said that being pulled out of the car and shot for no reason was a real possibility. I did not doubt it.

As we reached the outskirts of Burao, the turnboy held a bundle of cash out of the window. An urchin ran out to collect it. It was money for safe passage. We were stopped by a gang of child soldiers sitting on a tank playing with their AK47s, their fingers carelessly around the triggers. It was enough to turn my insides to water. My driver was interrogated, but he was surprisingly tough with them and we were allowed to move on. We never stopped again until we arrived at the hotel. The next day the Somali Red Crescent would pick me up at 9 am.

The hotel was a squat evil-looking place, perhaps also used as a brothel; there was nothing to eat. I went for a shower and was surprised to find running water. But as I took my shower, it was clear that the urinal next door ran through the shower tray. I went back and lay on my sleeping bag in the heat. At dusk the shooting began, single AK47 shots at first, but then heavy machine gun fire started outside in the street. Fire was now being returned, and I could hear the bullets smacking into the houses nearby. The wall next to my window was just one brick thick; it certainly wasn't going to stop a 12.7mm machine gun bullet. So I repositioned my sleeping bag and myself on the floor. This went on for a good two hours. I dozed off, woke at dawn, and waited three hours nervously. I regretted the improbable plan that had been made for me to reach the coast and began to think apprehensively of another way of leaving this extraordinary country. None came to mind. At least I had 7,000 dollars in my bag; a feature of travel in places devoid of banks, hotels or cashpoints, where credit cards were unheard of.

At 9 am, a Red Crescent pickup drove slowly up the main street, weaving around the rubble. I peered out nervously, but was disarmed by the huge smile on the face of the driver. I threw my bag in the back and jumped in. There was complete silence, not a soul in sight and not a single vehicle. We were soon back in the bush. The rains had failed and the camels and cattle looked miserable, their ribs showing; frequently we passed the skeleton of some beast lying near the road. Foreigners find rangelands difficult to read. In dry years, the Somalis point to starving stock as part of their claim to food aid. The truth is more complicated. In good years, and especially if they are sequential, the capacity of the rangelands to support stock increases hugely. In dry years, large numbers of animals die and this is presented as a calamity, which indeed it can be. In reality, the number of beasts has simply dropped to the long-term average. However, to a foreigner it looks like a disaster and they are encouraged in this view.

We began our descent towards the sea, still having seen neither a car nor a person. This was the famous route taken by the British explorer Sir Richard Burton in the 19th century. It was now a surprisingly good tarmac road, which wound through gentle hills. As we descended, the temperature began to rise. Finally, the port of Berbera came into sight; with its white buildings, flat roofs and the Indian Ocean behind it. It was a fabulous contrast to all I had seen. The last days had been surprisingly tense, but at the Red Crescent house I was warmly welcomed. Coated in dust and dehydrated to the point of alarm, I grabbed the offered cup of tea and sat down to discuss their programme. ODA was a major donor and they were looking for continued funding. One project was to improve the prison on the edge of the town, and the Red Crescent had organised a visit for me the next day. The project was important, as the treatment of prisoners in Africa at that time was medieval and a blot on the whole continent. However, I had another reason to see the prison – if the UK was to recognise Somaliland, human rights would be an issue, and the prisons would be expected to meet minimum standards.

In the event, the prison was worse than I could ever have imagined. It was dark, with very little natural light, and the heat was oppressive even this early in the morning. Worst of all was the disgusting smell. The prisoners were kept in metal cages, similar to those once used to keep lions in zoos, and there appeared to be no sanitation at all. It was difficult to see how any human being would last long in such conditions. I was told that the prisoners stayed there until their families raised enough money to secure their release. I emerged from the prison, into the bright sunlight, with the white city walls and sparkling Indian Ocean beyond, with a sense of relief, freedom and gratitude for fresh air.

I was driven out to the city airfield, a huge former Cold War base with a vast runway maintained by both the USA and the Soviet Union at different times. My weary-looking driver told me about the trials of working in Somalia. The Red Crescent had bought a generator for the hospital and a mass of other expensive equipment, which had all been looted and wrecked during the fighting. The International Red Cross were charged customs fees both on the export of their own equipment for repair and again for its return. He also told me that the Somalis were now exporting 120 million dollars' worth of cattle and sheep from the Port of Berbera to Arabia every year. Their entrepreneurial skills were renowned, so it was certainly possible.

The equally war-weary UN pilots flew me back to Hargeisa, their last flight before taking the aircraft back to South Africa. Hargeisa Airport was notorious. Gangs controlled the road to it and there were five checkpoints, on the principle that those arriving would have something to be stolen, and all those travelling on the road would have plenty of luggage. Negotiating our passage was an unsettling business. The one morale-raising sight at the airport was Boutros, a giant tortoise named after the UN Secretary-General Boutros Boutros-Ghali, who roamed freely. Boutros had his name painted on his shell in white and was the size of an office desk. He lumbered around outside the derelict terminal, hissing occasionally at the Kalashnikov-wielding youths. Fortunately, they did not appear to ill-treat him.

I went back into Hargeisa for a final meeting with the UN, during which a chicken was tied to a bush outside the window with great commotion. With one blow of a panga machete the UN cook sliced off its head. The headless body jumped about for a minute. After our meeting I was offered lunch, and the chicken reappeared. But even though I had not eaten properly for days, I suddenly found I had lost my appetite.

I had hoped to catch the Red Crescent flight back to Djibouti, but the aircraft was down for maintenance. It might arrive, it might not. For two days, I travelled back and forth to the airport – five checkpoints there, five checkpoints back – to meet a plane that stubbornly refused to materialise. I spent hours in the shade of the few derelict buildings that surrounded the control tower, staring at the blue sky and listening for anything that might be an engine. There was a total absence of other humans except the Somali militia who periodically fell out with each other. Violence was so close to the surface that even trivial disagreements could lead to loss of life. The enforced wait did give me the opportunity to talk to some young Somalis who spoke good English; some had relatives in England. Such family links, and the historical ties between the two countries, meant there was at least something to build on.

While I waited days for the plane, I had plenty of time to reflect. I really felt there was a possibility of bringing stability to this violent place. There was a good argument for recognising Somaliland. The union of British and Italian Somaliland had taken place after Independence, so there would be no change in colonial boundaries, a diplomatic principle in Africa. I would recommend recognition to Malcolm Rifkind on my return to London, but the timing of my visit had been unfortunate; things were going from bad to worse, and I knew there was no appetite now for any engagement in Somalia. I suspected the Foreign Office thought it more trouble than any benefit that would come from it. However, I thought failure to recognise Somaliland would be almost certainly the wrong decision. A stable Somaliland would have avoided the problems that later came to this unfortunate country. Once again, I observed, it was work at the political level that was most needed to solve humanitarian problems.

Back at the Sheraton Djibouti Hotel, the air-conditioned room, shower and food seemed fabulous luxuries. I had been eating goat and rice for weeks. When I got back to London I had only been away for a month, but it felt like a year.

9

Colonial Misfortune, Montserrat 1995

"How soon can you get to London?" Andy said without preamble. "There's a meeting about the volcanic eruption on Montserrat at 5.30 pm; can you make it?" It was 2 pm on a Friday, and I was two and a half hours from London. It would be tight.

I arrived at the FCO at the same time as Lt Col Nick Pounds, Commanding Officer of the Commando Logistics Regiment. Even in civilian clothes Nick was obviously military, his few comments indicating a delightful sense of humour. We were both equally surprised to be called to this meeting.

There were two middle-aged men with Andy. One was striding backwards and forwards, jacketless, his thumbs hooked around his braces. "The Americans will have to do something…" he kept repeating.

Montserrat, one of the few remaining British Overseas Territories, is a small island ten miles long and seven miles wide off the west coast of Antigua. The main mountain on the island, Chances Peak, had been dormant for centuries. However, recently there had been a series of shallow earthquakes, and ash from the crater had started to cover the cone of the mountain. Nearly 14,000 people lived on the island, but as seismic activity increased, half of them had left. Those who remained were anxious and the situation was chaotic. There were ugly rumours that some UK civil servants had abandoned the island and gone to Antigua (although Montserrat was self-governing, Britain retained responsibility for responding to natural disasters). It was now for London to decide what to do. Neither of us could understand why the Americans would "have to do something". Clearly, this was a British Overseas Territory, therefore our responsibility. Both Nick and I said so quite bluntly. Andy summed up the discussion with his usual consummate skill and suggested some terms of reference for Nick and me. We were to leave the following night and to report back in 48 hours by telephone with a sensible plan. His last words as we left were, "If I find 7,000 refugees at Gatwick, the pair of you will be fired."

The British High Commissioner in Antigua went out of his way to be helpful. Rooms had been booked at the very comfortable Blue Waters Hotel, which was in a small bay surrounded by palm trees, where tourists lounged on sunbeds beside the pool. Nick and I had taken rather a relaxed view of the mission. This wasn't a war, after all, and the contents of our rather small bags were more suited to swimming pools and beaches than yet another conflict. After Cambodia, Uganda, Iraq, Bosnia, Angola and Somalia this was a welcome change. During military training, Nick and I were both familiar with the military exercise that started, "There is a tropical island..." One was invariably given a C-130 Hercules, a company of infantry and a frigate to accomplish the mission. We flew out to Montserrat and there was an RAF C-130 unloading relief supplies. The frigate, the West Indies guard ship, had just arrived and Nick's company of Royal Marines were on their way.

The Governor of Montserrat, Frank Savage, was clearly delighted to see us, but looked exhausted, his kind face carrying every concern on the

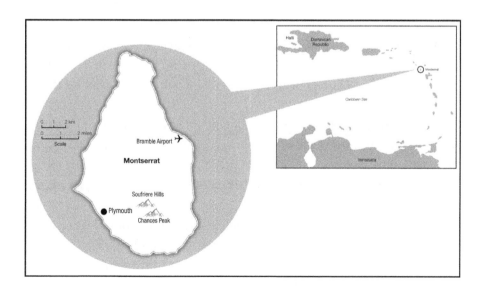

island. I suspected he had inadequate support from London and for the last two weeks had been unsure what to do. The Foreign Office deals with political problems, not natural disasters, and I could easily imagine the inability of the system to support him when he needed it.

In the middle of the day with blue sky and a shimmering sea it was difficult to appreciate how potentially serious the events of the last few weeks were. Frank began his briefing by describing the catastrophic eruption of Mont Pelée on the nearby island of Martinique in 1902, which destroyed the beautiful town of St. Pierre, killing between 30,000 and 40,000 people. Since the Montserrat emergency had begun, he explained, there had been activity from the volcanic cone, ash fell on the mountain and then the earthquakes had started. They were only five to six on the Richter scale, but were extremely shallow, no more than fifteen hundred feet below the surface, and extraordinarily violent. Caused by magma being forced up from the earth's core and the mountain widening at its base as a result, they were strong indicators of trouble ahead. We had arrived for the meeting feeling casual, almost flippant; we left feeling chastened and apprehensive.

The British Geological Survey, a world-leading geoscience centre, had already been deployed. As we drove to meet them, we were captivated by the island's charm. Its capital, Plymouth, was full of attractive 18th-century houses. Yet the roads were in a terrible state. This was a British Overseas Territory, and there appeared to be double standards here. I had already noticed at the airport that no two members of the Montserrat Defence Force unloading the C-130 Hercules were dressed alike; in the place of military boots anything went, high-top trainers, gym shoes, even flip-flops. It was becoming clearer by the hour that, despite the Union Flag flying over Government House, British subjects here were not treated like those back in the UK.

The British Geological Survey added details to Governor Savage's briefing and explained that the earthquakes could be followed by ash falling on the town and setting the houses on fire. Then the ash on the cone mixed with rain would flow down in lethal rivers of mud. Failing that, lava flows would wreak havoc. Worst of all would be pyroclastic flows, invisible clouds of super-hot gas racing down the mountain at hundreds of miles per hour, turning human beings to carbon as happened at Pompeii. In fact, the entire mountaintop could blow off, as it did in the 1883 eruption on Krakatoa, when a massive pyroclastic flow blasted out from the volcano, causing damage on other islands. The blast turned the seawater to steam, creating an almost frictionless cushion over which the ash, gas and pumice rock flowed. Our meeting ended, we sat mute after this description of the apocalypse.

Finally, there came a request for some very expensive equipment to measure seismic activity. I could see the politics in all the arguments, the role of responsible government to protect and penny-pinching leading to deaths. There was no doubt that ODA would have to buy whatever was needed, regardless of the expense.

Nick and I stayed on Montserrat, at a charming lodge. Sitting on the veranda under palm thatch with a gentle onshore breeze taking the edge off the heat, we started to plan. One company of Nick's regiment were already on their way. At the beginning of the crisis, several thousand people had left the island and only 7,000 remained, but evacuating 7,000 people in extremis would not be easy. Very little money was allocated to the evacuation plan. We decided to build one or two reception centres on Antigua to handle the evacuation and provide initial shelter. To evacuate the island by air was one thing, but the airport was in the most vulnerable area. A geological survey indicated that the north of the island was geologically different and potentially safer, so we needed to look at harbour facilities there, as evacuation by boat might be the only option.

That night we went out to dinner in Plymouth. The restaurant was an attractive wooden building open on three sides, with heavy overhead beams. Halfway through our calypso chicken, a grinding and tearing noise – the most alarming sound I had ever heard – rose from the centre of the earth, and the table began to buck. We grabbed our plates and glasses just in time; at that moment the left and right corners of the ceiling seemed to pass each other, screaming and shouting came from all sides and dogs began to bark. Then it all suddenly stopped. As the choking dust cleared, Nick smiled, holding up his glass, not a drop spilt. I said, "Well, it would be a shame to let something like that spill your beer." We continued our dinner, realising this mission was not going to be quite so simple after all.

The next day we were back on Antigua. We had already heard, before the High Commissioner told us, that a hurricane was on its way. A volcanic eruption, an earthquake and now a hurricane – this was for natural disasters what speed dating is to romance. People were scurrying about and boarding up windows. No one was now remotely interested in the volcano.

Nick and I were to stay at the High Commission, a fairly new building and, unlike most in Antigua, designed to withstand hurricanes. The ninety Royal Marines were to remain on the island in a bunker, rather strangely belonging to the Americans. As the storm approached, everything was surprisingly calm. Then the barometric pressure fell so low that the sea level began to rise and the wind started to pick up. From behind our hurricane shutters, we heard the roar of the storm. After several hours, there was a strange popping noise. We peeped through the shutters to see the palm trees on either side looking like streamers, and sheets of corrugated iron flying past at a hundred miles an hour. The house next door had vanished, and three people were clinging to a piece of brickwork. Nick and I decided that we needed to get them into the High Commission, so we crawled along the edge of a low wall and pulled them back into the building. Crawling was the only option as the air was full of flying coconuts and other debris. Shocked, wet and depressed at the loss of their home, the family were relieved to be safe.

There was the traditional calm as the eye of the storm passed over the island. After dark, it resumed. Nick and I slept on the floor in one of the offices. It was a delight to be safe and dry, but it was brutally uncomfortable. I hadn't expected the temperature to drop quite so dramatically, and was already regretting my failure to bring a sleeping bag; my teeth were chattering with cold. I used my wafer-thin blazer as a blanket, and heard Nick's laconic voice: "Note for the diary, be reminded of the thermal quality of a Guards' blazer." By late afternoon, the wind had dropped enough for us to begin our damage assessment. The biggest surprise now was rain, which fell like a curtain, an inch an hour. I was soaked to the skin in seconds, but at least it was warm again.

Nick had managed to contact his men at the bunker; they were ready with chainsaws and winches, and set about clearing roads, opening the airport and pumping floodwater from the hospital. The Blue Waters Hotel, where Nick and I stopped to get some dry clothes, was a sorry sight. Half the roof had been ripped off and the palm trees flattened. The swimming pool, formerly in the garden, now appeared to be on the beach, full of sand. Outside, sitting on their suitcases in the rain, was a dejected group of what I thought were tourists. One asked, "What are you going to do about us?" They were a group of ODA civil servants who had self-evacuated from Montserrat at the start of the volcanic eruption, seeking apparent safety in Antigua. I had heard about this on Montserrat and not been impressed. It was alleged that they had abandoned their duties. Along with the condition of the roads, a picture of the administration was emerging – it was shaming to hear those who should have been looking after the population in Montserrat demanding priority treatment to get back to the UK.

By 9 am the next morning, Nick's Royal Marines had completed the most essential tasks. We had achieved this on our own initiative as the telephone lines were down and the government offices were closed anyway. We thought it only correct now to visit Lester Bird, the Prime Minister of Antigua. The meeting was held at a bank close to the airport, a strange setting. The Prime Minister appeared flustered. He was a big man, rather undignified in jeans and a baseball cap. As he talked, he began to empty his over-full pockets. To Nick's and my amazement, the first thing that came out was a revolver.

A sycophantic civil servant gave him a briefing. It was pure fantasy; clearly, this fellow had only just got out of bed. Nick waited until he had finished, then with masterful understatement summed up the latest situation. The atmosphere was uncomfortable, but the Prime Minister, perhaps seeing some credit for himself in all of this, was not displeased. What we did not know was that relations between the UK and the Government of Antigua had been strained for some time. We heard that Antigua had large outstanding debts and repeated attempts to have them repaid had not been altogether successful. It was rumoured that someone at the FCO had intended to send the High Commissioner a line to take with Antigua. Unfortunately, a copy had been sent to the Antiguan government in error. It may have added to the mirth of the planet, but it was unhelpful to us.

No one knew when the C-130 Hercules would be back. The ground crew had stayed behind and were rumoured to be conducting community singing in some wrecked hotel. Nick wanted to get back to Montserrat and decided to chance a crossing with the Montserrat coastguard. He was lucky not to drown in the mountainous seas even on this short sea crossing.

I had the unwelcome job of trying to find potential sites for our reception centres. A major clean-up was now underway and the timing was inauspicious, but I did find something suitable. I was soon back on Montserrat, where the geological survey had uncovered evidence of a pyroclastic flow in the late 16th or early 17th century. This was unpropitious and added to the gloom that now pervaded the island. One felt that, however unlikely it was, one could dodge mudflows and lava, being turned to carbon instantaneously was an unspeakable horror.

An official at the Governor's office approached us clutching a file. It was a report commissioned in the 1960s about the probability of a volcanic eruption and the significance of this for planning and public safety. A map clearly showed where development was discouraged, in an area hatched green. The report had been filed and nothing done. Over time a new prison, hospital and government offices had all been built – in the area hatched green. All were now at risk. Little by little a shocking picture of incompetence, poor governance and complacency was emerging.

Nick and I had the bones of a plan, now the flesh had to be added. Meanwhile, volcanic activity on the mountain gradually increased. Curiosity got the better of us and we climbed up the mountain to have a look. The path was almost vertical with steps leading through thick vegetation, and we paused occasionally for the fabulous views of Plymouth below and the sea to the west. But above a thousand feet, ash mixed with rain covered the vegetation and coated everything with grey slime. As we approached the summit, the ground steamed gently, the rocks were hot to touch, and sulphurous gas made breathing unhealthy. Peering down into the caldera was a frightful sight – the crater seemed to be a thousand feet deep with clouds of gas belching up. Around us was a wasteland of ash, all life killed by toxic gas and sulphuric acid, which lay in pools around us. It was not a safe place to be. We took some photographs and began our 2,000-foot descent.

After almost a month the Royal Marines had done all they could in the short term and were returning to the UK. I had to hand over the evacuation plans to the government of Montserrat and return with the Royal Marines to London. However, the Governor was long overdue for leave, so I came back a few weeks later to take charge of the volcanic emergency during his absence. Sergeant Mitchell from the Royal Marines came out to join me in implementing the emergency plan. From the comfortable holiday house where we were based, we set off each day to encourage and at times cajole those involved. It was often more difficult than anticipated. The relaxed locals tended to take the view that all would be well. It was an attractive attitude and I found my natural optimism required daily suppression. For that, I only needed to visit the Geological Survey Team, whose prognosis was dire. More and yet more expensive equipment was bought to measure every seismic shudder, however small. One day I mentioned the earthquakes to an old woman, who just laughed. "Oh, we don't pay any attention unless the whole ground starts to ripple." My experience in the restaurant had been a mere hors d'oeuvre of what was yet to come.

I remained unconvinced by the role of the ODA civil servants who were on the island to support the government. They seemed to do the rounds between our remaining Overseas Territories, spending a few years on Montserrat followed perhaps by a few in the British Virgin Islands, and then a spell on Anguilla. From my brief observation, they were not hugely industrious. A government truck being driven around on tyres worn down to the canvas seemed indicative of everything that was wrong about our administration of the island. A rock had been knocked over and the creatures scurrying beneath it had been exposed to harsh sunlight. The British Governor was responsible for a self-governing Overseas Territory, but had no authority to do anything, and no budget, which made emergencies particularly difficult for him to manage.

Once it was clear that the situation was going to last months if not years, I flew to Barbados to visit the British Caribbean Development Division, ODA's Caribbean Regional Development Office. It was rather curious that this office was based on Barbados, an independent island, rather than on one of the remaining British Overseas Territories. They could have benefited from it economically as it had a surprisingly large staff. My meeting there was interesting; it was conducted with great politeness and sophistry, but the question – why nobody had come to Montserrat from the regional office while I had flown the Atlantic – was never answered. Nor were there plans for anybody to come to Montserrat.

It was unsettling being responsible to London for the evacuation plan. At any time of day or night the big moment might come. Volcanic activity was increasing, and ash was turning the pretty houses of Plymouth grey. The area of devastation was no longer restricted to the top of the mountain. On occasions intensive clouds of ash billowed from the cone and the mood was sombre. Many more families were wisely leaving, especially those that had relations in Antigua. ODA realised the situation was unlikely to quieten down and was setting up a permanent representation on the island for months and more likely years to come. Two months after I had first arrived, I returned to the UK. Yes, it had been different. At least I now knew something about volcanoes, earthquakes and even hurricanes. It was fortuitous; I was going to see many more in the coming years.

Within two years Plymouth would be no more, first burnt and then buried under nearly five feet of ash. Pyroclastic flows had raced down the mountain claiming nineteen lives and most of the island was now uninhabitable.

10

Winning the Peace, Bosnia 1996

"This one's right up your street," Andy greeted me. I had half expected a call after the Dayton Peace Agreement was signed before Christmas. The Balkans had been happily out of the news for several months and Andy began to outline some ideas how we might encourage continued compliance with the Dayton Peace Agreement.

American patience with the UN had finally been exhausted over Bosnia. In November 1995, the President of the Federal Republic of Yugoslavia, Slobodan Milošević (representing the Bosnian Serb interests due to the absence of Radovan Karadžić), the President of Croatia, Franjo Tuđman, and the President of Bosnia and Herzegovina, Alija Izetbegović, were invited to Wright-Patterson Air Force Base near Dayton, Ohio. They were kept there until they agreed to peace, and the resulting Dayton Peace Agreement. Formally signed in Paris on 14 December 1995, it put an end to three and a half years of war in Bosnia. The failed UNPROFOR peacekeeping years were finally over.

On 14 December 1995, UNPROFOR took off their blue berets, put on steel helmets, and made it quite clear that as the Implementation Force (IFOR) – the new NATO-led multinational peacekeeping force in Bosnia – they were in Bosnia to enforce Dayton. Suddenly, there was freedom of movement, with no more checkpoints, and a weary acceptance across the country that it was all over. This had been a truly bitter conflict and more than 100,000 people had died.

Major General Mike Jackson was given command of Multi-National Division (South-West), part of IFOR. His first job was to enforce the military annexes of Dayton, which stipulated that, within 60, 90 and 120 days respectively, heavy weapons would be corralled, troops returned to barracks and a multitude of additional military demands met.

Andy wanted me to join the Divisional Headquarters at Gornji Vakuf and put together a programme of civil assistance projects to support the military objectives and encourage compliance with Dayton. £1,000,000 a month would be made available by ODA. This was something I really felt confident I could do. Northern Iraq had given me experience of working at brigade level with 4,000 troops, but although the Multi-National Division (South-West) was over 12,000 strong, the system was identical. And because of the gruelling winter of 1992–1993, I had had experience of working in Bosnia.

I was thrilled to get the job. Ever since seeing the French helicopters efficiently dropping supplies in Uganda back in 1981, I had wanted to develop the role of the military in delivering humanitarian assistance. Now there was a real chance to show that the military could deliver aid more efficiently and quickly than their civilian counterparts. Yet I was apprehensive about returning after four years to Bosnia, where I had experienced some of the darkest and most dangerous moments of my life.

Luckily, there was no urgent need to start the very next day and I was able to take my family on an Easter holiday. Then I flew to Split from Zurich. I was told there would be a car for me, but I was surprised to find a tiny hatchback in the airport car park, a vehicle I suspected would be challenged by the roads through the mountains of Bosnia which had not been maintained for years.

As I left the coast and climbed into the mountains, Bosnia seemed to swallow me. The gloomy atmosphere, the shells of burnt-out houses, and the debris all over the almost-empty main roads were all so familiar. There was meant to be peace now, but it didn't feel like it. The absence of traffic or any human beings made the place feel desolate and hostile, and I could feel the evil of recent events all around me. It was impossible to know how safe I was as I travelled through these thick mountain forests.

After a few anxious hours, I arrived at Gornji Vakuf, the former British UNPROFOR base. Initially, Major General Mike Jackson had decided to stay here, and had already arranged to move forward to the metal factory in Banja Luka, but this would not take place for another three weeks. The centre of Gornji Vakuf was desolate, with severely-damaged abandoned buildings either side of the potholed high street, refuse was piled everywhere and wrecked military hardware lay where it had been destroyed during the fighting. At the headquarters I was relieved to find that I was expected. The Sergeant Major showed me to my accommodation, a Corimec container – a prefabricated flat-pack room – then took me to see Andrew Ritchie, the Chief of Staff. It was clear that Andrew's expectations of what I might achieve were high. I needed to put together a divisional programme for civil assistance, and a mechanism to deliver it. The first three weeks would be critical, and already the clock was ticking.

It was strange being back in Bosnia now the war was over. I could now drive straight down the main roads. This was often impossible during the war, and I frequently found myself taking the old route around what then had been the front line, or hopelessly overestimating the time it would take to get anywhere. Half a day of slithering over mountain tracks was now a fifteen-minute drive. ODA sent me a new Land Rover and a couple of weeks later, to my great surprise, my old Land Rover Discovery was dropped off at the headquarters, looking very dilapidated. No one seemed to know where it had spent the last three years. I was also equipped again with a satellite telephone, leaving me independent of military communications.

I spent the first week quietly exploring the divisional area trying to get myself into the minds of the people. It is easy for outsiders to think that the sense of euphoria felt at the end of a war is permanent. The brutal reality is that it is very short-lasting. When families are reunited and return home, they find that their situation is worse than even at the height of the war. Their home may be badly damaged; there is no running water, electricity, health services, public transport, food in shops or employment. The situation in Bosnia was now far worse than at any stage in the last three and a half years. It was clear that unless I could help to reverse this process within the next hundred days, the peace would be lost.

My days were spent driving around the divisional area by myself, establishing priorities and identifying what the army would soon refer to as the low-hanging fruit of quick wins. Each evening I returned to Gornji Vakuf with more of a plan, confident that within ten days I would be ready to present something to the General.

At that time, traditionally only two civilians worked in the military headquarters, the Civilian Secretary who ran the General's cash and dealt with civilian contractors and the POLAD, the Political Adviser. My role was initially a mystery to most. I came and went at any time of the day or night. I travelled alone, unarmed with my own vehicles and equipment and did not bother them for support. I had the necessary security clearance to be privy to the Division's secrets. Despite this, they could not have been more friendly or supportive.

It was already clear that economic recovery was going to be very different amongst the three ethnic groups. There were already more cars on the roads in the Croat areas, yet in the Serb town of Šipovo it felt as though the war had ended only a few hours earlier. The accumulated rubbish of four years was appalling, and a public health risk. Wrecked fighting vehicles lay in the middle of roads along with all manner of war debris that was not conducive to the image of peace. Although Mike Jackson's main focus was on the military aspects of Dayton, he was happy for any of his military units to get involved in clean-up operations if they had spare capacity. I had to explain to the troops that they were not required to do the work themselves, but to find and fund local people to do it through a series of what became known as QIPs – Quick Impact Projects.

I had finally designed a mechanism to implement my programme of civil assistance. There would be a single sheet of A4, on which were just four questions: What is the description of the project? What resources are required to achieve it? What is the cost? How long will it take to complete? Once I had looked at the project and signed the piece of paper, the project officer could use it as a cheque to draw up to £20,000 in cash from the Pay Office. When the project was complete, the receipts were stapled to the same piece of paper and handed back to the Pay Office with any change. The UK Ministry of Defence billed ODA monthly for reimbursement. The results were immediate and extraordinary.

I soon had a six-point Stabilisation Plan, starting with public health and ending with attempts to get everybody back to work. I worked with a small team in what had always been considered a backwater of the headquarters – 'Civil Affairs'. Commanding this little team was devoid of prestige and traditionally given as a wartime job to an officer from the Education Corps. Staff officers who worked in the prestigious 'operations' had nothing but contempt for 'Civil Affairs', and considered it fit only for officers not competent to be in charge of a fire extinguisher. All this was to change. My small group had just been handed money and the power to spend it, and our efforts would be targeted very carefully. The tail would shortly be wagging the dog.

Mike Jackson liked the Stabilisation Plan and it was to become his 'main effort' after Day 120, once all military annexes of Dayton had been completed. I knew he was open to unusual and radical approaches to problems. In time, our activities took centre stage and morale in our little backwater was transformed. The next step was to travel around the divisional area explaining what needed to be done. There were exceptions, but this proved to be a hugely successful tour.

The biggest surprise for the officers was that these projects were to be carried out by locals and not by soldiers. All the unit commanders had to do was appoint an officer or non-commissioned officer to manage the projects and then do as many as they could. I gave guidance on the type of project and the sequence of the various components of the overall Stabilisation Plan. Once projects were successful, they were repeated elsewhere. During the town clean-up phase one regiment, knowing Bosnia was famous for metal bashing, found a skip manufacturer, and within two weeks every town and village had a rubbish skip. Proudly painted on each one in Serbo-Croat and English was 'Gift of the British Government'.

The Royal Engineers found some projects to support local government services and others to help the electricity and water companies. These projects were sometimes simply to provide batteries and tyres for their trucks or salaries for their employees. The results were impressive. Water pumps were being replaced and whole parts of towns received water for the first time in four years. One water pump had been particularly critical and its repair caused a complete change of heart towards British troops in the area – an old woman who had carried a jerry can up four floors to her flat throughout the war cried with happiness.

New pumps were being ordered, along with transformers and transformer oil, and flown in from neighbouring countries. The speed at which the programme took off surprised us all. A cascade of projects, from infrastructure to schools, to hospitals and health clinics and finally projects to get people back to work, continued at lightning speed. In the early stages, there were no more than fourteen project officers across all 12,000 troops in the Division. Requests came in daily to Division Headquarters for me to visit and approve projects, but I thought it unwise to delegate responsibility for this. I had many years' experience and knew there were plenty of tripwires to avoid. Giving the projects to the military to manage was already controversial, and all the humanitarian agencies were watching with interest.

It was important to keep up the momentum and I tried to give a decision on a project within five days. I mainly drove to see projects, but on occasions there were just too many and I had to take a military helicopter to cover the ground, sometimes approving more than twenty in a day.

The whole mechanism was replicated at brigade and battle group level and the process became very efficient. Senior non-commissioned officers were often better at managing projects and less naive than the officers. I became keen to repeat successful projects. Once we completed one, we had a good idea of the costs and other units could always travel to have a look at them. 'A hundred days to win the peace' became an article of faith. The projects were soon to become the Division's main effort and were having the desired effect on the population.

Once all the rubbish and war debris were gone, I looked at other ways to demonstrate the benefits of peace. The streetlights did not work in any of the towns. It was a simple project to replace the broken bulbs. While other divisional areas remained in darkness, Multi-National Division (South-West) had streetlights that worked, and the change from war to peace, from darkness to light, was transformative.

On my return to the headquarters, the General – friendly and supportive as ever – mentioned that his boss, the Corps Commander General Mike Walker, had heard about the projects and asked that I go to brief him, which I did the next day. He seemed almost surprised that I was on time, and announced that *his* boss, the four-star Admiral Leighton Smith, was coming to the briefing. The fact I was a civilian made Mike Walker unsure about me in front of his IFOR Commander. "Gilbert, you're not going to waffle, are you?" I smiled. "Waffle, General? Good heavens – what a thought!" I replied cheerfully, despite being quite nervous. But the presentation glided to its conclusion, with the four-star Commander looking particularly pleased and me hugely relieved. All the other divisions were now encouraged to follow our lead.

It was time to move to Banja Luka. The metal factory, built in 1970, stood on a huge site on the northern edge of Banja Luka, a nondescript Serbian town of ugly buildings. Its management offices became the new headquarters building. A C-130 Hercules had flown in sixteen tons of wires for the computers alone, and a sea of white Corimec flat-pack containers was being constructed to accommodate the 800-strong headquarters staff. A massive helicopter landing pad had been built south of the main factory, which could accommodate two Chinooks simultaneously. Foul smoke from Banja Luka's main landfill site just to the west of the factory enveloped the site night and day. It was most disagreeable.

This was to be my new home for the next five months. I was now authorising twenty new projects a week and keeping to my objective of making a decision on any project within five days. This produced a relentless workload, given the size of the divisional area, over 600 square kilometres. The first projects had already been completed and it seemed that most would be completed within thirty days. Once a project was near completion, I let the British Embassy know in Sarajevo, and someone would come down to open it officially, so the embassy could bask in reflected glory. It was a joy to see the FCO, ODA and the MOD all working happily together. The opening ceremonies became carnivals. Happy locals brought industrial quantities of slivovitz, their homemade plum brandy and often there were regrets the next morning from some British soldiers who had not taken enough care with the mighty concoction.

Could it be that simple? was the question being asked in Whitehall, and there was a flutter of alarm about process and what the UK Parliament's Public Accounts Committee might have to say about it. Andy came out with his boss to review how things were going. This unfortunate fellow tripped over a giant metal peg getting out of the helicopter on arrival, tearing half the rubber sole off his shoe. He bound it up with gaffer tape and limped about in a rather undignified fashion for the duration of the trip, which did not help our credibility. However our reputation in the headquarters was transformed when Andy, fabled for his mathematical prowess, added up four enormous columns of figures upside down at a glance. He came with me to see a few projects and we went over every aspect of the project mechanism so he could defend it against the sceptics in London. I was given delegated authority to spend £250,000, after which I had to return to London for a further tranche. It did not really make any difference, but it gave the impression there was better central control of funds.

While Andy was at the headquarters, the Royal Engineers put in a bid for bridge repairs on Route Gull. This was the key main road south and spans of the bridge had been blown up during the war. Some refugees returning from abroad at night had driven round the barrier and their car had tragically tumbled down hundreds of feet into the gorge below. The route was economically important and the project cost was £150,000. Andy agreed immediately.

During these three months, the UN humanitarian agencies were completely absent. They had identified some projects for themselves, but in the weeks it took them to become organised the military had already completed them. This started a cascade of resentment, which, although muted, took another year to be fully expressed. This was the Quick Impact Project controversy, which in the following twenty years never really went away. The humanitarian agencies questioned the legitimacy of the projects as 'real' development projects and hence the ODA funding used for them. Some thought that if the projects were to support military objectives, the UK's Ministry of Defence funds should have been used. But peace was the goal and demonstrating the benefits of peace to get compliance with the Dayton Peace Agreement was the prize. Peace would in turn bring economic recovery.

Bosnia was a developed country and we were essentially putting together a miniature Marshal Plan. The water and electricity companies and the local government employees were all competent at their jobs. We were simply allowing them to do those jobs. Repairing and replacing equipment, setting-up local government services and paying their salaries were all part of this. There was a powerful multiplier effect and every week the increase in economic activity was obvious. The Corps Commander asked his staff to measure economic progress and they came up with what they called normality indicators that tracked the price and availability of food and household necessities. It was a simple and effective way of establishing a base line and measuring change.

One conundrum was the disparity between the ethnic areas. After six months, the bakeries were still not operating in Muslim areas, whereas the Croats were selling cut flowers and wedding dresses. The important thing was to demonstrate even-handedness in project allocation. We kept a close eye on both actual and perceived distribution of the number of projects, and I spent plenty of time discussing this issue with local leaders.

Preparing for the elections was a major task for the Division. Two towns in our area had failed to comply with some aspects of the Dayton Peace Agreement, and Carl Bildt, High Representative for Bosnia and Herzegovina, had sent down an edict saying that we should not provide assistance until the towns had mended their ways. It was a blunt instrument, and Carl Bildt's office made the decision without reference to us or without knowing exactly what we were doing. I thought delicate diplomacy might be more productive.

Mike Jackson sent me off to Sarajevo to see what could be done. My driver, from the Parachute Regiment, had little respect for the locals. As we drove along, he would point out evidence to support his rather extreme views and demonstrate with his driving skills his general contempt for other road users, sometimes making gestures to make his views entirely clear. My view that charm might be a more effective weapon than aggression seemed wasted on him.

As we approached Sarajevo, it began to rain. Under grey skies, with its blackened ruined buildings, and gravestones covering every available open space, the city was a melancholy sight. The wipers were scratching the glass and leaving thick smears across the windscreen. "For Christ's sake, Corporal, make sure you get a new set when we get back to Banja Luka!" I snapped in frustration. I had had enough of the aggression and the sod 'em attitude displayed over the last hour and a half. Outside the High Representative's office were four brand new Land Rover Discoveries. Major Patrick Darling, the ADC, aide-de-camp, met me and we went off for a rather lengthy, but not terribly productive, meeting. On the way home, I noticed the wipers were gliding silently across the windscreen. "Where the hell did you get those?" I asked innocently. "Oh, sir," he said, "I couldn't tell a lie. I took them off Carl Bildt's Discovery."

★★★

The Prime Minister, John Major, was to visit. The headquarters went into visit mode and we had no fewer than three rehearsals of the divisional brief. I was given a two-minute speaking part. As the whole brief was over in an hour, straying from the brief or even taking seconds longer than allotted was not tolerated. On the day, it went very smoothly and Mike Jackson walked on at the end. "Some thoughts, Prime Minister," he said, and then he summed up the four key points from the whole presentation with such care and precision it was a joy to watch.

The Prime Minister was to visit some projects over a few stage-managed kilometres. I was meant to play a leading role in this, but was rather surprised by the sharp elbows of others trying to hog the Prime Minister's time. However, I did drive him back to the helicopter pad and finally explained what we were trying to achieve. He seemed genuinely interested, and impressed by what had already been done.

★★★

The troops were only deployed for six months and it would soon be time for a roulement, with 3 Division being replaced by 1 Division. With only a few weeks to go until the handover, the advance party were already with us. I would be staying on and a seamless handover was expected. The new General was John Kiszely. John had won a Military Cross in the battle for Mount Tumbledown during the Falklands War. Had it not been for the modesty of the Scots Guards he might have been awarded the Victoria Cross. Like Mike Jackson, he was particularly interested in the activities of Civil Affairs. As we were in Bosnia to enforce the peace, not fight a war, soft power was going to be central to his command in Banja Luka. He made a big issue of raising the profile of our team and gave his Deputy Commander, Brigadier Freddie Viggers, special responsibility for everything we were doing.

The sixth and final stage of my Stabilisation Plan was encouraging employment and economic activity. This was tricky. Getting the wood factory back into production gave a hundred people their jobs back, but it almost certainly made the owner rich. There were rumours that some war criminals had cornered lucrative projects, and our group became increasingly vigilant. I had to remember that these were high-risk projects, but highly rewarded in making peace more advantageous than war. General Mike Walker's normality indicators were all going in the right direction.

The warlords, so powerful during the conflict, were visibly diminished by peace. Now, there was freedom of movement, the control of valuable resources and the source of their economic power had been taken from them. Those prospering through proper trade now sidelined them. There was political pressure to give priority to the immediate search and arrest of war criminals. However, I felt one side's war criminal was the other side's war hero and, at this delicate moment of peace building, it was an issue that could be approached quietly and wisely over the next few months, rather than plunge the country back into war.

***

It was summer, and the mood among the civilian population had clearly changed. Now in his third month as Commander, John Kiszely decided to send back some of his artillery, a decision based on compliance with Dayton. The extra cost of deploying the Division rather than having it sitting in barracks was £5 million a month. Any saving, justified on military grounds, was welcome and it was an accolade. For a relatively modest cost, our group's results had been impressive.

A study commissioned the following year found that while 10% of the projects had not achieved their aim, 90% had. One of the failures was a health clinic we repaired, but because of ethnic cleansing during the war no one came back to live nearby. There were notable surprises too. One project was a petrol station, which would particularly interest the Public Accounts Committee back in London. "Why a petrol station?" they asked. The answer was simple – we had managed to get the local textile factory back into production but, since there was no fuel within 50 kilometres, it was vital for the workforce to fill up their cars. The project was a great success.

***

The weeks tumbled by and my time was nearly over. I had been in Bosnia for nearly six months. The army were on six-month unaccompanied tours of duty and I felt I ought to do the same. My family was beginning to wonder when I would reappear. There was one last project to see through before I went home. At last the bridges had been repaired along Route Gull and I went to open them with the then Chief of Defence Staff, General Sir Peter Inge. It was a triumph for the engineers and the opening had a carnival atmosphere.

I then travelled further south to have a look at a problem project. A small hospital had been badly damaged when a mortar round removed part of the roof and importantly the parapet. The project officer took me up the concrete stairs to the roof. I was in a hurry; I tripped on the last step and took a dive. Ahead of me was nothing but a drop of four floors onto concrete. The interpreter and project officer by chance were in the right place at the right time and caught me as I was about to sail past them. It was a lucky escape and we all laughed. I had been continuously in war zones for years and managed to survive. Falling off a hospital roof would have been an ignominious end.

★★★

A few days later, after an absence of six months, I was back at home. "Hello, dear," said my wife. "Any adventures?" She took the view it was like being married to a criminal who spent most of his life doing time. She quietly got on with life so that, when I did reappear, my role was quite superfluous. I once even heard her say to friends, "He's quite useless, you know, can't organise anything." I suppose, from her point of view, it was difficult to find anything I had.

11

The Fires of Irian Jaya, 1997

I returned from Bosnia in September 1996, glad to be home after being away for the best part of five years. Over the following winter John Major's Conservative government stumbled towards a general election, and it became clear that there would be a change of government. I knew that if Clare Short were to become Secretary of State, things would be very different.

Working at ODA for six years had given me the opportunity to develop something I had seen in Uganda fifteen years earlier – the delivery of humanitarian assistance by the Armed Forces. First in Northern Iraq and then in Bosnia, I had provided the mechanism to make this work. But I suspected the coming changes would favour neither me nor the work I had been doing.

There was a relatively new organisation at the United Nations. It was United Nations Disaster Assessment and Coordination (UNDAC), part of the UN Office for the Coordination of Humanitarian Affairs (OCHA).

"There's a place on the next UNDAC training course in Lausanne," Andy said. "You should take it." I realised I was being handed a parachute, and readily accepted. Andy could sense even more clearly than me that the wind of change was not going to be in my favour. Furthermore, believing in mission command, I was ready to make decisions in the field without too much reference to my superiors. This was easily interpreted as being difficult to manage. The United Nations suddenly looked very attractive.

The day after the election in May 1997, I watched the Overseas Development Administration sign being taken down and the new Department for International Development sign being proudly installed. DFID was no longer part of the Foreign Office, but a new Department of State with a Secretary of State in charge, Clare Short. A new International Development Act defined its role – to eradicate world poverty and provide humanitarian assistance. Support for British foreign or defence policy was not allowed outside these two objectives. The cultural shift was noticeable within weeks. Gone were the suits; dressing down was the new norm. Soon there was a move to palatial offices in the aptly named Palace Street.

I could already see that, with a strong-willed Secretary of State at DFID and another at the Foreign Office, it would not be long before we had two foreign policies. Certainly having separate buildings abroad for DFID to demonstrate its new identity was going to be expensive. DFID's independence from the foreign and defence policy of the British government was something that sounded reasonable enough in the UK, but the people of North-West Frontier Province in Pakistan might find it difficult to believe. Even some years later, when I was there for the Pakistan earthquake, they thought I was really a spy searching for Osama bin Laden.

The work I had done in Bosnia to bring the Foreign Office and Ministry of Defence closer together looked doomed. Senior military officers had become accustomed to having ODA funding, seeing it as central to winning

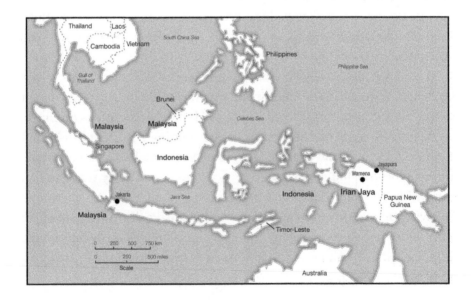

post-conflict peace, and they had demonstrated that it worked. They would be at a loss to understand how this support might now be withdrawn, and it was to take five years before the consequences were seen in the Second Gulf War.

I was never comfortable with the new International Development Act, which was a response to the Pergau Dam scandal in the 1970s, when British taxpayers paid for an excessively costly dam in Malaysia in order to secure a major arms deal. The new Act allowed funding only for humanitarian assistance and the eradication of poverty; spending to promote the national interest was excluded. The national interest was now only represented in the concept of John Donne's poem "No man is an island, entire of itself…" in that the reduction of poverty makes the world a better place for everyone.

I had my reservations, as the new Act really meant that UK taxpayers were funding charitable activities of the Secretary of State's choosing. I had seen enough development projects fail and knew that aid can destroy livelihoods as well as support them, and that the correlation between what is spent and what is achieved is a weak one.

A time would come when the British government would need to spend DFID money on activities that were neither development nor humanitarian, which would lead to a bureaucratic tangle. Watching later governments trying to get round this Act of Parliament with pooled funds was painful. Both the Act and the thinking behind it were to have calamitous consequences in the Second Gulf War.

My induction course at UNDAC took place later in the year and was a pleasant surprise. I had harboured a mild prejudice about the United Nations since my time in Uganda. I had all the usual criticisms of this vast organisation, driven by process, its plodding nature hampered by mandate, but what I encountered in Lausanne could not have been more different. The approach to natural disasters was essentially problem-solving and the talent impressive. Not least, with a lively mixture of United Nations and international foreign affairs staff at UNDAC, it was fun.

At the end of the course there was a role-play exercise; we were woken at 3 am and told to move immediately. Although this took place in a small hotel by Lake Geneva, we tipped out of our beds, blinking and disorientated. Some of my team were sent to collect a mass of satellite communications equipment from the top of the hotel and we were told to report to 'Immigration' in the conference room. My colleagues struggled in with a mass of enormous metal boxes, swearing just inaudibly. In front of us, stood a customs official in the type of uniform beloved by totalitarian states, the peak of his cap hiding his eyes. He immediately shouted at us to get back behind the yellow line, which had been taped to the carpet. The team leader stepped forward only to get a torrent of abuse in Spanish. She proffered her UN passport. "This! A passport?" he shouted in English. "You think you can come into my country with *this*?" After another high-volume rant to get back behind the line and move all the boxes to the other side of the room, he turned back to our poor team leader, held up her passport, then to our astonishment tore it in half. She was frantic; it would soon be Christmas and this was her only way of getting home. However, while ranting at us he had cleverly swapped her passport with an expired UN passport. Later we all laughed, but many of the points were well made and I often thought of him when faced by impossibly difficult officials in the years ahead.

On my return I dropped into the new DFID office in Palace Street. Andy had left and been replaced by his deputy, Mukesh Kapila. It was the end of an era. Mukesh called me into his office and, though friendly, he mentioned that I would never understand the principles behind this brand-new Department of State. He was right; perhaps I might not.

★★★

My first UNDAC mission was to Indonesia. Fires in the Indonesian rainforest had been started by illegal loggers, causing international outrage, and were so extensive they could be seen from space. Some estimated that the world's carbon emissions increased by nearly 40% in just one year. By 1997 environmentalism was the new international political issue and destruction of the planet's rainforest a focus of major concern.

The UN simply texted their team members to ask if they were available. Saying yes meant four frantic hours of grabbing kit, cancelling everything in the diary for the next three weeks, and dashing to the airport. There was always understanding on the part of employers, but less when it came to social engagements, and none whatever regarding family commitments. The list of absences at weddings, funerals, graduations and even school sports days would lengthen over the years, some never to be forgotten or forgiven. An erosion of marital harmony would be insidious and fateful.

The first leg of my journey was a 17-hour flight to Jakarta, a mega-city with – even then – more than 18 million inhabitants. A fetid tropical odour mingled with the exhaust from millions of vehicles, and driving in from the airport I felt I was breathing air that had already been exhaled a thousand times. The high-rise buildings discharged sewage straight into open drainage ditches, and I learnt later that sewage discoloured the sea for up to 25 kilometres offshore. My small hotel was a few hundred metres from the UN office. Just as the roads were choked with cars, the pavements could hardly contain the mass of humanity.

The other team members had been in the country for some time and were writing reports of their field trips. It was thought that illegal logging and a long period of unusually dry weather had caused the fires. The environmental damage was so immense it was seen as a regional problem, further complicated by accusations of political corruption; the situation appeared intractable. A previous UNDAC mission had covered Irian Jaya, the easternmost of the Indonesian islands, some weeks earlier and the team had since given priority to other islands. Mission Aviation Fellowship (MAF), who flew to the remote villages on Irian Jaya, had informed the United Nations that all was not well and requested another mission.

This was rather delicate, in that the earlier UNDAC mission, focused on the forest fires, had not spotted the major consequence – famine – and had not raised the alarm. I was to go to Irian Jaya with a consultant, David Lewis, to look specifically at this problem. The UNDAC team I had just met would stay in Jakarta to collate information and report to Geneva. David was an American academic with an encyclopaedic knowledge of Irian Jaya. He was also a very good travelling companion.

We would travel another seventeen hours to cover the 2,000 miles to Irian Jaya. We took an overnight flight, stopping at every island, where passengers clambered over the seats to get in and out. It was an exhausting process and made my destination feel like the end of the world, which by every indicator of poverty it was. I knew that the men in remote villages were famous for wearing only penis gourds and infamous for headhunting.

From the provincial capital Jayapura we took another flight to Wamena in an ancient Vickers Viscount turboprop airliner. The road only went some of the way, and petered out into a crocodile-infested swamp. The views were magnificent, with mountains covered in tropical rainforest, and ravines plunging down to rivers thousands of feet below. I expected to see spectacular waterfalls, but the riverbeds all appeared dry. Smoke from the forest fires swirled around us dramatically as we flew, and was a hazard for the pilot. I was not surprised that the fires could be seen from space.

A representative from Mission Aviation Fellowship took us to a charming old-fashioned wooden rest house on the main street, where he explained what had happened. The population were almost wholly dependent on the sweet potato crop, but drought, and severe frost in villages above 6,000 feet, meant that 90,000 people now faced famine. Alternative sources of food from the forest had been destroyed by the fires and many of the pigs, the traditional livestock, had died of disease or been slaughtered for fear they might become infected. At least 400 people were known to have died directly from starvation, but he thought the actual number was significantly higher.

People were walking long distances for water and some sources had become polluted, causing disease. With the decrease in infant mortality over the last two decades, the population had risen and malnutrition was endemic. This crisis was affecting a population with few reserves. Most unusually, local people had been arriving in Wamena every day from remote settlements, having walked for as much as two to three weeks.

"Can we get to any of these places?" I asked. "See that tarmac out there?" was his response. "Even that has been flown here. It's crazy, but there isn't a road from the coast to the capital. There are no roads at all to the villages, just footpaths, and it can take at least a week to walk to where you need to go. The only sensible way is to fly. I'll pick you up tomorrow morning at 6 am."

I had huge respect for MAF pilots. They would fly when nobody else dared to and were truly professional; but I was cautious too, as there had been a number of fatal accidents. We made an early morning start to mitigate the problem of density altitude in the tropics and to avoid the turbulent winds and thermal updraughts that would develop as the day warmed. We were strapped into a single engine Cessna 206 and ready to go, when the pilot turned to us and said, "In the name of Jesus." A brief incantation followed, to which we dutifully said "Amen".

We flew over the rainforest at between 11,000 and 12,000 feet. I was used to this type of flying, but not to what came next. After thirty minutes, we descended into a narrow valley. Ahead of us was a gash in the trees and a 500-metre track, which looked like a steep ramp running straight up the side of the mountain. This was our landing strip. We approached uphill; anything else would have been suicidal. As soon as the wheels touched the rough surface, the pilot applied the power again to avoid sliding back down the mountain, and we taxied upslope at high speed onto a tiny platform, stopping abruptly in a cloud of dust. I was very happy I was not at the controls and glad now of our pilot's prayer.

The missionary and his wife were in their early thirties, friendly and enthusiastic. I was surprised by how young they were. Their two small children with mops of blonde hair were playing outside their modest house perched on the side of the precipitous mountain. The forest crowded round three sides, but the views from the front, down into the valley thousands of feet below, were spectacular. There were no roads, they told me, and it took two weeks to walk the short flight we had just made. He had only recently taken over from his father, who had devoted fifty years of his life to this mission, which had just one development project – the villagers made Christmas tree decorations for sale in New York. He showed me some charming examples and explained that they brought in enough money to pay for medicines and basic essentials. What had astonished the two generations of this family was how long it had taken to get this simple project to work, effectively a lifetime of effort. Development is generational; I often thought of this when I was told in later years by DFID that nation building in Afghanistan would take just four years.

I asked about the forest fires. "Fires aren't the main problem here. There are just no roads, and it's impossible to build any. Without roads, the loggers can't plunder the timber. The problem has been one of the longest droughts I can remember. Children began arriving at our clinic with severe malnutrition six weeks ago and it's been getting worse and worse". I had stumbled onto a real natural disaster. The fires were only a symptom of a much larger problem – drought.

We climbed back up towards the tiny platform where the aircraft was parked, and saw a multitude of small men, pushing and shouting, dressed only in penis gourds. They were turning the aircraft around by hand under the watchful eye of the pilot so that it pointed downslope. I climbed into the rear seat and given the alarming cliff edge only two hundred metres away, tightened my seat belt further. After a quick prayer, the pilot gave the engine full power, released the brakes and we plunged off the platform. The point of no return was the starting point. It was as if we had taxied off a cliff; the nose of the aircraft dropped, the aeroplane was almost vertical now and all I could see over the pilot's head was the riverbed a thousand feet below. The descent was so steep that within 200 metres we were airborne and, with a gentle right turn, we climbed back into the main valley and up 11,000 feet to clear the mountaintops.

Back in Wamena, we spent two days helping MAF to design their famine relief programme. There were many parallels with my experience in Uganda and they were good people to work with, practical and resourceful. On my last night, I found a little restaurant on Wamena's main street. As I sat there writing my report for UNDAC, a man came in, naked except for a penis gourd, sat on the floor and watched the Princess of Wales on television on the far side of the world.

★★★

In the early days of UNDAC, we were required to return to our countries via Geneva for a debriefing, or 'backstopping' as the United Nations curiously called it, followed by lunch in a nearby restaurant. Afterwards there was always a presentation. All the missions to the United Nations were informed beforehand, and the presentations – though perhaps not in those early days very professional – were well-attended. They were certainly the ideal forum for drawing attention to breaking humanitarian emergencies and getting UN appeals funded, as indeed this one was.

Visiting Geneva really made us feel we belonged to our parent organisation, United Nations Office for the Coordination of Humanitarian Affairs (OCHA), whose offices in the magnificent Palais des Nations were always welcoming. They appreciated the hardship we endured on some missions and we were always treated with great courtesy. We were helped with tiresome admin and form-filling by Juliette de Rivero. She was the English 'mother' to the UNDAC members, and was responsible for breathing life into the UNDAC system. She knew everything about each team member, asked about our children whom she knew by name, flattered us, and generally made us feel valued. My first reaction when sent to Lausanne for the UNDAC training course had been sceptical, but I had warmed to this little organisation, with its mixture of national members and full-time UN staff. However much the UN members might protest about the lack of UN process, the national members were happy to use the protocols of their UN colleagues if it helped, but equally happy to ignore them when it did not. Perhaps the secret was that we were not beholden to UN bosses, as our national governments paid our salaries. Many of us were consultants and readily showed independence of thought. The result was a cadre of management for humanitarian emergencies, something that had been missing for all the twenty years I had been involved. Common sense might indicate that to take a multinational, multicultural team of six who had never met before, send them to the end of the earth to tackle an improbably complex disaster and return three weeks later having made a difference, would be less than ideal. Yet, as I was to find out over the years, seventy per cent of our missions were – by any measure – successful.

12

An Unusual Request from China, 1998

A few months later, I was watching television coverage of floods in China when a text message arrived from the UN. Apparently, 223 million people were affected by these floods, and the Chinese government was asking for international help. Such a thing had never happened before.

My flight over the North Pole to Beijing took less time than I anticipated and we arrived at 5 am, a little red-eyed. The small team was led by an Italian, Fabrizio Gentiloni, a United Nations staff member, and included a Norwegian, Terje Skavdal, and a Swede, Eva Johansson.

Our first hours in Beijing were an unfortunate start. A minibus collected us at the airport, and we set off through surprisingly deserted streets. It was still very early in the morning and I dozed off. Suddenly there was an alarming bang, and the minibus came to an abrupt stop, skewed across the road. We all jumped out. There was no traffic anywhere near us, but there was certainly a dent in the front of the vehicle. I gingerly looked underneath and to my horror; I could see a pair of feet. The front axle appeared to be on the chest of the victim. There was not a sound or a movement. We were now all gathered around the front of the minibus, our faces giving away our inner anxiety.

Suddenly, what looked like a garbage collectors' truck pulled up beside us, and two men in dark blue boiler suits got out. An animated discussion took place with our driver, who then asked us in English to try to lift the front of the vehicle. We managed this with some difficulty, whereupon the two characters in boiler suits pulled the man out unceremoniously by his ankles. I knelt beside the victim to see what I could do but within seconds, the garbage men grabbed him by his ankles and wrists and tossed him into the back of the pickup. Some more exchanges with our driver took place and then they were gone, but not before dusting off their hands as if they had got rid of something unpleasant.

Was the victim dead or alive? We tried to find out more over the next twenty-four hours, but failed to get any information, no matter how many times we asked. The only comment we got finally from our host was that "He was North Korean anyway". It was a strange introduction to China.

We were guests of the Communist Party of China and at our first meeting our host, a party official, briefly took us through our two-week field trip programme. There would be two teams, one to the south and the other to the north-eastern provinces of Jilin and Heilongjiang. Terje and I were nominated for the north-east and were to fly to Harbin later that day. The figures given to us at the meeting were astonishing. Overall, 223 million people were affected; nearly 16 million were homeless, 5 million houses had been destroyed and 21 million hectares of farmland were flooded. 3,000 people had lost their lives. In Jilin and Heilongjiang, the floods covered nearly 8,000 square kilometres. We met the Resident Representative of the United Nations Development Programme, Kerstin Leitner, before we left for the airport. She had a commanding presence and impressed on us the importance of our mission – this was the first time that China had ever requested international assistance.

The programme was ambitious. We were to fly to Harbin, the capital of Heilongjiang province. This region was what the BBC referred to as Manchuria, a term associated with the Japanese occupation during World War II and not popular with our hosts. At least twenty party officials were waiting for us at the hotel. I was not expecting such a large entourage. We discovered within hours that our Communist Party interpreters were decidedly unreliable, and strangers to the truth, but luckily, we had our two UN programme officers as interpreters. The organisation, however, was impressive and it was a delight not to have to struggle with transport and accommodation. This was just as well, as we only had two weeks to complete this massive task.

Like most of the cities we visited, Harbin, with a population of nine million, was a dreary place. A few old, grand buildings indicated its former Russian history. Each day we travelled to the flood-affected areas by minibus, stopping in the afternoon at some concrete municipal building for what our hosts described as a symposium. At these, Terje and I would be bombarded with statistics: the numbers of drowned or displaced, residential houses lost, farmland inundated, public buildings destroyed or damaged. It was extraordinary, but despite the torrent of information and the speed at which it was delivered, we did manage to capture most of it on our laptops.

Each day we travelled huge distances and there was not much traffic on the country roads. The floods were of truly biblical proportions. We arrived at the shore of what appeared to be an unnaturally green sea that stretched to the horizon. The army had some awkward looking diesel-engined boats ready, and we were issued with green army groundsheets to protect us from the spray. We needed them, as the combination of wind and the ill-designed hulls made it a very wet journey. For four hours there was no sight of land, and I thought of Noah and his dove. Eventually, we came to a massive dyke made of sandbags. We followed it for five kilometres, then six, then eight, but at ten kilometres, the dyke had been breached.

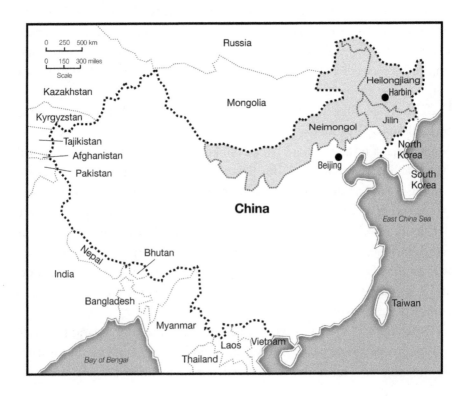

It had all been in vain. I was astonished at this mighty engineering feat. "Who built it?" I asked. "The army," our Communist Party minder said. To my next question – "How many?" – he replied, "A hundred thousand." I was duly astounded.

Occasionally we hit the roof of a submerged house, which nearly tipped us all into the two-metre-deep water. At one stage the engine broke down, which, given the state of maintenance, was no surprise. I had been keeping an apprehensive eye on the loose fuel line for some time; it finally came off, and a jet of diesel sprayed the hot engine. We were lucky not to have a fire on board. Eventually, after some frantic tinkering with the engine, we arrived back on dry land. When we handed back our groundsheets, we saw that the green dye had run, so we comically looked like leprechauns.

There was a great deal of activity, as those who had lost their homes were building shelters. These were most ingenious. Timbers covered in soil formed a 'tent' above shallow trenches topped with a layer of bricks that allowed heat from the cooking fire at one end to circulate underneath. Under blue skies, the temperature was now 20°C, but in six weeks' time it would be -20°C. Escaping my political minder and taking a UN interpreter, I went to chat to two old men sitting on a log. "Are you going to build a shelter?" I asked. They looked surprised. "No," they answered. "The logs are too heavy for us to lift." "Can't the young men help you?" I persisted naively. The answer was frank and brutal. "No," they said. "We're going to die."

On the way to the next city, we passed what looked like a prison. "What's that?" I asked my political minder. "An industrial park," came the bland reply. "With machine guns and watchtowers?" I enquired. He changed the subject. I was getting used to being told nonsense all day long by our political minders, but once we were out of earshot our UN interpreters were quick to tell us what was really being said.

Economic growth in China had been so rapid that some towns we passed through had over one million inhabitants. But they were yet to be marked on the map I had been given, which had been printed quite recently. The weather became humid and blue skies were replaced by grey. The long journey every day, the daily symposium and the nightly banquet organised by our hosts at some dismal municipal building were beginning to pall. Every night we had to make sense of laptops full of data, so we were very late to bed, and were off again at dawn.

The banquets were an uncertain pleasure. Once the food arrived, the clicking of chopsticks sounded like typewriter keys as elbows windmilled vast quantities of food into the mouths of our fellow guests. It was like a children's tea party; eating was the objective, not talking. At some point, our host would give a speech and we were expected to respond. Terje and I took it in turns to do this. We could not help adding to our speech each evening, and I must confess a small devil perched on my shoulder when it was my turn, the oleaginous nature of my praise for the hospitality reaching new heights. I was always scrupulously polite, but what was required was formalised nonsense. At the last banquet, the menu was translated into English for us and, to my disquiet; it read 'delicious dog's meat'. We had passed a lorry the day before, piled high with caged dogs. For an Englishman, it was akin to cannibalism. I just felt our hosts knew that.

Our last symposium was held at the main provincial office and there must have been at least a hundred people in the room. It was the final opportunity to be bombarded with information, and for them to gather our thoughts on solutions. We divided the task under the usual headings – water and sanitation, food, shelter and medical facilities – which seemed strangely novel for them. It was clear to us that deforestation at the headwaters had exacerbated problems downstream, so we suggested establishing a river authority. I was surprised by the reaction. The concept of a trans-provincial authority simply had no meaning for them.

Back in Beijing, we began the Herculean job of making sense of it all. The figure of 200 million people was a political figure, but it was clear that 5.8 million were severely affected. Even this was an enormous number, and we had to put together a sensible programme to support them. Terje's experience and mine were complementary, and his sense of humour actually made the immense task of writing the appeal entertaining. The massive task was complete within five days, including a briefing and organising a press conference for the Resident Representative. We put together an appeal for 139 million US dollars.

Meanwhile, our colleagues in the south were struggling. They had found the volume of data bewildering. Unlike them, Terje and I both had business experience and I was very thankful for my time at business school, where analysis under time pressure was highly valued. It was easy to be discouraged by the scale of this disaster.

I was soon on my way back to Geneva. My experiences in Indonesia and China had shown me that UNDAC provided a cadre of trained emergency managers that really could make a difference. We had taken only the first faltering steps but the potential was obvious. UNDAC had come of age. Even so, the concept was faintly implausible, and it was amazing that it worked at all. Sometimes it did not, as I was about to find out.

13

A False Start, Afghanistan Earthquakes 1998

In February 1998 a devastating earthquake, measuring 6.1 on the Richter scale, hit north-east Afghanistan, killing nearly two and a half thousand people. Takhar Province is a truly inaccessible place on the Afghanistan-Tajikistan border, and it would be difficult to find a more challenging place to provide immediate relief. The roads were either boulder-strewn tracks beside rivers or donkey trails in the mountains. There was no telephone network, and relief work would be hampered by snow and ice. Added to which, the earthquake was close to the front line of a bitter civil war between the Taliban and the Northern Alliance.

The earthquake occurred an hour after sunset, when most people were at home. The mud walls and flat timber roof beams collapsed, killing those inside, and overturned oil lamps and cooking fires, setting fire to the damaged houses. Many of the survivors suffered terrible burns. Villagers remained on the mountainsides without shelter in temperatures as low as -10°C. Aftershocks and landslides added to the confusion.

There was a UNDAC alert, and the next day I was on my way to Islamabad in Pakistan to join my team. It was raining torrentially and never stopped for the next two weeks. Within minutes of arriving at the UN building, I sensed that not all was going according to plan. There was no sense of urgency. The United Nations in Islamabad had taken three days to accept the offer of a UNDAC team and my three team members had only arrived the previous day. Speed is central to any earthquake response; with every day, hope fades for survivors buried alive. It was now five critical days since the earthquake.

My unhappy team listed the problems they had encountered in just twenty-four hours. As UNDAC was a new organisation, outlying parts of the UN had no idea what we were for, hence the delay in mobilising us. Our attempts to explain that we were deployed to assess and coordinate – a euphemism for 'manage' – fell on deaf ears. Frustratingly, we were seen as spare clerical staff, simply there to collate and manage information. This was depressing enough, but we could see that another issue was more challenging – we were in Pakistan, 400 miles from the earthquake, which was in Afghanistan.

The insecurity in Afghanistan after Kabul had fallen to the Taliban had led to a relocation of the Afghan UN office, the clumsily-named United Nations Coordination of Humanitarian Assistance in Afghanistan (UNOCHA), to Islamabad. These offices in exile never seemed to have their fingers on the pulse and they became immersed in international political manoeuvring. Furthermore, there was a civil war in Afghanistan and the earthquake was close to the front line between Rabbani's Northern Alliance and the Taliban. The Afghan Embassy in Dushanbe, Tajikistan,

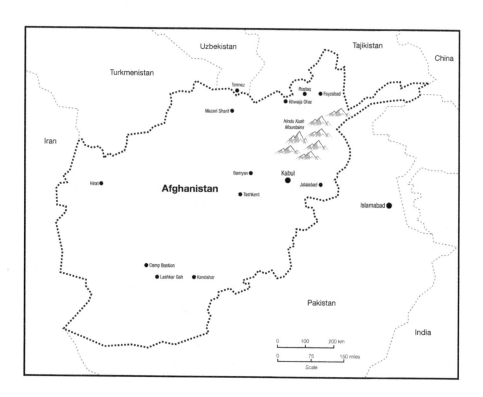

loyal to the Northern Alliance, had grossly exaggerated the number of lives lost and this had made the International Federation of Red Cross and Red Crescent Societies (IFRCS), and the UN, suspicious. Initially they thought that the area was not densely populated.

Terrain was our next problem. Between us and the earthquake was the Hindu Kush, a mountain range rising to over 20,000 feet. And between the earthquake in Takhar Province and Dushanbe in Tajikistan, a distance of only one hundred air miles, was the Amu Darya (Oxus) river, which had remarkably few bridges. Our small UNDAC team seemed to have insuperable obstacles ahead. We were going to do the wrong job, in the wrong country, and we were too late. I remembered the military aphorism about a plan never recovering from landing on the wrong beach.

We spent the next week in a cold office collating information and writing a UN consolidated appeal, but while it was only raining here in Islamabad, in Afghanistan it was snowing. As I lay in bed at night listening to the rain I thought of those we had come to help, homeless, in several feet of snow on the far side of the Hindu Kush.

At the beginning of the second week, I was sent to Peshawar to work with ICRC on the airdrop operation, which had just started. There was concern about the state of the runway at Khwaja Ghar airstrip in Afghanistan. The relief effort depended on air operations, the vital link with Rustaq, the town most badly damaged. I flew there on one of the relief flights to make an assessment. Communications had been hopeless; HF radio communications were very poor from Islamabad due to the mountains, and the early UN satellite telephones had worked only for a few days before power surges from portable generators rendered them useless.

The car journey to Peshawar in a Land Cruiser, 188 miles along the Grand Trunk Road (one of Asia's oldest and longest major roads), was enough to give the most carefree spirit a duodenal ulcer. My UN driver took the view that might was always right and overtook on every blind corner as a matter of course. Remonstrating had no effect whatsoever. Multi-coloured tinkling trucks missed us by millimetres and we passed two fatal accidents. At one, a blanket had been thrown over the victim's head, and a solitary shoe lay in the middle of the road.

I was hugely relieved when we finally arrived at Peshawar Airport, where an ancient Antonov was still being loaded. The skies looked menacing, but for the first time in two weeks it had stopped raining. I sat in the flight engineer's seat for the hour's flight over the Hindu Kush, a journey that reinforced my view that it was unwise to run this relief operation from Pakistan. We descended through thick cloud and the low foothills on the northern side of the Hindu Kush appeared beneath us. Visible now was the vast and desolate plain of the river Oxus sweeping north towards Tajikistan.

The gravel airstrip looked very wet, but we landed easily enough and taxied to a small hut. It was damp with a penetrating northerly wind only a few degrees above freezing, but Taco Mulder, who was managing the airstrip for the ICRC, seemed cheerful despite the cold. Apart from him and a crowd of fifty Afghans squatting out of the wind behind the building, the place was deserted. The Afghans set about unloading the aircraft manually; it had a busy schedule and would soon be off. I was to be collected later in the day by a UN Beechcraft King Air. This plan, given the weather, the war and the remoteness, had an unsettling improbability. With limited time, I tried to extract as much information as I could. The main problem was the practical difficulty of moving the relief supplies on to where they were needed. Rustaq was seventy kilometres away and trucks were difficult to find. Taco mentioned that the UN Resident Representative in Dushanbe had not been fully engaged, as it was 'not his patch' – although Dushanbe was only a hundred air miles away. I found this rather depressing, as I had just flown 400 miles over one of the most inhospitable mountain ranges in the world. An additional problem was soon to become self-evident.

We drove down to inspect the runway. There were some very wet patches where the gravel was so soft that the aircraft had left ruts over two feet deep. We marked them with a pile of stones on the edge of the runway so we could warn the pilots using the airfield. As we returned to the hut, an Afghan Antonov arrived; the landing was impressive, sending up huge plumes of spray. I had never seen an airliner land on wet gravel before. The Russian pilot asked about the condition of the far end of the runway, and my colleague warned him not to taxi beyond the marker – the pile of stones we had made earlier. The pilot was a man of few words and was soon off. As he passed the marker, one wing dipped giddily, and we heard the roar of the engines as he applied full power, then silence. The huge aircraft was truly stuck. I began to assess the prospects of leaving this forlorn place. I was in Afghanistan, close to the frontline of a brutal civil war; it was already late on a winter afternoon with less than two hours of light left, the weather was closing in, and now Homo Sovieticus was blocking the runway, his main wheels up to their axles in mud. He did not seem remotely bothered that the main gear was at the bottom of a three-foot trench. Within minutes, the fifty Afghans who had been unloading our aircraft appeared, carrying long-handled shovels – this was obviously routine – and silently got to work digging out the airliner. The pilot climbed back into the cockpit, ran up the engines and gave full power. To my amazement, in a manoeuvre that would have torn the undercarriage off any airliner built in the West, the aircraft churned its way out of the boggy ground, and he was gone. In less than an hour, my aircraft approached from the south, and we took off in the dusk, with me relieved to be climbing once again over the snow-covered Hindu Kush, to Islamabad 400 miles to the south.

Our UNDAC mission was only for two weeks and it had been a frustrating experience. The UN Office in Islamabad did not really understand what UNDAC was for, hence the late deployment and the idea that we were emergency clerical staff, there to manage information and write consolidated appeals. The idea that we were to get on the ground, assess and coordinate an international response was horribly threatening and we never got the point across. It was an attitude that we encountered in the early years of UNDAC. Eventually, however, the country UN teams, who had very little experience of managing emergencies, realised that once we were deployed they were no longer responsible for the outcome, and attitudes changed. It was incredible that, despite all the problems, the 32,000 earthquake victims did receive some supplies and the airdrops made a significant impact. Amazingly, 700 tons were eventually delivered.

The limitations of trying to run emergency operations in Afghanistan from Islamabad in Pakistan had been exposed, but this was only part of a greater tragedy. As often happens, another devastating earthquake hit Takhar Province four months later, in May. This one measured 6.9 on the Richter scale, which, being a logarithmic scale meant it was substantially bigger than the February quake. This time 5,000 people were killed and 160,000 affected, five times as many as in February.

We were mobilised quickly and I joined two other UNDAC members, Simo Wecksten and Peter Swartling, for the flight to Islamabad. Our team leader, Rudolph Muller, was already there. Within hours of arrival, we were on a charter flight to Fayzabad in Afghanistan.

As the wheels touched down on the runway, there was an alarming metallic whine and a mechanical clattering; the Russians had built an all-weather runway during the war in the 1980s by pegging perforated metal sheets to the boggy ground. Even now, the remains of Russian military vehicles littered the field, lying where they had been abandoned. The terminal was a roofless hut with scorch marks down one side from a fire. Most of the airfield buildings had been looted of their roofs, doors and windows and, as I was soon to discover, the only covered space was home to several dozen journalists who had arrived the previous day from Tajikistan. We were in a narrow lush valley with the small town of Fayzabad lying in a fold of the hills at the eastern end, but I was so surprised by the journalists milling about that I hardly noticed the astonishing beauty of the place.

A UN staff member asked me to accompany her to one of the destroyed villages, Dawlat Kol. We climbed into an ageing UN M18 helicopter full of tents, blankets and water containers. I luckily found some earplugs in my jacket to moderate the noise of this ancient machine. Only fifteen minutes later, we arrived at one of the worst hit villages, and I soon had a helpful overview of the situation. There was hardly a building left standing. The heavy earth roofs had collapsed and only mounds of earth were left, with wooden roofing beams poking from them. The survivors were camping outside the ruins of their homes, listless and paralysed by shock.

I soon discovered to my surprise that I had been brought here to triage patients for the Médecins Sans Frontières surgical team in Fayzabad. It was a daunting task, as there was limited space on the helicopter. There was every sort of injury and everyone had been forced to sleep in the open since the earthquake, and had been soaked by the spring storms. The decisions I had to make were particularly hard – burns versus fractures and lacerations, walking wounded over stretcher cases – as it was probably a case of now or never. Helicopter fuel was limited, and I knew there might be no further flights to this village for some time.

While I was there, there was another aftershock. The terror was pitiful. I was told there were up to four aftershocks every day, severe enough to cause further damage to buildings. As we flew back to Fayzabad, I could see where the earthquake had sent entire hillsides sliding away into the steep-sided valleys.

Back at the airfield, we met our team leader, Angus Fraser, who worked for the World Food Programme. Seeming unsure what to do with us, he briefed us in the open air against the roar of helicopters so it was difficult to hear him. It was equally unclear what he wanted us to do. Like his colleagues in Islamabad, he had the firm idea that our role was only to collect and disseminate information. Before we could ask questions or clarify anything, he was off in a helicopter, where to and why was never explained. We did not see him again for three days.

The only available covered space on the airfield was occupied by the crowd of journalists. There were no latrines, refuse lay scattered everywhere, and everything needed to run a major relief operation was absent. There was no operations room or tent, no office or equipment, and no logistics management. There was nowhere to sit or write and – considering the airfield was half an hour from the town – there was nothing to eat or drink. Worst of all, now that Peter Swartling had left for Rustaq with the generator, we had limited battery life to our satellite telephones and laptops. It was also unclear who was in charge, as our team leader had disappeared without delegating authority.

It was not just these basic requirements that presented such a challenge. As the UN, we were the coordinator, yet we were second, if not third, fiddle to two other humanitarian organisations working on the airfield. The International Red Cross had chartered three helicopters from Dushanbe and had more of a presence than the UN with only one. Médecins Sans Frontières had now arrived, and began to assemble a 1,000 square metre Rubb Hall, a large relocatable tent-like structure.

With no clear instructions, we started to set up our operational headquarters. By the end of our second day, the remainder of the team had arrived and, with their help and equipment, we were able to set up a radio room, meeting room and operations room inside one of the derelict buildings.

I was concerned about landmines on the airfield. All military targets were traditionally mined and there was no reason to think this one would not be. I went to see Commander Mohammed, the local militia leader, and the next day – astonishingly – a local team turned up to clear the areas we wanted to use. As I learnt later this was probably pure theatre, a service that generated a fee. He probably knew these areas were free of mines.

With the arrival of so many foreigners, some enterprising locals set up a mini bazaar at the airfield entrance selling Pepsi and cartons of Iranian cherry juice. They even provided petrol at 45 US dollars a litre. The runway proved to be quite a hazard to incoming aircraft; after each landing, it had to be inspected and huge jagged pieces of metal hammered back into place. The four helicopters were now delivering to as many of the eighty-four badly-damaged villages as they could, but a shortage of fuel and bad weather were major constraints. They flew back to Dushanbe each night and, until an Antonov flew in with a delivery of drummed fuel, flying hours were limited.

We stayed in Fayzabad about ten kilometres away. The road was a mud track strewn with large rocks along the side of the river. It took at least forty minutes to drive it, and I could see why the locals preferred to ride. Horses would have been significantly more comfortable than the dilapidated Russian jeep we hired, which wheezed its way to town on three of its four cylinders, bouncing over boulders, our driver doing everything in his power to shorten its remaining life. Along the side of the road were fields full of opium poppies, all in flower.

One day a black cloud appeared over Fayzabad, an impending thunderstorm. Within minutes, there was a stampede to Fayzabad. Simo and I carried on working and left at our usual time, just before last light. We soon discovered why the others had left in such haste. The dry riverbed had been transformed into a two-metre deep fast-flowing torrent so powerful that huge boulders were being carried down the mountain. We sat on the bank for two hours before we could cross safely.

In town, we slept on the floor of a grim concrete building with a huge crack through one wall caused by the earthquake. During the aftershocks, I did wonder how safe it was. But at least during the thunderstorms, it was dry and relatively clean. One evening an Afghan member of our UNDAC team invited us to supper at his house. It was a great honour to be invited into an Afghan home and I was hugely impressed, despite the ascetic lifestyle, how well the Afghans lived. There were no women present and we chatted about many things. The cultural collision of attitudes towards women did come up in conversation, but our host, working for the UN, did not hold the conservative views of the majority of Afghan men, although he was worried about the West trying to enforce social change from outside.

One incident that demonstrated the gulf that separated UN office staff from fieldwork was the delivery of fuel for the helicopters. The UN office in Islamabad told us an Antonov was on its way with ten tonnes of aviation fuel. It would arrive just before sunset when almost everybody had left the airfield and the UN office were concerned we would not be able to unload it. For insurance reasons, the aircraft had to have a quick turnaround time and be out of the war zone before dark. My message back to Islamabad that this would not be a problem was met with blank incomprehension. How could two people unload ten metric tons of fuel without assistance in less than thirty minutes? Fortunately, both Simo and I had handled 200-litre drums of fuel for most of our adult lives. In the event, we just tipped them onto their sides and rolled them down the rear cargo ramp. The job was done in fifteen minutes and the happy pilot was on his way back to Pakistan.

By the time our team leader reappeared, we had a functioning coordination centre. Simo was a Finnish firefighter, and very resourceful. He was not the only one. A young French woman was in charge of the construction of Médecins Sans Frontières' warehouse on the airfield. She made no concessions to Afghan modesty, wore T-shirts, with her bare arms showing, and never covered her hair. She took no nonsense from Commander Mohammed's men, who were clearly in awe of her. If I needed the Afghans to do anything, I just had a word with her and it would be done immediately.

The helicopter operations were a source of constant disappointment. On a good day, they delivered an impressive payload, but fuel was always a problem. I would have travelled by helicopter to make some assessments but my eighty kilograms was eighty kilograms of assistance in lost payload, enough to save more than one life. The operators were unwilling to leave their valuable aircraft in a war zone overnight, so every evening they flew one hundred miles to Dushanbe where they were based, to return at first light, a huge waste, as these ancient Soviet machines guzzled 1,100 litres of fuel an hour.

Unlike the February earthquake, the weather was warm and improving by the day, though violent thunderstorms were not uncommon. It was on such days that we appreciated the importance of the donkey teams organised by the Red Cross, which delivered a substantial quantity of relief. Sometimes low-tech solutions suit a low-tech environment, and the donkey teams were surprisingly effective.

Towards the end of the second week, I spotted five military helicopters parked near the government rest house in Fayzabad. The Pakistani Army had flown in with humanitarian assistance, and I assumed that the government of Pakistan had sent them to assist us in the mountains. However, something didn't feel right. Pakistan had leanings towards the Taliban, and here the

Northern Alliance were supported by Iran. Humanitarian assistance should override politics, but I suspected it might not.

I found the Colonel, a tall impressive-looking character, strangely wearing a UN baseball cap with his military uniform. I asked about the helicopters, but his answers were evasive and his manner hostile. "They have brought humanitarian assistance," he said, "and we shall shortly be returning to Pakistan." I mentioned the 160,000 people camped out in the mountains. He categorically refused to assist us. I told him there were two dozen journalists at the airfield and I suggested the positive things they might say about Pakistan if he joined the relief operation. I then foolishly mentioned that fuel had recently been delivered to the airport. If he could help us, I said, we could refuel his helicopters. For a moment, he looked more positive, but for the wrong reason. What I did not know was that the ousted Afghan President Rabbani had promised this delegation aviation fuel and had none to give. Whatever they had really come to do – and the humanitarian element seemed spurious – they were stranded without fuel.

Clearly, the last thing the Pakistanis expected was to find the international media in Fayzabad. Bringing a few hundred kilos of assistance by helicopter was meaningless when the airfield was open only a few miles away. Yet as we left Fayzabad the next morning, we heard the helicopters heading for the airport. When we got there, there was chaotic pandemonium. The Pakistanis were attempting to take the UN fuel and having to be physically restrained, and the journalists were hounding them. I demanded to see the responsible Pakistani Representative. The Colonel, still wearing his UN baseball cap, walked up with a slightly-built man, allegedly an official from the Ministry of Foreign Affairs. They arrogantly stated their claim to the fuel. By now, we were surrounded by journalists. Seeing that de-escalation was required, and UN diplomacy would be better served by discussing this privately rather than in front of the world media, I asked the Colonel and the official to follow me to the blackened ruin that served as our operations room. Twenty minutes of high-intensity diplomacy followed. My options were extremely limited and would inevitably mean a loss of face for the Pakistanis, despite my attempt to portray this diplomatically as a simple misunderstanding. This, I knew, could only end badly. There was nothing to negotiate and their aggression and threats against me personally were unpleasant.

There was something deeply depressing about their stance. They had the power to do good, but they had chosen to prevent others from doing good. Seeing that an unfavourable interpretation of this event might bounce around the world's capitals, I decided to get a statement from the UN Coordinator in Islamabad, Alfredo Witschi-Cestari. When this came through, supporting my decision to deny them fuel, I handed it to them and they retreated to the other side of the airfield, pursued by journalists. Eventually, they siphoned some fuel from the wing tanks of President Rabbani's Antonov, and were gone. The encounter had been bizarre but intriguing. Politics were never far from the surface in humanitarian emergencies.

The response to both earthquakes had been chaotic. However, many things made this mission particularly difficult. It had occurred in one of the most remote places in the world. There were hardly any roads, or even telephones to raise the alarm. Having the UN Coordinator based in Pakistan had been unhelpful in both cases, and the contribution from the Dushanbe office had been minimal. It was clear that the operation should have been run from Tajikistan. It did not help either that we were operating in the middle of a war. Despite this, Geneva was pleased with what UNDAC had achieved. It had performed better than any of us imagined, and as a result of the difficulties there were many changes. We never again deployed without a support package. In time, this included taking an IT team with us as well as our own team leaders, not relying on them being provided by other UN agencies. Frustrating as the problems had been, the mission was a major step forward for the organisation.

This was the first time helicopters had been used in a major humanitarian emergency. It would take another seven years, until the Pakistan earthquake of 2005, for their use to be routinely expected. I also observed that substantial delivery of humanitarian assistance never really happened until the beginning of the third week of any emergency. Twenty years later, this remains the case.

This mission had been a case of one step forward and two steps back. However, lessons were learnt and substantial changes were made. I had yet to be made a team leader, but had seen the challenges that involved. The hierarchy of the team was flat, and often the skill sets of the members were unknown, as were their temperaments under stress.

14

In a Strange Country, Albania 1999

The flames in the Balkans had been extinguished in Croatia by the Vance-Owen Peace Plan of 1992, and in Bosnia eventually by the Dayton Peace Agreement of 1995. However, the underlying political fault line had a habit of producing unpleasant aftershocks. This time it was Kosovo. The Serbs had fought the Battle of Kosovo in 1389, giving Kosovo, for them, almost sacred status, and in recent years they had refused to recognise the rights of the majority ethnic Albanian population. By late 1998, the Kosovo Liberation Army was mounting attacks on Yugoslav authorities, and the violence escalated when President Milošević ordered his paramilitary police force and army into Kosovo. After a campaign of terror, nearly a million Kosovar Albanians had fled into neighbouring Macedonia, Montenegro and Albania. NATO's response was to launch an air war against Serbia, which began on 24 March 1999 and continued for seven weeks.

Although the UNDAC system was designed for natural disasters, we were to be deployed on a conflict-related mission for the first time. I was joined by Fabrizio Hochschild, one of the most talented of the UN's younger generation in New York, and Niels Munk, a senior Danish diplomat. After a six-hour flight on a Danish C-130 to Albania, the three of us made our way to the UNHCR office in the centre of Tirana.

I was struck by the strangeness of Albania. Forty years of isolation under the bizarre dictatorship of its Communist leader Enver Hoxha had made Albania truly different. If anyone were to wake up disoriented after a heavy anaesthetic in Albania, they would remain disorientated, in both time and place. There were no visual clues except one – Hoxha's programme of bunkerisation. The dictator became so convinced his small state would be invaded at any moment that he built bunkers in every corner of Albania, from mountain passes to city streets. Perhaps as many as 750,000 are still dotted across the country. These extraordinary one- or two-person concrete pillboxes, with gun slits to defend the country against an imaginary enemy, were ubiquitous, and so ludicrous that journalist black humour suggested they could be used to house the similar number of refugees shortly to arrive in the country. Beyond this, the language and appearance of the population were unlike those anywhere else in Western Europe, and a time warp placed the country at best at the beginning of the 1970s. Since then, it had remained the poorest country in Europe. In 1997, the failure of a large-scale Ponzi scheme not only prompted the country to fall into financial ruin, but also sparked a mass rebellion that toppled the government, adding to the country's woes. Anarchy and looting broke out and 2,000 people were killed. The disturbances were so serious that the UN authorised the deployment of 7,000 Italian troops to restore order. With this unhappy legacy, I was not surprised that it was the oddest place I had ever visited.

UNHCR had been wholly unprepared for the arrival of over 290,000 refugees, and it was obvious the organisation was floundering. Worse, all the Head of Mission could do was tell us how to claim our daily subsistence allowance. However, he did mention that the Albanian government planned to run a coordination centre from the Prime Minister's office; at least we knew immediately where we would be best placed to work.

In an effort to find somewhere to stay, we tried the main hotel. However, the reception was full of media – among them the journalist Sam Kiley whom I had not seen since Angola six years previously – and the receptionist was trying to placate those who thought they had booked rooms and whose disappointment was turning to anger. When it came to us, she said rather cryptically, "Meet me in the car park at half past five and I'll see what I can do."

At 5.30 pm, with no better option, we met her in the car park. With her were two young men wearing leather jackets, mirrored sunglasses and flashy gold watches. I didn't exactly warm to them. "Go with them. They have something for you," she said. They led us to a brand-new red BMW with no number plates. We were in a place known for violence, extortion and criminal organisations, and I was about to get into a car with two strangers. It began to rain heavily and in an hour, I knew, it would be dark. "You want apartment – no?" was the only attempt at conversation.

We drove down unpaved refuse-strewn streets, past rows of shabby houses. There was a rumble of thunder; the sky was now black as ink. Feeling extraordinarily foolish, I watched everything, the two men in the front, and every detail of the streets, in case I needed to make a hasty exit. Suddenly, we stopped. Incongruously, a newly-built apartment block stood proudly above this poor neighbourhood. We went in and, to my amazement, found ourselves in an impressive flat. Within minutes a deal was done. In the days to come, when we mentioned our apartment to the UN drivers, they went pale. Although UNHCR did not say anything, I could sense that they considered the neighbourhood distinctly unsafe. However, when Daniel Mora Castro, UNHCR's Senior Water Development Officer, took accommodation nearby our fears were somewhat diminished. He also gave us a lift to work every day in his UN Land Cruiser.

The new Emergency Management Group at the Prime Minister's office was in a solid, rather grand building on one side of a square near the parliament. For the next month, we were engaged in an extraordinary struggle to coordinate the response to a humanitarian emergency affecting a million people. The scale of the outflow of Kosovar Albanians from Kosovo had surprised not only UNHCR, but the rest of the world. On our first day, there were already 290,000 refugees and by the end of the fourth week there were 977,000. To begin with, most were absorbed by the generosity of host families. Four weeks later, it was difficult to find even enough flat ground for people to lie down. On a good day, there might only be 3,000 refugees arriving in Albania, on a bad day 50,000.

Fabrizio and I hardly left the Prime Minister's office for the whole month. It was the most frantic, most arduous and most political of all the missions I had experienced. This deployment was important for the UN because, for the first time, the old ideas of coordination were finally being replaced by new ideas of management. Coordination for the UN had always been an Achilles heel. No one wanted to be coordinated, and in any case the UN Coordinator had no authority to tell any organisation what to do. This was all about to change, and what happened was revolutionary. Firstly, the Albanian government gave OCHA the authority to coordinate the international response. As we were now doing this on behalf of the government, at least we had the authority we needed. Secondly, instead of the feeble coordination meetings traditionally held by the UN, we now had the 'daily brief' and separate sector coordination meetings, which only involved the organisations engaged in those sectors. It was now clear what the meetings were trying to achieve.

It was always the same agenda, at the same time and place. We would provide the latest refugee situation to an audience of between 150 and 200. The agencies responsible for food, health, shelter and logistics then updated the meeting on what was happening. This meant it was easier to hold them to account. The Albanian government chaired the meeting, which avoided the usual problem of international agencies ignoring the government of the country. The meetings only lasted an hour, a radical change from the typical UN meetings which rambled on inconclusively for four hours. Embassies and donors who always attended also saw the daily brief as useful. It became the daily gathering place in Tirana; everybody could conduct their business before or after the meetings. With most major donors – the EU and embassies from rich countries – present, we could make a pitch for things that were desperately needed, and they, seeing the operation properly managed, were more inclined to give them. The Albanian government was pleased as, in a very public way, they appeared to have everything under control. The real coordination work was done by only four sectors, which given the scale of the emergency was enough – water and sanitation, shelter, food and medical assistance – under the auspices of a government ministry with the help of the UN. We were struggling to provide even those basic needs.

More than 500 NGOs had arrived in Tirana and were complaining they were not properly represented. Next to the Prime Minister's office was a strange glass pyramid-shaped building, a museum of the late dictator Hoxha. I suggested it should become the NGO forum, which was readily accepted. The NGOs then chose a representative to join our management meetings. This quickly sidelined dissent, otherwise it would have been impossible to manage so many people with diverse and often quite strident views.

Fabrizio and I spent every morning running the meeting and every afternoon preparing for the next one. The office swarmed with donors, ambassadors, journalists, and politicians. My experiences in Cambodia and Uganda, when field trips were a vital and central part of the job, now seemed to belong to a different life. Then I was out amongst the people, trying to see problems through their eyes and adjust accordingly. Here I was incarcerated in the Prime Minister's office, almost never getting out. However, I was very aware that the appearance of good management was unlikely to be mirrored in the field. An analogy I used at the time was: the pedals may be flying round, but the chain might not be on the back wheel. I decided to go on a field trip and take a look for myself.

The next day I set off in a UN vehicle for the town of Kukes in the north-east, 150 kilometres away. I immediately realised it was going to be a slow day. It was not that there was a huge volume of traffic; it was just there were very few tarmac roads, and the majority were simply tracks. A vintage Puch-type moped passed us as we left Tirana, ridden by a chap wearing an equally vintage open-face helmet. He was still ahead of us when we reached Kukes four hours later. I felt I could have reached our destination quicker on a bicycle.

Everything looked half-finished or prematurely abandoned. Even attempts at farming looked half-hearted. We were going to need water for the refugee camps, yet I was told that Albania had the most polluted groundwater in the world from mine tailings of heavy metals. Nothing surprised me in this, the oddest of odd places.

As we arrived in Kukes, the atmosphere was as dark as its reputation for gang rivalry and murder. We stopped at the only hotel, where I met Lieutenant Colonel Trefor Williams, who I had last seen in Banja Luka. He had subsequently left the army and was now working for an NGO. He ran up the steps of the hotel almost out of breath, and warned me that only a few streets away he had witnessed a murder. As he was passing a road junction, two shots were fired from a car at a man on the pavement, who fell to the ground screaming in agony. One of the occupants of the car had jumped out and shot the man in the head at point-blank range. I was silent for a moment. Some gunshots could be heard in the distance. Trefor continued to describe the chaos on the border, as each day thousands more refugees arrived from Kosovo.

Feeling unsettled by his stories, I went to the border to assess the tide of desperate humanity arriving in Albania, and the valiant attempts by UNHCR to look after them. The UNHCR field officer told me that whatever they had was woefully inadequate for the numbers arriving each day and that the system they had in place to receive people had effectively broken down. From the coordination room in Tirana all seemed well, but my suspicion was correct – the chain was not on the back wheel. The relief operation was faltering and complete chaos was not far away.

The international humanitarian agencies could manage 250,000 people easily, and 500,000 with difficulty; at 750,000, cracks would appear in the system, while at over 900,000 it would collapse. I was glad to get away from the fractious atmosphere of the Prime Minister's office for a day. There was no substitute for getting out in the field, yet Kukes was not a place to spend a moment more than necessary. On the return journey, the driver pointed out a huge unfinished motorway. This project had, in the way of all things Albanian, been abandoned a decade previously, its bridges forlornly but rather gracefully spanning several valleys that could be seen from the main road to Tirana.

The next day I heard that the British Army was about to be deployed on Operation Allied Harbour. They were coming to help us with the refugees, the first time that NATO had been deployed on a humanitarian mission. I knew the Commander, Lieutenant General John Reith, from my work at the Permanent Joint Force Headquarters two years earlier. The advance party was soon with us and a Canadian staff liaison officer was appointed to the Emergency Management Group. Charming and positive, he was delightful to have with us. The key to the military deployment would be the de-confliction of logistics. Deploying a force of this size with contributions from twenty-five countries would block all air and seaports. A UN Joint Logistics Centre was set up, with both UN and military logistics officers, to make sure this did not happen. This turned out to be such a success it has been used subsequently whenever the UN and military units have to work together. Most Albanians saw the deployment of NATO as a positive development, one that might provide some stability, while for others it was a business opportunity.

The humanitarian emergency generated plenty of discord. There was unhappiness between agencies, and disagreements between strong-willed individuals, donors and the Albanian government. People were exhausted and stressed, and our job was to defuse difficult situations, calm fevered brows, smooth ruffled feathers and prevent diplomatic ripples. We had two meeting rooms and at times had to change rooms after a particularly bad session to escape the tension palpable in the room. It was exhausting. At 9 pm we would stagger out to a restaurant we called the Carlsberg, after the advertising sign outside and the beer we found inside. We definitely needed it.

By the third week in April we had 750,000 refugees, and it was becoming increasingly difficult to find anywhere for them to go. There were now plans for NATO to help with the construction of camps for 200,000, but it would take a month for these to be ready. Finding suitable sites anywhere had been seriously difficult. The low-lying areas had been flooded by recent heavy rain, the high water tables made sanitation difficult. Even the groundwater was polluted with heavy metals and Lindane, an agricultural pesticide. It was impossible to do anything quickly. There was confusion over public and private ownership of land; where local government had decided on sites, there had been subsequent disputes. Even where the sites had been agreed, farmers objected to the construction of gravel tracks across their land. Most of the sites were small and inaccessible, and supplying a large number of small sites with food and relief supplies was a huge logistical task. This was Albania and, with any disagreement or dispute, violence was never far away.

Host families had taken in most of the earlier refugees, but this was a poor country and it was an increasing burden for them. I looked at ways of supporting these host families financially as well as with food aid. Many public buildings belonged to government enterprises that had ceased trading or been looted during the Albanian Rebellion following the failed Ponzi scheme in 1997. If renovated, these could provide desperately needed shelter. After the success of the Quick Impact Projects in Bosnia, this was something the NATO force might do. I had one other more adventurous idea, to build camps along the unfinished Tirana-Shkodra motorway. It had many advantages over other sites, not least that it was actually owned by the government. It was also near the seaport of Durres and very accessible.

Fabrizio and I had another concern. The former Communist love of mind-numbing bureaucracy had brought the import of humanitarian aid almost to a standstill, causing a cacophony of complaint from donor governments and humanitarian agencies. Agency vehicles were blocking the port of Durres because the Albanian customs would not release them, and even health NGOs were being harassed for being in possession of medical drugs, which was evidently illegal. With ministers never available, the discord was vented on me, Fabrizio and the Emergency Management

Group. It was an unusual experience, to be seen to be responsible for a failed bureaucracy in a failed state. Into this storm of protest came our saviour, the European Customs Assistance Mission to Albania. I chaired various meetings involving the Ministry of Labour and the Ministry of Public Order, I dealt with donor certificates, packing lists, proforma invoices, consignees and the State Reserve, and even became the expert on authorisation certificates. Fabrizio and I told the Albanian government bluntly to change the laws that were causing such a hideous mess. We got the EU Customs Mission to write a simple guide for the NGO forum and dispatch them to Durres Port. At least this was one less problem for us.

However, another issue was an increasing worry. NATO had been bombing Serbia for a month and there was no end to the conflict in sight. There was now a real chance that the refugees would have to remain in Albania over the winter. Within sixteen weeks, at least 450,000 refugees would need winter accommodation, which would be difficult to achieve in the time. No one had really accepted how much this would cost and my estimate was at least 500 million US dollars. The continued capacity of the Albanian economy and infrastructure to sustain the refugees without massive international support was also in doubt. There was no proper infrastructure, no tarmac roads, and land reform and privatisation remained unfinished. It was a country that had a 50% food deficit, where factories lay abandoned and looted, where only 20% of farmland was being used, and tax revenues were negligible.

My month's mission was almost at an end. For most of it, I had been inside a building and very far from the fieldwork of twenty years earlier. This had been an intensely political and diplomatic role, but also a major milestone for the UN. We had designed a management system for enormous numbers of refugees, and we had been well-supported throughout by the new Head of UNHCR, Jacques Mouchet, who had arrived soon after us. Whether the UN would adopt the new coordination method in the future was another matter.

As the UN car took me back to the airport, the sun was out and the month of torrential rain had finally come to an end. I felt I was leaving a job not even half-done. There were now nearly a million refugees in this broken country, and no solution in sight. I took the UN charter flight to Rome and made my way home.

A week later, I received some tragic news. One morning, after we left, our neighbour Daniel Mora Castro had been car-jacked by unknown gunmen. As he handed over the keys, he went to release his seat belt. Thinking he was reaching for a gun, they shot him in the head. He was the kindest of men and much admired by us all. Perhaps it had not been the most suitable place for us to stay after all.

15

Not Much of a Solution, Kosovo 1999

I had only been back home a week when Hugh Hanning, a journalist with an interest in humanitarian relief, rang. He had arranged a meeting with the Chief of Defence Staff, Charles Guthrie, to discuss a Safe Haven along the Albanian border, and wanted General Robin Ross, who had commanded British troops in Northern Iraq in 1991, and me to join him as we were considered the experts on Safe Havens. I had my doubts, as the concept of Safe Havens had been horribly compromised ever since July 1995, when it failed to prevent more than 8,000 Bosnian Muslims, mostly men and boys, being massacred by Bosnian Serb Forces at Srebrenica. The plan now being proposed seemed rather feeble. Its only merit was that it would take the economic pressure off Albania and the political pressure off the Former Yugoslav Republic of Macedonia – there was a real risk that both countries would collapse. There was another issue; there were only fourteen weeks left to prepare the refugee population for winter, and there was grave doubt that even this was possible. The estimated cost was 500 million US dollars, which was yet to be found.

NATO's response to the Kosovo crisis, apart from sending troops to Albania, had been to bomb Serbia. The bombing had now been going on for six weeks and, judging by the number of refugees, had only exacerbated the crisis. It was unclear what to do next from either a military or a political point of view. I was never convinced by the bombing. I had heard the Serbs described as a 'terrier' race, happy to take on an adversary ten times their size quite fearlessly. If this was the case, the campaign would only make matters worse.

Hugh, Robin and I assembled outside the Ministry of Defence Main Building in London. Grotesque monumental female statues of Earth and Water flank the northern entrance, and I remembered being told at Sandhurst that, at the MOD, "You'll find bigger tits inside". Charles Guthrie's unshakable charm would disarm an enemy at a hundred paces. I had not seen him since 1976, when he was the Brigade Major, Headquarters, London District, but he welcomed me as if we had seen each other just the day before.

I realised that even at this level there was still no clear plan of what to do next. The bombing had produced a massive refugee crisis and nothing else. A land war against the Serbs seemed a high-risk venture, and even the thought of it frightened the politicians. Yet doing nothing was not an option either. I pointed out the danger of political and economic collapse in neighbouring countries, and as we left, thoughtful and slightly subdued, I was not sure our meeting had really been very helpful.

★★★

The following Tuesday evening, the UN rang from Geneva. I was to be at Manston Airport in Kent by noon the next day. I had to cancel everything in my diary for a month, delegate, pack and travel to Kent, six hours' drive away. Even taking the train would not be much quicker. However, I could fly there in an hour. So I rang the chief pilot of my local aero club at Staverton Airport and easily persuaded him to come with me and fly my aircraft back.

I had been home from Albania about a month and it was now 15 June. Three days earlier Milošević had suddenly agreed to the Kumanovo Peace Plan and NATO troops had moved north from Skopje, the capital of Macedonia, towards Pristina, the capital of Kosovo. The UN had been authorised to set up an Interim Administration Mission under the leadership of the Special Representative to the Secretary-General (SRSG), Sérgio Vieira de Mello (who would later die in the bombing of the Canal Hotel in Baghdad in 2003).

Our mission was to support the SRSG. I was one of a team of three, and our terms of reference were delightfully wide. From Manston Airport we would be flown in an Ilyushin Il-76 air freighter with our vehicles and equipment to Macedonia. My fellow team members were Guillaume de

Montravel and Richard van Hazebrouck. Richard and I knew each other well and he had a well-deserved reputation for being hugely competent.

Guillaume and I had yet to meet. But as I landed at Manston and taxied over to the enormous air freighter, he bounded over to greet me despite a recently-broken ankle, and his broad grin raised my spirits. Within half an hour, he had demonstrated a total disregard for any authority and his boundless enthusiasm was infectious.

The sullen Ukrainian crew, who had little English, did not inspire confidence. I inspected the Ilyushin's undercarriage bays, having always been taught that this was the best way to assess the standard of maintenance of an aircraft. There were no shiny components here, just thick grease, dirt and corrosion, and the tyres were bald right down to the canvas.

We flew sitting in our Land Rover as there were no passenger seats. No one was remotely interested in seat belts or any of the rigmarole that accompanies commercial flying. Before long the inflight catering began. To our astonishment one of the crew fried onion rings on an electric hob just in front of our vehicle, as we watched like dogs through the windscreen. The onion rings were, it turned out, only for the crew and not for us. While we flew, Guillaume briefed us on our mission between amusing anecdotes of internal politics at the Palais des Nations in Geneva, where he normally worked.

Thirty minutes before arriving at Skopje in Macedonia, we flew into a thunderstorm so violent that it curtailed any enthusiasm for inflight catering. It was an unusual sensation being bounced around the sky sitting in the front seat of a Land Rover. One of the Ukrainians clung to the wing mirror to steady himself and observed in English, "Weather, no good," as if we had not noticed. As the aircraft took a great lurch, he grabbed at the windscreen wipers. Such was the violence of the storm, I was surprised the wings did not come off.

It was a relief finally to be on the ground; the sky was ink-black and it was raining torrentially. It was already late and the weather discouraged any activity from customs; it would be another frustrating twenty-four hours before they cleared our vehicle. The communications equipment was another matter and an unhelpful customs official announced that it might take a week, which it did. We decided to continue without it.

We joined a small band of UNHCR and UNMIK (UN Interim Administration Mission in Kosovo) personnel for the inevitable security briefings and the distribution of body armour and helmets for the road journey to Pristina the following day. The next morning, under blue skies, after inevitable yet inexplicable delays, we climbed up the famous Kacanik Defile into Kosovo. Progress was slow since thousands of refugees were returning to their homes. The congestion was so bad that we had to act as traffic controllers. Our 96-kilometre journey took over three hours.

Pristina was an ugly town. Damage had been caused by the NATO bombing, but what caught the eye were the shabby abandoned office buildings in the centre belonging to Serbs. Most Serbs had been intimidated into leaving. This would prove a problem as they had a disproportionate role in the running of public services, administration, utilities and most businesses.

UNMIK's temporary headquarters were in a small residential house. This was only D+5, the fifth day after the troops had moved forward into Kosovo, and arrangements were still being made to accommodate the interim administration in proper offices. We were hugely relieved that, with the Deputy SRSG Martin Griffiths, we were able to find the ideal role for our team. Working as a team of three, we would assess public utilities and design mechanisms for small-scale infrastructure repairs over the next twelve weeks. We would travel throughout Kosovo and report directly to the SRSG. We were also asked to provide advice to the new UN civil administration.

We had time before dark to visit General Mike Jackson's tactical headquarters. He had moved here from Macedonia and now commanded from a collection of military trucks in a nearby car park, dominated by a large satellite communications dish. His two deputies were the French Major General Thomann and the German General Olshausen, so by chance all three of us had a fellow national as a point of contact.

I had prepared a paper on how we would restore essential services for the thousands of refugees returning to Kosovo every day, and General Mike agreed to send it out as a Fragmentary Order, or FRAGO, to all troops under his command. It was a wonderful start to our mission.

Then we set off to find our accommodation. In a very 18th-century way, we were to be billeted on a local Albanian family. They were a delight and I think enjoyed having us as much as we enjoyed staying with them. Guillaume, always gallant, immediately found a present for our hostess.

The next morning, we found an abandoned office fifty metres from the SRSG's office and installed ourselves in it. Guillaume left us sweeping out the broken glass and disappeared for an hour, returning triumphantly with some desks and filing cabinets on the back of a lorry. Within an hour, we had a fully functioning office, even down to a box of Serbian paper clips. Macedonian customs had finally cleared our communications equipment and Guillaume drove to Skopje to collect it. It completely transformed the SRSG's office, giving him a reliable satellite link to the world, and our reputation soared.

A dangerous situation had arisen in the hospital on the southern edge of Pristina. Returning Albanians wanted their jobs back, and were causing an ugly confrontation with Serb staff. The massive hospital, which must have had at its height nearly a thousand beds, was built a quarter of a century earlier, a prestige project for President Tito in an optimistic Yugoslavia. Now it had an air of decay and chronic under-maintenance; the concrete was stained and there were cracks in the render, which like much else had remained unrepaired for years.

Waiting for me at the entrance was a British KFOR (Kosovo Force) soldier who led me upstairs. I could hear the raised voices before I reached the room. The Kosovo Serbs in white hospital coats and Kosovo Albanians in leather jackets were facing each other angrily, and between them stood an exasperated British Army officer from the Royal Army Medical Corps. My entrance distracted everyone for a second and there was a brief moment of calm. The officer summarised the position of each party. This started the antagonism once again until I intervened, suggesting that this dispute should take place elsewhere, so as not to compromise patient care. This was grudgingly accepted, but not before another burst of invective from the Albanians – death threats to all of us, I later learned.

This ugly scene was intensified by the fact that the hospital was full of weapons. I drove back to town with two conclusions: we had to provide a forum to resolve this type of dispute, which had become commonplace across the province; and since Belgrade no longer paid salaries or funded anything in Kosovo, the hospitals clearly couldn't continue to provide clinical care. With nearly one million people returning to the province, hospitals would need both funding and management support.

I suggested to the SRSG that we should set up 'Joint Civil Commissions' to deal with the reintegration of Kosovo Albanian staff. The high expectations of returning Kosovo Liberation Army soldiers, the frustration of the Albanian population, and the fear of the remaining Serbs made for an explosive mixture. I wanted disputes about the future structure of the administration removed from the workplace where they were highly disruptive and led to violent situations. They also meant that KFOR were spending too much time negotiating over trivia, while the hospitals and utilities were paralysed. The idea was that five of the key government ministries of Albania should adapt a process to make negotiations more manageable and KFOR's intervention less likely. I also suggested we should establish 'Reintegration Boards' in the workplace under KFOR chairmanship. This was agreed within twenty-four hours, and was a great step forward. We now had to get the message out to the general public as quickly as possible with a robust information campaign.

Richard was working on the public utilities and especially the two power stations. We faced every sort of problem – bodies found in deep wells, an alarming eight metric ton spillage of mercury from a factory bombed by NATO, water shortages in Pristina caused by a lack of electrical power, unpaid salaries and missing Serb engineers. Obvious everywhere was two decades of chronic underfunding. At my first Reintegration Board at the hospital, KFOR asked if they should search the participants before the meeting, and I reluctantly agreed. However, they did find ten AK47s, 600 rounds of ammunition, a rifle, two pistols, three bayonets and a hand grenade.

At the weekend, we set off on our first field trip. The flow of refugees was relentless. A million people were on the move and residential housing was a major concern for UNHCR and the SRSG's office. I was not convinced by their argument that most houses had been destroyed. All three of us took the view that although the Serbs' attempts to burn Albanian houses had been industrious, they had not been very successful. Many would still be habitable, if only in a rudimentary way. However, we did pass industrial estates where the bombing had been very accurate and hardly a building remained. The activities of the military-civil affairs units varied hugely among the different nationalities of KFOR, but they had all received the FRAGO and were making their assessments. There seemed to be a functioning hospital in each Brigade area, and it made sense to ask the British, German, Italian and French governments to sponsor a hospital in areas where their troops were deployed. They quickly and happily agreed to this.

Late one afternoon we were returning to Pristina from our field trip through a very rural area. Guillaume was map reading. As we turned off into a small lane, I immediately felt uncomfortable. Small branches lying about, and gravel on the sealed road, indicated there had been no traffic for some time. We were also close to the border. Discomfort was turning to apprehension, and I was about to suggest we turn back when we came upon the remains of a blown-up truck lying on its side. The cab had been wrenched from the chassis by the force of the blast and was lying in an adjacent field. In a tree overhead a human arm complete with hand dangled from a branch and higher up still, caught between some branches, was a boot with part of a leg still attached. We reversed ever so slowly back to the road junction, simply relieved to be alive.

The security situation showed no signs of settling. The Serbs who remained were certainly not safe, and revenge murders were commonplace. The need for my suggested Joint Civil Commissions was greater than ever. One afternoon a large crowd gathered in a dangerous mood outside one of the main public buildings. Anticipating violence, I was sent out by the SRSG to investigate and de-escalate the situation, if needed. To get into the building I had to walk in front of a crowd of at least a thousand. This stimulated hostile shouting. Once inside, I was met by some UNMIK officials who told me that the municipal workers had not been paid. Negotiating wages for them was the easy part; the next issue was more complicated. Reintegration of Kosovo Albanian staff was never straightforward, as some of them had not worked in Kosovo for many years. And without the Serbs, there would be no technicians to run the utilities or the hospitals. Sensing danger from the increasingly hostile crowd, I asked the UNMIK officials to allow five people in to talk to me. How they were selected I have no idea, but it seemed to calm the crowd. These hastily-appointed tribunes of the people seemed so surprised to be consulted, and so clearly flattered by their new position, that their anger evaporated. I explained my plan for the Joint Civil Commissions and the Reintegration Boards, to which I am sure the interpreter gave suitably grand titles. The five went outside to show off their apparent victory, and the crowd dispersed in a better mood. As I travelled back to the office, I noticed Albanian flags hanging from many government buildings. It was clear that UNMIK needed to occupy these buildings if they were to have any chance of establishing an interim administration, a point I made very bluntly to the SRSG.

Something that really concerned us was that, just as UNHCR had been unprepared for the exodus of refugees into Albania, so they were equally unprepared for their return to Kosovo. The people had returned en masse in remarkably few days. UNHCR had asked donors for millions of US dollars to improve domestic housing, but it was now obvious that it was unnecessary. The SRSG called us to an urgent meeting with Kevin McNamara, Head of UNHCR, who asked us bluntly, in front of UNHCR, whether the appeal for housing was needed. We stated clearly that it was not.

At the end of the second week, Guillaume's boss came on a visit from Geneva. Although a senior UN official, she had not spent much time in the field and I detected a degree of humanitarian tourism behind the visit. We took her to the north of Kosovo, where the Serbs were still in charge. Now 50,000 troops were deployed and equally vast numbers of police soon followed them, all for a province the size of Dorset. This massive security force was not going to sort out the underlying political cul-de-sac we now found ourselves in.

On our way back, not far from Pristina, we stopped at what once had been a café. One wall was missing and many of the tables and chairs had been mangled in the blast; however, the proprietor, an elderly Albanian with a tremor in one hand indicating Parkinson's disease, was happy to see us. I asked our guest from Geneva what she would like. To my astonishment, she said, "I'd like a cappuccino." I quickly told the interpreter she wanted a Turkish coffee. Her naive but innocent request demonstrated the vast gap that divided office staff in capitals from fieldworkers for whom observation was key to staying alive. Yet it also touched a much bigger reality – it was not only senior international civil servants who were out of touch; the politicians were too. The UN administration was doubling its head count every week, and it was apparent that the over-deployment of troops and police would now be followed by that of civil servants. Kosovo was a small province, not a country, but it was getting an administration for a continent.

It was now time for me to leave Kosovo, but not without misgivings. The political entity created was unstable and would cause hostility towards the Serbs for generations to come – this was a country that still celebrated the Battle of Kosovo Polje in 1389. The UN, who still had an anti-colonial unit, had demonstrated that they were struggling to govern even a small province. The power stations still were not working properly and many of the international police seemed to travel around the various KFOR units in search of free food. There had also been a tense stand-off at the airport between KFOR and the Russians, which Mike Jackson had skilfully de-escalated.

There was something wholly unsatisfactory about the whole intervention, which was difficult to articulate. The bombing, the exodus and now the return of one million people marked only the beginning of Britain's new ethical foreign policy, which was values-led, not interest-led, our Foreign Secretary Robin Cook informed us. Two years earlier, he had made a now-famous speech in which he announced, "the Labour government does not accept that political values can be left behind when we check in our passports to travel on diplomatic business".

It was not clear how a 'values-led' foreign policy would be expressed in a war zone.

16

Paper Tiger, East Timor 1999

It was getting dark and much of Dili, the capital of East Timor, was in flames. Single shots could be heard periodically as the militia and Indonesian troops raped and murdered anybody unfortunate enough still to be in the city. Indonesian soldiers were looting on a grand scale and had brought in army trucks to plunder anything of value. It was not a time to tarry and we were weaving through the streets at a good pace. The buildings on either side of us were on fire and the heat was intense enough to blister the paint on the vehicle.

I turned right into a street that I thought would take us towards the Australian Consulate. Ahead of us, I spotted an Indonesian soldier firing through the open doorway of an abandoned house; I could hear the spent cases bouncing on the pavement. Bob Churcher's laconic voice came from the passenger seat, "Perhaps not this way." Such massive understatement was almost reassuring. I turned the car round as another soldier scurried out of a doorway carrying an armful of looted property. Bob, holding the tourist map as if we were sightseeing in Florence, guided me back to the city centre. In a few minutes, we had found our way to the compound of the Australian Consulate.

★★★

For more than half a century the former Portuguese colony of East Timor had suffered, first at the hands of the Japanese during World War II and then, after

167

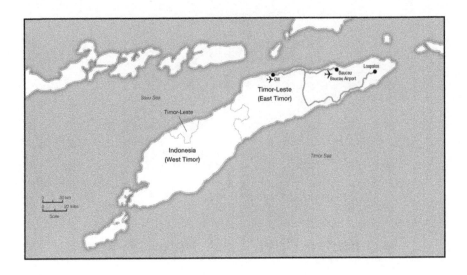

the Portuguese revolution in 1974, when it was invaded by Indonesia. This was unopposed by the international community; the Vietnam War was coming to its unhappy conclusion and they feared another state falling to communism. Australia was happy to go along with the unification of the island after a shabby oil deal was agreed with Indonesia in the South China Sea.

Over the subsequent 30 years, the Roman Catholic population of East Timor did not accept the domination of their Muslim neighbours from West Timor. A guerrilla war was then waged by FALINTIL, the military wing of the Marxist-Leninist political party FRETILIN, from their mountain hideouts. When President Suharto of Indonesia suddenly and unexpectedly resigned in May 1988, the United Nations Mission in East Timor conducted a referendum on independence from Indonesia. On 4 September 1999, when the result was a clear victory for independence, a campaign of violence, looting and arson was conducted by the pro-integration militias and departing Indonesian troops. Around 80% of the population of 890,000 were displaced, as many as 150,000 fled into West Timor, and another 400,000 took refuge in the mountains and jungles of East Timor. An unknown number were deported elsewhere in Indonesia. As East Timor dissolved into anarchy, Australia organised a multinational force and invaded the island.

I was deployed as part of the UN Military and Civil Defence Unit to provide a link between the military intervention force and humanitarian agencies. I had flown to Darwin in neighbouring Australia to join our team leader Michael Elmquist, and Ernie Chamberlain, a former Brigadier in the Australian Army. This quiet tropical city, 400 miles across the South China Sea, felt far removed from East Timor, the centre of world attention.

Personnel from the humanitarian agencies were now arriving in Darwin, which was quickly becoming a hub for the arrival of humanitarian supplies. It was hoped that, once the Australian Brigade had moved into Dili, supplies could be flown directly from Darwin. There was a real need to coordinate the deployment of humanitarian agencies, their equipment and the military. Yet, our first meeting with the Australian Army was unpropitious. Isolated from military conflicts since the end of the Vietnam War, the Australians were surprisingly unaware of developments in civil-military relations brought about by the war in Bosnia. They were reluctant to discuss any detail of the operation in East Timor apart from its name. Yet we did leave with a small victory; we were going to move forward from Darwin to East Timor the next day by C-130 Hercules.

★★★

The flight from Darwin to Dili had been uneventful – the usual very early start, then the endless rush to wait, until finally towards the end of the day we were in Dili. The small airport was already overloaded with military equipment and overwhelmed by frantic activity. I was delighted that Bob Churcher, whom I had first met earlier in the year in Albania, had been sent by the Foreign Office to support us. Standing at least six foot three, and often seen in a white linen jacket, he had a commanding presence. His greatest weapon was charm.

A cascade of events unfolded after we left the airport, culminating in us finding a trove of fifty Land Rover Discoveries abandoned by the United Nations in their hurried evacuation three weeks earlier. The British government had supplied four hundred of these vehicles for the elections, and they now lay scattered about the island. Bizarrely, Bob had been fortunate to meet a man carrying a bucket of Discovery keys, a trivial encounter that was to change the course of the war.

We navigated our way through the burning capital in a brand-new Land Rover Discovery with smashed windows – looters had attempted to steal the radio and anything else detachable – to the Australian consulate; I beeped the horn and the steel gates opened cautiously. Inside the consulate, someone or something occupied every square metre of the small building, which was temporarily the home of the UN Civil Administration of the island. It had its own generator; the brightly lit interior was a striking contrast to the neighbouring buildings, all now without power.

The UN Humanitarian Coordinator was Ross Mountain, a large New Zealander known in the UN as the Bulldozer, with a reputation for being friendly but tough. He had met with Major General Peter Cosgrave, the Australian Commander of the International Force East Timor (INTERFET), earlier and was not happy with the outcome. The General planned to deploy the entire Brigade of over 5,000 troops first, and only when the island was secure would he address the humanitarian situation. The deployment would not be complete for another three weeks and the plan to move troops out from Dili was expected to be painfully slow.

Ross explained that the main government food store in Dili containing 10,000 tons of rice was being looted, and that satellite photographs showed that most of the small diesel power stations were on fire. In the absence of a national grid, these power plants generated power for the small towns across the island. With nearly a million people displaced, our first task was to persuade the General to provide security and humanitarian relief at the same time rather than sequentially.

Finding somewhere to sleep that night was a case of finding space on the floor. I was thankful to find some cardboard boxes nearby, as a sleeping bag on a tiled floor is about as bad as it gets. We settled down to eat whatever we had brought from Darwin. I had a bottle of warm water, and ate my muesli bar in ascetic silence. At least it was dry, but the tropical night was rather warmer than I would have liked, and mosquitoes whined constantly, eager for a meal.

The British government had sent a support team, which was a new idea to overcome the lugubrious deployment of the UN. Rapid deployment and procurement had always tested the bureaucratic endeavours of this vast organisation. The support team were to provide food, accommodation, communications and transport for the whole of the UN team. There was already a team of fifteen, and within days this would increase to over fifty.

Having acquired the wrecked Discoveries and the bucket of keys, we now had over thirty vehicles, most with more than half a tank of fuel, to add to the two that we had managed to fly in from Darwin. The support team had brought with them both HF and UHF radios. Everything was beginning to fall into place.

We were soon to have somewhere of our own to live, too. One night in the Consulate was quite long enough. The next morning we started setting up our new headquarters in an abandoned school nearby, which would be our home for the next month.

Meanwhile, I went to meet Major Stoddard, the Australian Civil Affairs Officer. I felt he was not impressed by the role he had been given. All staff officers wanted to be part of the headquarters that dealt with Operations, whereas Civil Affairs had no status. He told me there would be a delay until the whole brigade was deployed from Australia to Dili, and that it would probably take another three weeks to move them out from Dili to take the rest of the island. I was most concerned about the security of the main government food store in Dili, which was being looted daily, and of the fuel farm, which contained 3 million litres of fuel. If anything happened to that, I pointed out the nearest fuel was 400 miles away in Australia. I also wanted the brigade to secure the power stations and to open the other airfield at Baucau. But I seemed to be getting nowhere. The war in Bosnia had made such discussions between military and humanitarians quite normal, but in this backwater the area of operations belonged to the military force and there was to be no discussion.

The British Military Headquarters was in an unfinished school building but, unlike the Australian Headquarters, it was hyper-organised with not a scrap of rubbish anywhere. It was obvious within minutes that the Brigadier, David Richards, would help me in any way he could. David had a company of Gurkhas from Brunei, some Special Forces, a C-130 Hercules aircraft and a frigate, and the whole headquarters gave the impression they could take the island immediately. It was the second time I remembered the desktop military exercise at Sandhurst that started, "There is a tropical island..." and required us to take the island with remarkably few troops. This was precisely what David was intending to do.

Like me, David was already frustrated by the Australians' caution. He considered the militias no more than small town bullies, inadequates who had been given automatic rifles and mopeds. His main problem was transport. The Gurkhas used helicopters to get around the jungles of Brunei but had arrived without their helicopters or even vehicles. I remembered our thirty blue Discoveries. Though hesitant about making a rather irregular contribution to the campaign, I said, "I've managed to salvage thirty of those Discoveries at the airport. They're a bit bashed about, but…" David was delighted, and within an hour, they were sitting outside his headquarters.

The support team had also found their box of UHF radios, which they loaned to the military headquarters. With vehicles and their own radio frequency, David's Gurkhas were less dependent on Australian support.

Agencies and NGOs arrived every day, and the numbers grew. Ross Mountain got on well with the Australian Commander General Peter Cosgrave, and we went to see him. His office was in a partially burnt-out building and we sat on boxes in semi-darkness. It was brutally uncomfortable. As Dili airport was congested with the military deployment, I explained the importance of opening up the second airport for humanitarian flights and securing the road to it. The General reluctantly promised us a military escort the next day.

It had taken four exhausting days to persuade the Australian Army to take us to Bacau. An enormous armoured column was deemed necessary. With no experience of NGOs' rebellious ways and unhelpful attitudes, they had difficulty getting the military vehicles and a ragbag of agency vehicles on the road. When we finally set off, the six-wheeled armoured cars thundered ahead.

Jon Swain, the veteran *Sunday Times* correspondent, had asked if he could join me. He was charming and highly respected for his coverage of the fall of Phnom Penh in Cambodia, so I was delighted to have him with me. The week before, Jon, with his driver, photographer and interpreter, had been detained by Indonesian soldiers outside Dili. Three of them managed to escape under fire, but the interpreter was never seen again. This event eradicated any residual complacency we might have felt.

The main road was hardly wide enough for armoured cars and badly neglected. The road ran along the coast; amidst the chaos and violence, I had failed to see I was on a very beautiful island. The remains of charming Portuguese villas and the sea were almost always in view.

At the first little town we came to, the whole population came out to wave and we stood a real chance of being kissed to death. A jubilant population was all we saw the whole way to the other end of the island. Yet despite the friendliness of the local people, we remained cautious. A hit-and-run attack by the militia remained a real possibility. The convoy was now strung out over several miles and we were surprisingly vulnerable.

It was not long before we saw the first of the burning diesel power stations. The building that housed the great generating sets was still burning, and the blackened hulks of the vast engines could be seen inside. It was immensely frustrating; if only a few platoons had been deployed by helicopter, all this could have been avoided. We struggled on, stopping and starting. In some places, we were more vulnerable to attack and our escort was sensibly cautious. I was driving one of the two British government Land Rover Discoveries that had been flown in from Darwin, listening to the radio chat as I drove; the Australians were certainly taking the threat very seriously. Driving along the coast in this balmy tropical climate was certainly no Bosnia, yet it was only a week since Indonesian soldiers had killed Jon Swain's interpreter. Despite the smiles we met along the way, there was a distinctly menacing atmosphere and it was very uncertain what lay ahead.

It took all day to drive the 124 kilometres to Baucau and was sunset when we arrived. On the deserted airfield another fifty Land Rover Discoveries still stood, parked haphazardly on a sea of broken glass, where the UN had hurriedly abandoned them as they fled after the elections. Jon and I set off to the terminal building, which looked an inviting place to stay the night. We had not gone far before an Australian soldier shouted, "Wouldn't go in there, mate – might be booby trapped!"

We heated up our military rations on hexamine stoves and settled down for the night. Some opted to sleep in the destroyed cars, despite the seats being covered in broken glass. I rolled out my sleeping bag on the apron under a magical full moon. From time to time, I could hear the whinnying of wild horses, descendants of the ones brought by the Portuguese in the 15th century.

The next morning we broke into small groups, with the different agencies doing their own assessments. The main task had now been achieved, as we had reached the airfield safely. Despite mutterings from the military headquarters about wild horses galloping across the runway, we decided it was serviceable. The important thing now was to get the first flights on their way. The return journey was swifter and easier, but the tension had not completely disappeared. Again, the column stretched over several miles. Security discipline had dissipated and it was already dark as we trickled into Dili. As I counted the vehicles back into the camp, it appeared that we were one vehicle short. James Brown, from the support team, volunteered to go back for it in the dark. It was dangerous and courageous too, since we seemed to have lost our armoured escort and our radio coverage was minimal. Happily, he returned an hour and a half later with a vehicle that had failed to keep up.

Now that we had succeeded in getting the road proved, I wanted the Australians to open the airfield. At 'Camp Caution', Ross Mountain pushed his fellow antipodean as far as diplomacy would permit. However, it was clear that nothing was going to happen quickly.

My regular meetings with Major Stoddard were equally unhelpful. To every request, the answer was almost always "No." This caused the diplomatic ether to buzz. I called London, London called Canberra, Canberra called the Australian Headquarters and the General summoned me for a fireside chat in the burnt-out building that was his headquarters – he was a real warrior and relished the sparse and uncomfortable surroundings. Happily, I was in good company and found myself in the naughty corner with Brigadier Richards. Our meeting with the General was difficult and had a 'headmaster's study' feel to it. "You two," he said, "have caused me more trouble than all 12,600 men under my command." With a burst of his natural charm, David pointed out that our trip to Baucau needed to be followed up, and presented a plan to send a platoon of Gurkhas back, this time travelling along the south coast.

Although this was grudgingly approved, two Australian liaison officers were to accompany the tiny force as the General's eyes and ears. David asked me to join them as an unarmed non-combatant in order to assess the humanitarian situation. This was unusual. We were to accomplish our mission with just one platoon of Gurkhas and, at the briefing the night before, the Brigade Commander's last words were, "Be bold." I certainly thought it was a very bold plan.

The liaison officers got a double surprise when they arrived at dawn to find a fleet of new vehicles, looking rather strange without windows, and a platoon of Gurkhas speaking only Gorkhali. I drove my white Discovery at the rear of the column. As we approached each settlement, I had to wait beside the road while they 'fought' through. Fortunately, no fighting was required and I was soon called to rejoin the platoon.

At midday, we arrived at a small town and I waited for over an hour before being called forward. I drove through the deserted streets until I found the Platoon Commander at the hospital, a typically charmless 1960s concrete building that appeared to have had no maintenance since it was built. The walls were stained by damp, the light fittings were missing, the glass in the windows was broken, and the floors and walls were filthy. The few remaining staff looked tired.

There were still a few patients, and the Platoon Commander wanted me to do an assessment. The first patient I saw was a woman with a large advanced tumour on her face. It was a terrible sight and she was horribly distressed. In the next ward was a child who had been admitted with severe abdominal pain and was badly dehydrated. I discussed the case with the doctor, concerned he had peritonitis. Then I was shown an exhausted sunken-eyed young woman with a suspected ectopic pregnancy.

All three needed to be taken to Dili, but road travel was out of the question, as it was obvious that very little traffic had come this way for a considerable while. However, organising a helicopter would take time.

It was already past midday and we planned to reach the town of Lospalos at the east end of the island by dark. I hated getting involved in individual medical cases when on military operations like this. A normal hospital assessment followed a logical procedure. I would check the building was usable, that it had water and electricity, and that the basic medical equipment was functioning. Next, I would make sure there was an adequate supply of drugs and surgical supplies, and see if the staff were still present. Lastly, I would look at the five most common hospital admissions and the numbers being admitted, and take a view on what support was needed. This was all quite different from looking at individual clinical cases. Clinical triage, though important for the patients, risked distracting us from our primary objective.

Once the request for a helicopter had been made, there was endless chat on the radio about suitable secure helicopter landing sites. We waited and waited as the daylight hours slipped by. Eventually, the helicopter arrived and the patients were loaded on board to the visible relief of the hospital staff.

We had assumed that once we reached the south coast the road would be in reasonable condition, but it had hardly been used since the Portuguese left twenty-four years earlier, in 1975. Undergrowth crowded the road, which was now only half its width and tropical downpours had washed away some sections completely. Steep gullies ran down to the sea, which had to be crossed with great care to avoid rolling the vehicles and getting them stuck.

It was dark. When it came to navigating the gullies, the sergeant shone a torch exactly where he expected the driver to place his left front wheel. It was precarious stuff, and there was always the chance that we might be attacked at any moment. We navigated a long section with multiple ravines and were making good progress. Then we were halted by several fallen palm trees. Within moments, the Gurkhas were out with their characteristic kukri knives, furiously chopping at the trees without much success. Our two Australian liaison officers made easy work of it with axes, after which they stood aside, leaning on their axes with smug satisfaction.

At about midnight, as we were getting close to our destination, suddenly there were shouts and a single shot rang out. We had just driven through a militia position, but not from the direction that we were expected. The not-so-brave militia had fled into the darkness. We finally reached Lospalos where we broke open our military ration packs. We had not eaten since dawn and it had been a long day.

Then a message came from the Bishop of Lospalos that the militia were holding a number of hostages on a jetty without food or water some kilometres away. Plans were made to rescue them at first light. Attempts to contact the Australian Military Headquarters initially failed, but Major Tim Warrington of the Royal Gurkha Rifles was able to receive instructions using my HF radio. The Gurkhas set off at dawn. It was not long before I got a message that the rescue had been successful. After a brief firefight the militia had released the hostages and now we had four prisoners. We also had some extremely happy local people. The incident caused a media storm, and the Gurkhas became the stars of the East Timor campaign, to the discomfort of the Australians, who began to feel that their Brigade in East Timor was to support the Gurkhas rather than the other way round. At first, the Gurkhas were mistaken for Indonesian troops, which caused apprehension, but good news travelled fast, and after the first few days everyone knew who they were.

On the way back to Dili, I had the chance to visit Falintil's Headquarters. Leaving the main road, I plunged into the bush down a dry riverbed. I had driven off-road for years, but this precarious track strewn with vast boulders was challenging, and I wondered if any vehicle had ever travelled this far into the mountains.

Chapter 13 – The Team Leader briefed us in the open air with
the roar of helicopters behind us, Afghanistan 1998

Chapter 13 – With local villagers unloading the UN helicopter near Fayzabad,
Afghanistan 1998

Chapter 13 – Airfield catering, Fayzabad, Afghanistan 1998

Chapter 13 – With Simo Wecksten in our Ops Room at Fayzabad airport,
Afghanistan 1998

Chapter 15 – Ethnic cleansing in process, Kosovo 1999

Chapter 16 – Fighting through. The road to Baucau, East Timor 1999

Chapter 16 – Leaving with the Gurkhas en route to Lospalos, East Timor 1999

Chapter 16 – Taking a short rest against my Discovery in East Timor, 1999

Chapter 18 – The quality and quantity of weapons handed-in were impressive, Macedonia 2001

Chapter 19 – Over the mountain passes to Bamyan, Afghanistan 2001

Chapter 19 – Arriving at Karim Khalili's fort in Bamyan, Afghanistan 2001

Chapter 20 – Defence diplomacy 2002 – L to R: ADC, GG, Lt Col Carleton-Smith, Alexander Crown Prince of Yugoslavia, Maj Gen Mike Jackson, Prince Philip of Yugoslavia, Brigadier Bill Rollo, HE Charles Crawford HM Ambassador to Serbia, British Defence Attaché.

Chapter 23 – FCO Compound at Kandahar camp, Afghanistan 2010

Chapter 23 – I'm right behind you, sir, armed with a pencil, Kabul 2010

Chapter 23 – Muktyala Fort, Lashkargah, Afghanistan 2010

Chapter 24 – Passports returned in Choucha camp, Tunisia 2011

After the riverbed the track wound through a ravine until eventually I arrived in a clearing on a plateau, where I found shelters with bamboo roofs, defensive positions and groups of armed men of all ages. I was surprised to see that the Commander was flanked by two soldiers from the Australian Special Forces. We all sat under a bamboo canopy and discussed the humanitarian situation. Thousands had fled into the mountains; they were apprehensive and wanted reassurance that all would be well if they returned to their villages. The shocking revelation was the number of cases of malaria, which the Australian Special Forces had not reported as they felt it was neither a military task nor their responsibility.

For European armies, winning the peace had become just as important as winning the war and the civilian aspects of the battlespace were much discussed by military Commanders after their experiences in Bosnia. Yet time had stood still for the Australians since the Vietnam War.

My main objective, to get Baucau airfield open, was realised a few days later. The east end of the island was now secure and I was back to the more mundane task of assessments and delivery of humanitarian assistance. Though there were only 800,000 people to look after, I felt the UN was making quite a meal of running this small country. That same year, I had watched them failing to administer Kosovo competently. This was an only slightly more demanding task.

Liaison between the Australian military and the humanitarian agencies had been a failure. I succeeded despite this by going behind their backs and shamelessly exerting pressure wherever I could. It was also my good fortune to work with such a forward-looking Commander as David Richards. Military success in this micro-conflict was always going to be the easy part; winning the peace was more complicated. Despite the lesson of the Balkans, the majority of military commanders still saw military and civilian tasks as entirely separate things. This would have unfortunate consequences three years later, in the Second Gulf War.

I visited the hospital in Dili to see how the three patients were getting on. The woman with the tumour had been flown to Australia for surgery and I was much relieved, as this was something that could not be achieved on the island. The two patients with abdominal pain had died – the child was only eleven. It was clear that the military policy of excessive caution had its casualties too.

17

Legal Challenge, West Bank and Gaza 2000

"What you have to understand, Gilbert, is that anyone exposed to Gaza and the West Bank tends to lose their objectivity," Kevin Kennedy, a senior official at the UN in New York, told me over lunch. Almost all those dealing with the Israelis and Palestinians adopted this weary voice of caution in the end. The war of attrition was not limited to the warring factions, but affected everyone who over the decades had poured their energy and enthusiasm into trying to find a solution.

I had returned the day before from Gaza, the most surreal city in the world. Twenty-five miles by five, Gaza in 2000 was effectively a vast prison incarcerating 1.5 million people. The city was a collection of hideous half-finished concrete box houses and precarious apartment blocks. Broken pavements made it look particularly unloved, and rubbish provided the only colour.

Only the sea behind the city raised one's spirits. The Mediterranean should have offered at least the hope of freedom, but not here. Armed Israeli naval vessels patrolled offshore, guns ready. Yet, in Gaza city there was vitality and enthusiasm. Half the population was under fifteen.

Hostilities between the Palestinians and the Israeli Defence Force (IDF) had flared after Ariel Sharon visited Temple Mount on 28 September 2000, and I was sent by the UN a month later to look at two problems in the West Bank and Gaza. The main problem was a medical emergency caused by 'internal closures', which the IDF used to combat what they considered acts of terrorism. They were imposed intermittently, completely isolating zones in the Occupied Territories, limiting freedom of movement, hampering communications, and severely affecting the local economy and delivery of food. Most critically, medical supplies were obstructed, patients were denied access to hospitals, and uncollected rubbish started to pile up, all affecting the general health of Palestinians young and old.

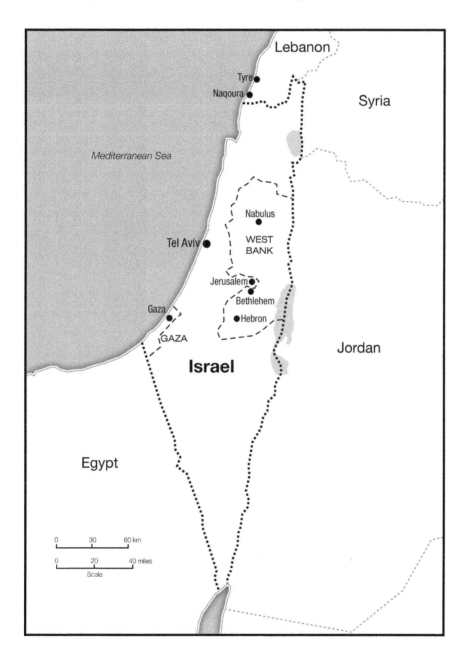

The World Health Organization stated that since the beginning of the Second Intifada a month earlier, approximately 120 Palestinians had been killed and 5,000 injured. Of a health budget of 100 million US dollars in the West Bank, 50 million had come from health insurance paid largely by Palestinians working as day labourers in Israel. But since they could not travel, this was no longer available.

In Salfit City on the West Bank, 49,000 people had been unable to move freely since September and were continuously harassed by Israeli settlers. The water supply was repeatedly cut off. In Hebron, 20,000 lived under continuous 24-hour curfew. These settlements had few resources, since as much as 80% of family income had previously been earned by day labourers in Israel.

Palestinian ambulances could not travel freely and large quantities of medical supplies were blocked at the border for what appeared to be spurious security reasons. The policy of the Israeli government had raised serious questions about breaches of international law, matched only by accusations from Israel that the Palestinians were using the ambulances illicitly to aid the war effort. The results – growing frustration and increasing levels of violence – had been predictable.

I was sent to deal with this medical emergency, though what I was going to do about it was not clear. The UN wanted me to find ways of improving humanitarian access, and it was obvious that this would be an intensely political mission. I was also asked to improve the coordination structures and the humanitarian database, assist contingency planning, and even launch a flash appeal.

The second problem I had to look at was an internal UN issue about the roles and responsibilities of United Nations Relief and Works Agency for Palestine Refugees (UNRWA) and United Nations Special Coordinator for the Middle East Peace Process (UNSCO). The former, one of the original UN agencies, had been set up in December 1949 to look after Palestinian refugees; the latter was the Office of the UN Special Coordinator for the Middle East Peace Process, that coordinated all UN work in Gaza and Israeli-occupied territories. UNSCO was a Norwegian initiative that had raised hopes in its early days, but now, despite the energy of its young team of UN diplomats, had become just another roadside carcass. The terms of reference of these two UN organisations had become tangled and each accused the other of undermining their work. There was enough conflict without a divided United Nations.

All this meant shuttling between Gaza, the British Consulate and the American Colony Hotel in East Jerusalem where most UN staff stayed. In Gaza, I stayed in a pleasant modern hotel facing the sea near the UN office. The fact that such a decent hotel existed at all was one of the curious contrasts in this strange city. The staff were extraordinarily hospitable and the sound of the waves breaking on the beach was a joy, but the claustrophobia of the city quelled any positive emotions I might have brought with me, while Gaza's friendliness and good humour were steadily eroded by daily violence. At each flashpoint where violence flared between the IDF and the Palestinians, I quietly listened to the arguments of each side and did my best to broker humanitarian access. On the whole, I was spectacularly unsuccessful, but carefully documented each apparent breach of humanitarian law.

On Fridays, I went to the UN office to write our 'flash appeal' and from a nearby mosque heard the faithful being exhorted to support a day of rage. The haranguing began quietly enough, but after four hours crowds were pouring out into the street, suitably enraged. Each time I re-entered Israel, I had to wait, often for hours, as my UN passport was passed backwards and forwards for inspection, the car was searched and I was interrogated. Section III of the Privileges and Immunities of the United Nations had no meaning here. I was always relieved to be finally out of Gaza, but bizarrely felt equally alien in Israel.

At the American Colony Hotel, a popular meeting place for the UN, NGOs and journalists, I met by chance the British lawyer Lee Marler, the United Nations' Chief of International Law based with UNRWA in the Gaza Strip. Amongst many other human rights initiatives, Lee designed and implemented the Operational Support Officer Programme, which to this day continues to operate in Gaza and the West Bank as an effective human rights verification regime. I had last met him when he was working as a military lawyer with the British Military Headquarters in East Timor. He had devised an emergency Rule of Law system when no such system existed and the country risked descending into lawlessness. He had left the army the following year and joined the United Nations. He told me that he had already prepared the case against breaches of international law, but UNRWA were not presently going to take it up.

Over the next few weeks, my attempts to make any progress on the internal closures were a complete failure, and I found myself in increasingly dangerous situations. The concept of neutrality was long gone, and the IDF did not see the UN as helpful to their cause. On one occasion, UNRWA trucks were held at a crossing point into Gaza for five hours and I went to see what I could do. A young IDF Captain, who spoke faultless American English, tried hard in a 'between us friends' sort of way to win me over with the most effective weapon he had, charm. It was difficult not to succumb. "I can't think what all the fuss is about," he said. "The trucks were here for half an hour, forty minutes at most." "Nine hours by now, for the record," I said, correcting him before this went into the minutes of the meeting. This unsettled him. The rest of the meeting was riddled with inaccuracies, with two very different interpretations of what had happened.

By now, I was used to everything being distorted in this strange territory. Even something as simple as how long a truck waited at a checkpoint could become a matter of spin and distortion. But as I drove from Gaza and approached Jerusalem, the city was glowing in the setting sun – truly 'Jerusalem the golden'.

Since diplomatic work with the Israelis was so disappointing, the UN in New York wanted me to hire a press officer to present our work in a more positive way. Always an optimist, I hoped this might help. I met the only candidate for a breakfast interview the next morning. He was a British journalist, Jewish, who had lived for a while in Israel. All went well until I asked how he would feel if he had to be critical of the government of Israel. The conversation became awkward and I knew instinctively this was not going to work. He declined the post, and there were no further applicants.

The next day I had to travel to Hebron, but the main road to Jerusalem was shut due to a demonstration. I took a side road towards Bethlehem and almost immediately came to an IDF checkpoint, where I had to wait for a good half-hour next to a battle tank. A tarpaulin had been rigged up on one side and in its shade four soldiers were playing cards. Eventually, one came and looked at my UN passport, which he passed to the others to inspect. More time passed, then a soldier laconically made a rather odd statement, given the tranquillity of the immediate surroundings. "Not a good road to take today," he said with now-familiar bluntness. "You will find it noisy. Best take another road to Bethlehem." But, irritated by the pointless delay, I was naively determined not to be rerouted a second time, so I politely thanked him and continued on my journey.

The sun was glaring down on the rock-strewn landscape. I could see Bethlehem ahead, and could not get the tune of *"O little town of Bethlehem"* out of my head, nor the last line about *"The hopes and fears of all the years"*. Suddenly, about a kilometre behind me, there was an explosion, a huge cloud of dust rose into the air, and panic broke out. The few cars on the roads accelerated with all speed into the outskirts of Bethlehem, and civilians ran for cover. It was not a moment to hesitate, and I slammed my foot to the floor. Once safely in the town, I pulled over to see what had happened. An IDF helicopter hovering fifteen hundred feet above the town had just fired a missile at a minibus travelling on the road behind me, killing nine people, including two passers-by. There were no survivors.

I had been told I would never understand the problems of the West Bank until I had been to Hebron. Working for the UN there is a real requirement to be objective and try to see the situation from both sides, but here I struggled. Carlo Fazzina, Deputy Head of the Temporary International Presence in Hebron (TIPH), took me on a tour and described the daily torments inflicted on the Palestinians by their Israeli neighbours. It was a dismal catalogue, ranging from the petty – shooting holes in plastic rooftop water tanks, or throwing urine and human excrement down onto market stalls – to the very serious, such as seizing houses left unoccupied by their owners even for one hour. As I stood above the market in the old town, I witnessed verbal abuse, and a group of people pushing each other about which only just stopped short of violence.

It would have been impossible to leave Hebron without a jaundiced view of humanity. It was easy to respect the existential threat to the state of Israel, but the West Bank settlements and the behaviour of the Israeli settlers seemed to be major drivers of the conflict. I learnt early on to be wary of these settlers in civilian clothes with assault rifles slung over their shoulders. Israel prides itself on the rule of law, but this was not demonstrated in what I had observed in the West Bank. I drove back to Jerusalem in a rather sombre mood, feeling that the only way ahead lay in the application of international law, a set of rules to be obeyed by all. I was totally unprepared for the reaction to my pursuing this course of action.

I explained to the kindly British Consul in Jerusalem that I had failed to make much of an impression on the internal closures and that trying to use the media to voice reason had been equally unsuccessful. I suggested the use of international law. He looked cautious but did not dismiss the idea. I explained that Lee Marler had already done some work on this and that there were no other options if we were really serious about improving the situation in Gaza and the Israeli-occupied territories. He warmed a little and I left feeling I had a toehold, but no more.

In Gaza, the situation grew darker by the day. UNSCO calculated that the internal closures were costing the Palestinian Authority eight million dollars a day, which would soon halve Palestine's GDP. Unemployment had increased from 70,000 to 250,000, a third of the population were living on less than 600 dollars a year and depended on humanitarian assistance. One million people required food aid.

I had designed a new coordination structure for what had been our internal weekly meetings, to make them shorter, more business-like and effective. The issues were different in Gaza and the West Bank so two sets of meetings were required. Progress was painful and the new style of meeting, which had worked so well elsewhere in the world, was clearly falling on stony ground here. After one tortuous session two Palestinian doctors took me aside. "It's not going to work, is it?" said one. "Why not?" I asked hesitantly. "Well, you see, it's not our way," said the second. I swallowed my pride, took the hint, and resumed the old way. Things improved.

I went to see Lee Marler, still clinging to my view that international law was the only weapon to deploy in this intractable conflict. He was upbeat about the approach and we discussed Section III of the 1946 General Convention on the Privileges and Immunities of the United Nations and the Fourth Geneva Convention, which defines humanitarian protection for civilians in a war zone, and Article 59 in particular. This states: *If the whole or part of the population of an occupied territory is inadequately supplied, the Occupying Power shall agree to relief schemes on behalf of the said population, and shall facilitate them by all the means at its disposal.*

Driving through Gaza city, I saw a platoon of IDF with armoured personnel carriers, and a bulldozer demolishing a house. The evicted family were standing with their pitiful pile of possessions on the pavement. This was retribution for stone throwing or some other provocation. It was deeply depressing, and I wondered whether the cycle of violence and terror would ever end.

In my last week I revisited the British Consulate in East Jerusalem, where I immediately detected a change of mood; the cautious welcome I received a few weeks earlier had vanished, and my idea of using international law to resolve the internal closures was no longer a consideration. British foreign policy, I concluded, swung between Tony Blair's special envoy to the Middle East, Lord Levy, and the Foreign Secretary Robin Cook. I assumed one drove pro-Israel sentiment while the other gave succour to the Palestinian cause. I may have just visited the consulate on the wrong day, but I was not going to get any support.

I had one last visit to make. In the extreme south of the Gaza Strip there had been an increased level of violence over the last few days, and there was still sporadic shooting when I arrived. I was taken to visit a family who showed me bullet holes in the walls of the room where the children had been sleeping. There was an air of both desperation and despondency, but there was little I, or anyone, could do. It was a sour note on which to end my mission.

I felt these previous months had been very fully lived and I was exhausted. At the airport, I went through security, but even before I showed my United Nations passport I got the feeling I had attracted special interest. My laptop was brand new and a label on the keyboard indicated it was the property of the United Nations. The security official rubbed his finger over the blue UN label then disappeared for a moment, returning with what looked like an electromagnetic wand, and waved it ceremoniously above my laptop. Then followed the usual twenty questions most people are subjected to when they leave Israel. The entry and exit stamps for Gaza in my passport excited my interrogator, but my UN passport seemed to make most of his questions superfluous. Finally, I was allowed to proceed. I sat down at the boarding gate and switched on my laptop. It didn't work. In fact, it never worked again.

18

Brinkmanship, Macedonia 2001

"The next one will bite," Father Basil told me. He was an amiable and kindly man, with the slight stoop common amongst the very tall, and was padre to 16 Air Assault Brigade. We were chatting at our headquarters outside Skopje in Macedonia. He went on, "We went to Bosnia, we shouted boo and they ran away. We went to Kosovo, we shouted boo and they ran away. We went to Sierra Leone, we shouted boo and they ran away. But the next one will bite." How prescient he was, a lone voice of caution in the exuberant period of Tony Blair's 'Force for Good' policy. This was 2001; Afghanistan and the Second Gulf War were yet to come.

The Brigade, commanded by Brigadier Barney White-Spunner, had been deployed to Macedonia. Violence had spread eastwards, the latest repercussion of the break-up of Yugoslavia ten years earlier. War in Croatia had been followed by conflict in Bosnia and Kosovo, and it now seemed inevitable that Macedonia would be included as well. EU politicians had had enough and, after the horrors of Srebrenica, a decision was made to deploy 4,000 British troops for one month to show resolve and prevent further conflict.

Attacks had been launched by Ali Ahmeti, political leader of the former Albanian National Liberation Army, against the security forces of the Republic of Macedonia. A string of villages along the Albanian border were severely damaged during the short-lived conflict, which had ended with a precarious peace known as the Framework Agreement. The idea was that British troops should keep the peace. Thirty-one days seemed a very short time for such a large task. I could understand the padre's scepticism.

Also surprising was the lack of any budget for civilian projects. In Bosnia, I had been allocated £1 million per month to spend on civilian projects to win the peace. But this deployment mission, Operation Essential Harvest, was limited not only in duration, but also in terms of reference. The gloomy script read, "...*specifically tasked with weapons collection, Operation Essential Harvest will not engage in civilian activities external to the Commander's mission.*"

I had been back and forth to the Balkans for nearly a decade, but now I flew to Skopje with some misgivings. The Brigade was being deployed to collect weapons after a flimsy peace agreement, yet could do nothing about the 110,000 people affected by the conflict. It was August, and thousands had been without electricity since March. The delivery of humanitarian assistance was, according to my terms of reference, the UN's job; I was merely there to monitor and report on their performance. However, there was also a mention of confidence-building measures, and this did seem something I could work on.

Unhelpfully, the UN had designated the conflict area as 'Security Level 4', which limited their activities to essential humanitarian assistance. UN civilians were required to adopt complicated security protocols; they had to give two days' notice of travel, had to move around in armoured vehicles, wear helmets and body armour. Since there were remarkably few armoured vehicles available and the restrictions were so onerous, very little was happening.

There was a further twist. Humanitarian assistance for Albanian villages in the former conflict areas was highly controversial. The Macedonian government and ethnic Macedonians generally were of the opinion that the Albanian population harboured terrorists. The injudicious delivery of humanitarian aid could raise political tension rather than improve the situation. The years since 1999 had been unhappy for the Macedonians. They had seen their territory used for NATO attacks on the Serbs, their fellow Orthodox Christians. The new political and military arrangements in Kosovo, and empty promises of economic support, had made ethnic Macedonians think that the EU and NATO, and the Framework Agreement, favoured the Albanians. More than 100 million euros of EU assistance promised to Macedonia had remained unpaid since 1999.

The peace agreement was extremely fragile and dependent not only on the collection of weapons but also on a tortuous path through the Macedonian parliament before its ratification. Strong, visible and unequivocal support for the Macedonian government would be essential if the Framework Agreement was to hold. It would be impossible to provide humanitarian assistance in the former conflict areas without first demonstrating such clear support. I was concerned that, with Skopje so close to the conflict area, if the Framework Agreement broke down and hostilities resumed, the potential for serious population displacement was very real. However, this was all hypothetical. With the mission timeframe set to one month, I had only days to grasp the politics.

The military headquarters were in an empty factory on the outskirts of Skopje. The Brigadier, Barney White-Spunner, was a large man with a commanding presence, known for his courtesy and friendly nature, which were almost at odds with his military persona. He spoke very precisely and words were not wasted. He seemed pleased that I had been sent to join him. I explained my rather dismal role in monitoring the UN effort, but when I mentioned the second part of my job he became more interested. I read out the relevant terms of reference: "...*identifying and promoting confidence-building measures that might make a central contribution to the success of the Framework Agreement.*" I was also rather relieved when he said, "There are plenty of hotel beds in Skopje. No point in making yourself uncomfortable here."

It is always a matter of courtesy to call on the Ambassador or the Chargé d'Affaires when one is working on their patch. It was doubly important for me to call at the British Embassy as this was clearly going to be a very political mission, and I needed to make an initial assessment within a few days. So I needed to speak to as many people as possible – diplomats, heads of agencies, and local people. Once I had a feel for the politics, I could challenge any hypothesis again and again until I was reasonably confident that it held some truth. I also needed to travel to the conflict area and, given the UN's caution, I needed to work on this straight away.

The Chargé d'Affaires was an astonishingly energetic diplomat, Dickie Potter. I received an enthusiastic welcome and was made to feel part of the embassy team within minutes and given a set of embassy keys. He gave me a summary of recent political events, and his descriptions of the main characters involved were wonderfully entertaining. His political assessment was a huge help and his judgement turned out to be both prescient and astute. My security clearance, unusually for an outside consultant, had recently been upgraded; this gave me access to information that made my work easier and meant Dickie could discuss the situation much more frankly. A rented car was arranged, a gold Ford Focus; it was an odd vehicle in which to set off into a conflict zone and caused much amusement back at the headquarters.

Assessing the contributions of the UN agencies was not difficult. 'Masterly inactivity' – as the maintenance of the status quo with Russia was known in the 19th century – was definitely the approach here, rather than the Forward Policy favoured by expansionist British India officials at the time. It was immediately clear that the UN unanimously disapproved of the NATO deployment, seeing it as high-risk and an impediment to progress. My suggestion, that once British troops were deployed in the conflict zone they might provide a security window where real change could be achieved. It was dismissed without discussion. However, I did manage to secure myself a place on the humanitarian convoy into the conflict zone the next day. But I felt this had more to do with their hopes of continued British government funding than any desire to be helpful to me.

My low expectations were realised. Three hours and considerable energy were taken up complying with UN security regulations, including a briefing by the security officer on radio procedures and convoy drills. It was a good three hours before we finally moved off.

It was a beautiful summer's day. The conflict area being only thirty kilometres from the capital, our long convoy of white 4x4s from most of the UN agencies in Skopje soon arrived at the first checkpoint. Here we passed some Macedonian irregular soldiers, known for their brutal suppression of the Albanians. I could see that bringing succour to their enemies was hugely unpopular.

The villages lay in ruins, mainly from artillery fire during the conflict; weeds grew everywhere and the roads were littered with debris, which made me a little apprehensive. Being shot at was something one could do something about, but landmines were a less visible threat. As in Kosovo, any houses untouched by shelling had been set on fire.

After the first checkpoint, we travelled for nearly half an hour without seeing a single human being. Ethnic cleansing had been at the centre of all these Balkan conflicts. We stopped to talk to a small group of old women, who pleaded for assistance. Looking at their ruined houses it was difficult to see how they managed to live here at all. It was still August, but in ten weeks' time the first frosts would arrive. I was amazed that this was the first visit by many of the UN agencies. ICRC and a few NGOs had been almost alone in providing humanitarian assistance. We snaked through ruined villages for another hour, then it was time to return to Skopje. It had been hugely helpful for me to get a view of the situation, but I was not overly impressed by inter-agency trips like this one. I got the impression that for some of the agencies this was no more than humanitarian tourism, and unlikely to produce results.

It was clear that the UN was cautious of the NATO deployment from the start and, by overtly helping the enemies of the ethnic Macedonians, this field trip might make matters worse. From what I had seen, there was no humanitarian emergency here. Most of the displaced people were living elsewhere with host families, which allowed the UN to justify caution. There had already been anti-NATO protests and it was possible that the UN agencies feared that too much sympathy for the Albanians might see these protests replicated outside their offices in Skopje.

When I got back to the embassy Dickie was writing a report for London. He showed me a paragraph, which was witty and challenging, written in the robust style of diplomatic missives of an earlier century. Upstairs in what was now my office I found clouds of concrete dust and a builder with an enormous drill installing an eyebolt into the centre of the floor. He did not speak a word of English, so I went to find one of the local staff to interpret. After a long conversation, she pointed to a bag behind the door. "There is only one door out of the building. This could be the only way out in an emergency." I looked rather baffled. "The crowd might come to burn down the embassy," she explained. "So you have a harness and a rope to abseil out of the window." She looked none too sure about this herself. "Of course," I replied. One needed to remember that the FCO Property Services Agency had to think of everything. I could not really see how abseiling down the outside of the building on a rope clipped to an eyebolt was going to be very useful in the circumstances. But no doubt this satisfied someone's risk assessment back in London. Meanwhile, I made a mental note not to trip over the eyebolt every time I came into the room.

The Brigade POLAD Roland Hayes, Dickie and I had discussed the merits of a diplomatic pre-emptive strike. It would only be a matter of time before I was summoned to account for our attempts to support the enemies of the Macedonian State. So the next day I went to see the Deputy Prime

Minister, a decent, solid individual, whom I instinctively and immediately liked. This was fortunate in the circumstances and it did not take long before he started a diatribe against the EU. The list of complaints was predictable. There was of course the name FYROM (Former Yugoslav Republic of Macedonia) that we used to placate the Greeks who objected to the use of the name Macedonia. Then there was the use of their country to attack their old friends the Serbs. And, of course, there was the 100 million euros promised to Macedonia but not yet delivered. This was merely an *amuse-bouche*. To my relief, the main course, the subject of Kosovo, was left for a subsequent meeting. My diplomatic skills were severely challenged, but he was impressed by my decade of experience in the Balkans and my quiet arguments in favour of containing the Albanian problem. I explained that the UN in Skopje were expecting the displacement of as many as 600,000 people as a result of counter-insurgency operations by Macedonian troops near the cities of Tetovo and Kumanovo. I said that although I thought the collection of weapons from rebels in Macedonia would be of limited importance, real improvements to security would be provided by the deployment of the brigade. He had his doubts, but I felt the meeting had been a success. What was abundantly clear was that without the release of essential EU funding, the whole operation would be in trouble.

At the Commander's 'bird table brief', I was able to observe the progress of the operation. Within the first few days, a concrete block had been dropped from a motorway bridge, killing a British soldier. It was a bad start, but thereafter things had rapidly improved. The confidence-building measures were now firmly part of the plan and two staff officers were assigned to work with me. To show how important Barney considered this task, we were even given a speaking part at the brief and were expected to keep him informed of any progress we were making.

At my second meeting with the Deputy Prime Minister, it was obvious that Dickie's diplomacy with the Macedonian government had been successful. The meeting seemed constructive from the start. I explained that the key to success lay in improving the lives of those in the conflict areas. Water and electricity supplies had been cut off for months and restoring them, I suggested, might be the most productive measure to allow a return to normal life. Also, reconnection was a neutral intervention as it affected friend and foe alike. It was just a matter of releasing the EU funds to pay for it. But as relations with the Macedonians improved, intelligence reports indicated unsurprisingly that the Albanians were now less than happy.

Barney told me he had arranged for me to meet that afternoon the Albanian leader, Ali Ahmeti, who commanded what were called the Albanian Armed Groups. I had little time to prepare. A Lynx helicopter was waiting at the headquarters and, escorted by Special Forces, I flew thirty or so kilometres into the conflict zone, reflecting that I knew very little about this fellow, and even less about what I was going to say. After a twenty-minute flight across a desolate and wrecked landscape, we landed in a field of unharvested wheat near a crossroads and all five of us sprinted to the tree line. There was a steep bank ahead of me and my escorts climbed it effortlessly. I considered myself fairly fit, but for the first time I noticed I did not quite have the agility of my younger companions.

Two black Mercedes were waiting for us. They were dreadfully battered; even the laminated windscreens were cracked. We were greeted brusquely by four Albanians in the usual outfit of the insurgent fighter, a curious mix of military and civilian clothing. Despite the ostentatious and unambiguous pistols tucked into their belts, their rather pointed civilian shoes rendered the whole image rather underwhelming. We were driven at speed to a sizeable village, considerably more knocked about than anything I had seen during my UN field trip the week before. Whole houses had collapsed, piles of rubble lay in the road, and electricity and telephone cables were draped mournfully across our way. Not a soul was in sight. We were escorted on foot down a narrow alley between two destroyed buildings. There in front of us, holding their Kalashnikovs in an arch for us to pass beneath, were twenty insurgents dressed, like our escorts, in an odd arrangement of military and civilian clothing. Large hunting knives looked incongruous with the military webbing stuffed with improbable numbers of magazines for their automatic rifles. It was pure theatre, and more was to come.

It was clear that the house for the meeting, like the village, had been specially chosen to emphasise the scale of destruction. We had to step over beams, piles of broken glass and mangled furnishings. We entered a large room, with a sizeable portion of one wall missing, where fifty people assembled to greet us. We took our seats and were given Turkish coffee. There was now a long wait. A headless doll lay near my left foot.

I was used to the protocol of Balkan warlords. It was customary for them to demonstrate control and gravitas, so it was important that we should wait for the arrival of the big man. Eventually, a loud and extravagant man appeared and harangued us for nearly half an hour. My interpreter struggled to keep up, but this was of course the mandatory history lesson that preceded most meetings in the Balkans, an opportunity to relate the outrages of many centuries to justify the action currently being taken by our host. I had assumed the imposing speaker was Ali Ahmeti, as formal introductions played no part in the protocol. In the pre-internet era, photographs were uncommon, but such was the ego of most warlords that they found it difficult to understand that they were not universally recognised. However, this was just a warm-up act and, to my surprise, a diminutive figure now appeared from the back of the room. The great terrorist leader was of small stature and quietly spoken, yet his alert gaze indicated a sharp intelligence. He spoke in a flat monotone and much of his speech only reconfigured the sentiments of his Chief of Staff. He finally came to the point: what was I going to do to help his people? Since the Kosovo war he knew that the West had favoured the Albanians, and now was a good opportunity to extract as much as possible from us. I explained that the British government had already agreed to spend £2.4 million through the Red Cross and the UN. This was pure flannel, unlikely to stir any terrorist's heart, but I continued, "The real prize, if hostilities ceased, would be the reconnection and even the improvement of water and electricity supplies to the Albanian villages." I could see that he thought this was something he could take back to his people.

If I could match the reconnection of water and electricity with the release of funds to the Macedonian government both sides could feel there was merit in the deployment of NATO troops.

In former times this might have been easy, but gone were the direct operations I had been accustomed to for the last decade, where, once broad objectives had been set, we were left alone to achieve them. Things now were to be multilateral. DFID would provide the funds and it was up to the EU, UN and the NGOs to achieve the results. This, I felt in the circumstances, was unlikely.

In mid-September, I received a copy of a long fax written by a senior British civil servant to Kenzo Oshimo, Head of OCHA in New York. In the most brutal terms, it said that having received funding from the British government it was time for OCHA to perform. I felt that this was hopelessly naive. Imagining that the UN could do anything quickly indicated a failure to understand the organisation. As a bureaucracy, the UN deals with process and has a structure that is inimical to management. It is risk-averse, with a procurement system of imponderable lethargy designed to avoid fraud. To think that during our month-long deployment a nimble UN would be able to take the initiative, satisfy both sides and produce a lasting peace was hugely misplaced. Rude letters to New York were only going to make matters worse.

The UN in New York had declared the conflict area in Macedonia 'Security Level 4', which was hugely restrictive, so the Heads of the UN agencies in Skopje had the perfect excuse to do as little as possible. Matters were no better at the EU. The dirty laundry of the European states had been cruelly exposed in the Balkans, and the legacy of World War II and ancient alliances during the 19th century had all been stirred into a hideous broth. Now tensions between the EU, NATO and the UN made clear, unequivocal action difficult.

Despite these obstacles, successful efforts were being made by the British Embassy in Skopje to keep the Macedonians happy. My shuttle diplomacy on humanitarian issues was delicate, and only one thing mattered – I had to deliver. Operation Essential Harvest, to everybody's surprise, had become a real success. The quantity and quality of weapons handed in for destruction were impressive. Security in the conflict area had been transformed by the Brigade's deployment and 54,000 refugees had returned from Kosovo. This meant nothing to the humanitarian agencies in Skopje who were quite convinced that progress was an illusion and that continued contingency planning for the 600,000 people who would inevitably be displaced by the conflict was still necessary. For the Framework Agreement to be a success there needed to be progress at all levels, political, military and humanitarian. Dickie had made real progress at the political level, Barney at the military level, but at the humanitarian level, I was feeling increasingly uncomfortable. With no budget, and terms of reference forbidding me to actually do anything, I had little room for manoeuvre. My only hope was to get the EU to release funds.

During the war in Bosnia, the EU had funded a small organisation called the International Management Group, which had been very successful at repairing the electricity network during the conflict. Now, in Macedonia, it had been tasked with helping with domestic housing. Throughout the Balkans, domestic housing was an acutely sensitive subject. The wars had been fought about who lived where, and it was profoundly unwise to be tangled up in this; the result was usually seething resentment. The key to keeping both Macedonians and Albanians happy was to work on the more neutral subject of power and water supplies.

I needed to go back to the conflict area for another look at what had to be done. With two junior staff officers from Brigade Headquarters, I set off in my gold Ford Focus for the Tetovo Valley, to meet some of the Brigade's weapon collectors and make a more detailed assessment. After the fuss created by the UN on my original field trip three weeks earlier this was a welcome change, and no different from my experience in Bosnia. It was interesting to see how attitudes to risk had changed over the decade. What was considered normal then was now considered reckless.

As we passed burnt houses and destroyed villages, I realised that one of my passengers was uncomfortable, and heard him fastening his body armour as we passed a checkpoint. Happily, it was unmanned, but a dubious group of Macedonians soldiers were sitting on an armoured vehicle nearby. I gave a friendly wave, but received none in return. Fifteen minutes later, we came to the crossroads where I had agreed to meet our soldiers, a desolate spot, with abandoned fields all around. Within minutes, they had arrived and there was a great deal of military banter, with my gold Ford Focus at the centre of it.

We spent the day looking at water and power supplies. Towards evening we made our way back towards Skopje, and met a large group of vehicles from what appeared to be an important delegation. Curious, I got out to look. Standing in front of the group was Chris Patten, the EU Commissioner, and Ed Llewellyn, his Private Secretary. I knew this was probably my only chance to obtain the EU funding so desperately needed to make the fragile Framework Agreement work, and this was exactly the opportunity I needed. I introduced myself and briefed the Commissioner on the Brigade's confidence-building measures whether he liked it or not. It seemed to have the right effect, for I spent the rest of the afternoon travelling with him and discussing all the issues. He stopped to talk to an old woman outside her house and chatted to her in front of the cameras, with a consummate display of political charm.

★★★

Our month-long deployment was coming to an end. Although the harvest of weapons had surprised everyone, the major contribution was the real improvement in security brought about by the British deployment. We had not overcome the curmudgeonly disapproval of the UN, but the idea of reconnecting the power and water supplies had become central to strengthening the Framework Agreement.

The electricity distribution grid was part of Macedonia's sovereign territory and the psychological impact of reconnecting the former conflict area was enormous. During my final week, I heard that Chris Patten had authorised the release of 26 million euros for infrastructure repairs in the conflict area. Tetovo and Kumanovo were to have their water supplies repaired, and road access to the Tetovo valley was to be improved. I had also been working on getting the railway open to Tetovo and this was to be included. It had been an extraordinary month; we had started with the death of a British soldier and the universal hostility of the Macedonian government, the Albanian Armed Groups and the United Nations, and thirty-one days later, there was a real chance of lasting peace. The UN remained unconvinced, but they had been sidelined by the release of funds for the Macedonian government.

The humanitarian agencies were still approaching problems with a 'developing country' mindset – a blanket and a water container for everyone. Restoring urban power and water was the best way of reaching the majority of the population in mid-income countries, and had the benefit of being the most neutral way of delivering humanitarian assistance. Thousands could be reached by the flick of a switch; but this was a lesson that even twenty years later had still to be fully appreciated.

I drove back to the British Embassy to find no one at their desks. The place was deserted, I sensed alarm. Everyone was in the conference room, watching in stony silence as the television broadcast news of attacks on the World Trade Center. For an hour, we watched the devastation until we were summoned back to our desks by a cacophony of telephone calls. The consequences, and the war on terror announced by the Americans, were going to change the approach to the delivery of humanitarian assistance in conflict zones. As I left Macedonia a few days later I reflected how, little by little, the appetite for risk on the part of governments and humanitarian agencies had been decreasing over the years. The 9/11 attacks were to herald a step-change. Within fifteen years, humanitarian agencies would be paralysed by risk aversion.

Operation Essential Harvest had been a huge success. Both the Macedonian government and the Albanian Armed Groups felt they had benefited, and further conflict had been avoided. I had been wholly sceptical about the weapons collection, but everyone had been surprised by what was handed in.

Military success was one thing; DFID's new approach was another. I felt it was unlikely to be successful. I reread the letter sent to Kenzo Oshima. The general message, 'We have paid you several million, and you will perform to our expectations,' could only be an irritation. I remembered Andy Bearpark's advice about the United Nations: "Go there; find out what plan they have. If they don't have one, help them make one. If they have problems with procurement, let me know what people and equipment they need and we'll get them within a week." This had been very effective, and made us friends all over the world.

But it was going to be very different now. Andy had left DFID and Mukesh Kapila was the new Head of Department. He had told me once again that I would not understand the principles behind the new policy. I, however, understood them only too well.

19

Support and Influence, Afghanistan 2001

"The solution to any problem here, Gilbert, is industrial-scale application of the perceived remedy." I was being briefed by Brigadier Peter Wall at the United States Central Command (CENTCOM), the vast military headquarters located at MacDill Air Force Base in Tampa, Florida, where the British Contingent Headquarters was in a trailer park just outside the main CENTCOM building. The issues were deadly serious and would dominate world politics for a generation to come.

Since the destruction of the World Trade Center in New York five weeks earlier, an enraged United States had been looking for someone somewhere to punish. Central Command, for the US Armed Forces, is responsible for Central Asia and it was the training camps in Afghanistan which had spawned the 9/11 terrorists. These were now the centre of attention. A bombing campaign had started against both the training camps and the Taliban in Afghanistan, but this was not without complications. The long-running civil war between the Taliban and the Northern Alliance had displaced a large proportion of the population, who were dependent on humanitarian assistance. In addition to the conflict, Afghanistan is prone to natural disasters and this time it was drought. The UN had been providing Afghanistan with over 350,000 tons of food aid every year from a huge railway depot at Peshawar in Pakistan. However, UN aid convoys and the bombing were not hugely compatible activities.

I had already travelled twice to Pakistan to try to de-conflict the civil and military activities in Afghanistan. This meant preventing civilians being caught in the crossfire. The US-led Coalition efforts in Islamabad to soothe UN nerves about civilian safety had been a disaster. From the start, there were problems of protocol. The two British military staff officers were only majors and the heads of agencies they met were, in military rank equivalent, generals. Having known such a good relationship between military and civil humanitarian agencies in Bosnia, the two staff officers were not prepared for the reception they received in Islamabad.

This was no Bosnia where, during the UNPROFOR years, the military had been UN peacekeeping troops and even after the Dayton Peace Agreement were peace enforcers. Here, the military were party to the conflict. Many humanitarian agencies had had a working relationship with the Taliban government in Afghanistan for some years, and were outraged by the bombing, believing it would only make matters worse. They wanted 'humanitarian space' and felt that the failure of the military to understand their plans and operational constraints was inexcusable.

The Coalition had airdropped humanitarian daily rations, which exacerbated an already difficult relationship, especially as it was done without consulting the UN Humanitarian Coordinator and without any thought for the target population, the number of beneficiaries or even the identified need. It was clear that the Coalition Humanitarian Liaison Team (CHLT) should have been larger, more experienced and engaged with the Humanitarian Regional Coordinator from the start.

While I was in Islamabad, the Coalition bombed a Red Cross warehouse by mistake, causing international outrage. As I knew the ICRC delegate and was working for one of the countries in the Coalition, I added my apology to what I thought would be many. I was astonished when he said that mine was the first. He mentioned wearily that none had come from the military in person and that he was not used to apologies by press release. As a result of the strained relations with the Coalition, a British Air Commodore, David Walker, was put in charge of the Coalition Humanitarian Liaison Team (CHLT) in Islamabad and a humanitarian cell was established in the trailer park at CENTCOM. Since I had pushed for humanitarian representation at CENTCOM, I got rather more than I wished for – I was sent to Florida.

Central Command is in a huge building at MacDill Air Force Base. In the adjacent trailer park were all the Coalition partners, among them the British Contingent Headquarters commanded by Air Chief Marshall Jock Stirrup. The British delegation numbered eighty-three and we, uniquely among the

Coalition partners, were allowed inside the headquarters building. Each day we were invited to planning meetings, and I saw and heard a range of plans aimed at anyone who might have been responsible for 9/11.

There was a profound ignorance of humanitarian issues in the headquarters. Unlike the British Armed Forces, the US did not see the management of civilian issues as part of any overall military operation. They were only interested in the military 'projection of force' in a very rigid fashion. This headquarters was on an Air Force Base and the place was all about bombing; the bigger the bombs the better.

The US military command displayed little communication between staff functions, which was made worse by excessive secrecy within the headquarters. Little thought was given to the wider effects of actions, or the fact that the vigorous pursuit of one objective could be inimical to the successful outcome of another. The presence of our British National Headquarters, I felt, was crucial, so soon after 9/11, in asking the right questions, in damping enthusiasm for less wise courses of action and in modifying strategy and operations. Much of the credit was down to the easy relationship that Jock Stirrup and Peter Wall had with the Americans and the friendly and good-humoured way we were treated.

One meeting I attended had a distinctly *Dr Strangelove* touch. The intention was to bomb a hapless country where some of the inhabitants were guilty by association with the 9/11 plotters, which seemed to justify punitive retribution on a medieval scale; it involved bombing until all known life was extinguished. Finally, the Brigadier General turned to me. "Dr Greenall, what do you think of that?" Indeed, what did I think? I said confidently, "I'm afraid this will require a little more planning", the standard British euphemism for "We should bin this one." Then a young staff officer, all square jaw and enormous biceps, jumped up. "Yes, sir!" he shouted, although I was no more than five feet away. "I have fifty more planners!" I groaned inwardly.

The ground war had now started. British and US Special Forces had joined the Northern Alliance in North-east Afghanistan and the Taliban were retreating rapidly to the Pashtun strongholds in the south-west of the country. Kabul fell within days and the humanitarian agencies that for so long had predicted an emergency were keen to move back into the country.

As soon as I returned to London, I discovered that I was to lead the DFID team in Kabul. The team had already flown in a chartered Russian

IL-76, with forty-six tons of equipment, to Termez in Uzbekistan. From there we would proceed overland to Kabul.

Termez is a scruffy settlement on the north side of the Oxus River; I flew there via Moscow and Tashkent. As I was driven from the airport, I could see to the south a line of low hills and the mountains of Afghanistan beyond. As soon as I met the DFID team, I realised quickly that frustration had given way to extreme exasperation. Like all the other humanitarian agencies in the town, they were waiting to cross the Freedom Bridge into Afghanistan; however, the bridge was closed and showed every sign of staying closed. The reason given was security, as there had been fighting involving British Special Forces in Mazar-i-Sharif on the other side of the bridge. I sensed that there was more to it. At a meeting that night it was clear that wider political considerations would need to be addressed before the bridge was opened, and this was not going to happen in Termez. Some of the humanitarians displayed an unattractive self-righteousness and self-importance in their dealings with the Uzbek officials. The sentiment was 'How can these unfeeling people not understand the good we are going to do'. As far as the Uzbeks were concerned, we were just a crowd of meddling foreigners with nothing to offer the people of Uzbekistan. We could wait.

Clearly nothing was going to happen for some while. I contacted London and was told to make my way to Peshawar in Pakistan – no small task. First, I had to get back to Tashkent, but there was only one daily flight and I was told it was fully booked for weeks. However, I knew that little had changed here since the fall of the Soviet Union, when a row of seats was always reserved for the *nomenklatura*, so it was just a matter of a 100 dollar supplement to the ticket price. Within the hour, I was on my way back to Tashkent. The next step was a little more complicated. The only international flight that day departed at midnight for New Delhi. From there I would fly to Karachi and from Karachi to Islamabad. After a dash up the Grand Trunk Road – two nights and three days of travelling – I would finally reach Peshawar.

With the whole day ahead, I reported to the British Ambassador, explained the situation at Termez, and asked if I could approach the Uzbek government about the bridge. He seemed delighted, and summoned the Third Secretary to join me. Soon we were waiting in a Soviet-style concrete government building. Eventually a man in an ill-fitting uniform appeared, his peaked cap pulled firmly down over his eyes. I started an introductory ramble and, feeling that a little competitive needling might be necessary, I talked of fictitious plans the US had in neighbouring Tajikistan, of the billions of investment in roads and even a new bridge over the Oxus that might go to the Tajiks if the Freedom Bridge remained closed.

The Colonel's face remained impassive except for a twitch at the corner of his mouth at every mention of the Tajiks. Rather abruptly, I came to a halt. He pulled down his cap. "Dr Greenall, we understand each other very well. The subject requires some consideration." Some mumbling in Uzbek now took place and the Third Secretary looked delighted. We had not mentioned the bridge, yet now we had the beginnings of a deal, which we could triumphantly present to the Ambassador. However, on hearing our story, he simply looked weary. It was clear that he found this aspect of living in Central Asia deeply disagreeable. "Oh, must they?" was his only response. After three weeks, the bridge did finally open.

★★★

Whatever the dangers of being in Afghanistan during a war, they were nothing to driving up the Grand Trunk Road from Islamabad to Peshawar. It was not very different from my last trip up this road; this time I saw no fewer than three fatal accidents in a mere 173 kilometres.

Kabul had been taken by the Northern Alliance, supported by British and US Special Forces a few days earlier, and the fighting was now in the Pashtun strongholds in the south-west of the country. The Red Cross flight from Peshawar with twenty of us on board had arrived at the former Soviet Air Force Base at Bagram just after dawn, and it was an extraordinary sight. The vast base was abandoned and littered with the debris of present and past conflicts. Armoured cars sat wheel-less, jet fighters lay wingless, jauntily at odd angles, buildings roofless and rubble-strewn acres of concrete indicated two decades of neglect. It was dangerous too, littered with thousands of anti-personnel mines. The Russians had laid some on the perimeter before 1989, but more were scattered by whatever faction had held the base over the last twelve years. To walk anywhere except on the taped paths was to lose a limb or one's life.

Although four million people were living in Kabul, life in the city seemed muted. There was an atmosphere of uncertainty, of fear. People were still in survival mode, watchful, unsure, and the Pashtuns amongst them resentful. Change had come quickly and the city was coming to terms with it.

My first call was on the British Ambassador, Stephen Evans. I had known Stephen since the First Gulf War and I could not have received a more enthusiastic welcome. He was based in an annex of the old British Embassy, which had been the subject of a long dispute between India and Pakistan after partition and had fallen into ruin. The adjacent annex was a small friendly place with portraits of Edward VII and Queen Alexandra flanking the hall. The building had not been used for years, but once the Ambassador returned, so did all the staff. It had been an emotional time, especially as they were all now quite old. They and the Edwardian furniture gave the embassy great charm. We drank tea out of the best bone china and relaxed on the sofas in the anteroom of a former age.

My terms of reference were refreshingly broad – I could do anything that might improve the humanitarian situation. This was helpful in that I could go anywhere I wished and could work with any of the UK's civil or military personnel, in the country or not. Yet I knew from experience that I needed to present London with a humanitarian strategy that was both simple and effective. This was no Kosovo. Afghanistan is the size of France, with over 20 million people, a huge number of whom were affected by a severe drought. It was not just about a humanitarian response; the goal was political stability, and I needed to recommend things that would demonstrate the benefits of peace and support the political process.

My recommendation to fly the DFID team direct to Afghanistan after the fruitless wait at Termez was accepted, and they duly arrived. While I was at the embassy, the team looked for an office and accommodation, and found a house in a residential street not far from the centre of Kabul. It was a modest, ugly modern house of rendered blockwork, set back from the road with large metal gates and a small garden. The area was considered safer than the more densely populated area near the old embassy.

The first thing we unpacked was a large diesel fuel stove. The important thing was to be warm, but by complete chance we also had hot water. This made our house rather popular during the freezing cold Afghan winter that lay ahead. Kabul in winter is muddy, as cold nights are followed by sunny days that thaw out frozen water. A shower and clean laundry were very precious. The transformation of this empty house into an office and accommodation for all six of us – with satellite communications and a full complement of local staff, including an excellent cook – was completed within twenty-four hours. After the delays at Termez we could hardly believe our good fortune to be here in Kabul and fully operational.

While the equipment was being unloaded, one of the drivers reversed a brand-new Land Rover into a generator, breaking the rear window. The driver was profusely apologetic and, through the interpreter, there was talk of going to the bazaar to find a new window. I thought the probability of finding such a thing highly unlikely. Someone observed that as we were so well set up all we needed now was a gin and tonic. I dispatched the driver to look for the window and as a parting gesture told him to bring back some tonic water. Within the hour he was back, with a window for the Land Rover and a box of rather ancient Schweppes tonic water. This told me much about Afghanistan. The country had been at war for twenty-two years, yet the survival mechanisms were remarkable. I reflected on the predictions of the humanitarian disaster that had been much mentioned in Islamabad. There were certainly many extremely vulnerable people, but watching this city come back to life with each passing day made me focus on the political implications of any programme I put together.

There were now almost twenty of us in Kabul, including Special Forces. A last-minute decision had been taken for our Special Forces to operate in civilian clothes, which had been sent out from a sports shop in Poole. With their beards, Afghan scarves, checked shirts and anoraks they all looked as if they had adopted a new uniform. Every evening there was a meeting at the embassy, after which I drove back across the city alone to be at the house before the 9 pm curfew. I was still unfamiliar with the route and on one occasion I got lost. All the empty streets suddenly looked the same. I retraced my journey and tried another route, as I now had only minutes before the curfew. I was still on the street at the magic hour. A sentry rushed out from the shadows screaming at me and put his rifle to my head. I could only smile and gesture for calm. He spoke no English, and I had not a word of Dari. I rang the house on my mobile, got the local staff to explain the situation, and was finally escorted home, feeling rather foolish.

Mixed messages were coming from DFID in London. The new broom in this newest Department of State was increasingly evident. Bilateral action was out, multilateral action was in. Mission command, the ability of an official to choose how to achieve given objectives, was disappearing fast. Now that we had email, London tried to control the minutiae of daily life; any movement out of Kabul had to be authorised by London, and I was even told which building to sleep in. I suggested this might be an operational decision better taken in Kabul, only to get a sharp rebuke. One edict was that any Quick Impact Projects identified should be jointly managed with the United Nations. This immediately threw up a problem. The UN were only just setting up their offices, had very few staff, and certainly did not have the operational capability to do anything at this stage. They couldn't understand why we didn't just get on with our own projects and stop bothering them. One UN official said, "You chaps are big grown-ups; you don't need us holding your hand." This was not a message easily conveyed to London.

As my terms of reference covered the whole of Afghanistan, I had been wondering how I would travel. I discovered at an embassy meeting that the UK's military Support and Influence Team was preparing a mission to the town of Bamyan, 250 kilometres north-west of Kabul in central Afghanistan. The population there were Hazara, and had been persecuted by the Taliban. They were an ethnic minority widely discriminated against and easily identified because of their distinctly different looks. Living in the mountains, they were also particularly poor and amongst the most vulnerable in the country. I was asked to join the mission to make a humanitarian assessment.

Six of us set off at first light in two Toyota Land Cruisers. They were black with tinted glass and I thought they looked particularly sinister, as I was used to driving in white vehicles, the chosen colour for humanitarian agencies. The sun was just appearing over the mountains, and it was cold and dry with not a breath of wind. We were to meet Karim Khalili, then leader of the Wahdat political party of Hazara, at his headquarters in Bamyan, a journey of five to six hours. With hardly a vehicle on the road, we were soon out of Kabul and up in the mountains. My colleagues in the front were silent types and long periods went by without hardly a word.

The checkpoints seemed friendly enough, but continuing our journey involved our leader making lengthy satellite calls to the next Commander up the road to guarantee our safe passage. I got out of the car at these stops to stretch my legs. It was minus ten degrees, and very young children, gloveless, were mending potholes in the road. This was a brutally tough country and the people had clearly been shaped by their environment. The process of stop and go continued all day as we snaked our way through the mountains. We approached Bamyan from a high pass, and I could see the aquamarine lake in the valley below. It was dusk when we arrived at a mud fort with massive metal gates, which were opened by two Hazaras armed with AK47s. The gates banged shut behind us, and we were in a courtyard full of armed Afghans. It was clear there was no easy way out of here should things turn ugly.

We were led into a mud building with low beams and a fire at one end, which was welcome after the cold. Our host, Karim Khalili, looked like everyone's favourite grandfather, genial, kind and charming, yet I saw behind this an iron will and wolf-like cunning. The conversation was in Dari and, not understanding a word, I watched the body language. It was reassuring; little else was. Six of us were in a mud fort in the middle of Afghanistan as a guest of the Hazara leader, outnumbered five to one by armed Afghans. I just hoped the support was going to get the influence we hoped for and that any disappointment would not turn to anger.

After a few minutes, half a dozen men appeared carrying trays of food; a banquet had been prepared for us. Our leader once again engaged with Khalili in an animated conversation in Dari and I was reassured by the friendly gestures being exchanged. My taciturn colleagues remained alert but impassive, their hands folded over their torsos. It was getting dark, and paraffin lamps were lit. With the fire and the wood smoke it was warm and I felt, after such a long and uncertain journey, rather drowsy. Then the banquet ended suddenly and we found ourselves alone. We laid our sleeping bags on the earth floor, but despite being exhausted I slept fitfully, not entirely convinced this would all end well.

In the morning, Khalili returned. This time I was involved in the discussion, our leader acting as interpreter, and was able to ask a myriad of questions about the civilian population, availability of food in the province, the conditions of roads and bridges, the destruction of houses by the Taliban, whether the markets were open and whether health services still existed. Khalili explained that not much had changed for some time and that, despite the shortages, there was no new emergency. I was impressed by the resilience of the population who, after decades of war, managed to survive on next to nothing. It showed that despite all that had happened, they were not facing the humanitarian catastrophe predicted by the UN.

We were waved through checkpoints on our return journey. I had a wealth of information and my anxieties about us being murdered in our sleeping bags had been unfounded and, given the hospitality we had received, rather uncharitable.

***

Each week life returned to Kabul. The journalists Sam Kiley and Janine di Giovanni were in town, and both occasionally dropped into the embassy where we would sit on the magnificent sofas in the Edwardian time warp chatting as if in a grand country house in England. Sam was a very useful contact, as he knew many local people, so I was much better informed than any of my colleagues. The DFID office was always full of people, perhaps attracted by the warmth of our very effective stove; in the afternoons, a few cheeky individuals would arrive with towels under their arms, hoping to use our hot shower. We were able to keep London happy with an impressive flow of information, but whenever we actually tried to do anything, it was another matter. No one at the UN was ready for our multilateral projects and bilateral action was forbidden by London.

Meanwhile, I produced a strategy paper with five objectives. The food aid programme should be continued, and key roads improved. We needed to organise high visibility Quick Impact Projects in Kabul to demonstrate the benefits of peace. The Hazarajat region needed to be given priority as the Hazara people had long been marginalised politically and economically. Lastly, the Pashtun areas south-east of Kabul were not to be forgotten. I was very aware of Thucydides' view on how to treat the vanquished by being magnanimous in victory. The Pashtuns were losing the war and it was vital they were not marginalised. They made up 46% of the population and it was important to readdress the political centre of gravity if there were to be lasting peace. Disaffected young Pashtun refugees would be returning from the north-west of Pakistan, and they needed attention. There was a practical point too; these areas were closer to the regional humanitarian and logistic hubs of Islamabad and Peshawar. The military could provide assistance in two other areas – the repair of airfields, especially Kabul's which had an unexploded bomb in the middle of the runway, and the two key supply routes from Mazar-i-Sharif, Afghanistan's third-largest city, to Kabul and from Kabul to Jalalabad on Pakistan's border. These routes linked central Asia to the subcontinent and were essential if Afghanistan was to prosper.

The trip to Bamyan was considered a great success and another, to Herat, was planned for the following week. This sounded precarious, for many reasons. Mohammad Ismail Khan, the Governor and self-styled Emir of Herat, was a colourful figure who commanded great influence. It was thought he was close to Iran and that their support might carry more weight than ours. Moreover, getting to Herat was a lot more complicated than our recent drive through the mountains. We were to be dropped by a C-130 Hercules, where exactly was less than clear. I was driven at dusk to Bagram Air Base, up the Najibulla Road across the Shomali Plain. Mohammad Najibulla, the former President of Afghanistan and a Soviet puppet, lasted four years after the withdrawal of Soviet troops in 1989. With increasing insecurity, he had constructed this road to Bagram Air Base to bypass troublesome villages along the old road should he need to make a hasty exit. But all that effort failed to save him and he met a brutal death at the hands of the Taliban.

The plain was now a desolate place. Before becoming a front line in the battle for Kabul, it had been a fertile area with an abundance of water, where fruit and vegetables were grown, and where Kabul's residents picnicked at weekends. Yet it was here that the Taliban had dug in to defend Kabul and where Coalition bombing had taken place only a few weeks before. It caused a huge loss of life and broke the Taliban resistance. Rumours were circulating that many of the Taliban, facing certain defeat and wishing to change sides in the time-honoured way in Central Asia, had sued for peace. But this had been denied them.

Now the debris of war littered the landscape, vast craters had churned the ground, and military hardware lay scattered along the road. At Bagram Air Base, much had changed since I was here three weeks earlier. At the back of the Soviet concrete hangar were now some Portakabins, where I met the British Commander and was told there was a briefing at 2100 hours. We rolled out our sleeping bags on the concrete floor of the hangar. The roof at the far end was missing and snow was blowing in. On one wall was a vast radiator, and two British servicemen, one very tall and one very short, were arguing about who was going to sleep next to it. The pipes that once supplied this metal tribute to Soviet engineering had emptied their contents onto the floor decades ago, leaving a dismal red smear.

The briefing was a cursory affair. We were to leave at 3.30 am, but – alarmingly – we were to be literally dropped at our destination, which meant driving down the ramp at the back while the aircraft was flying close to the ground. There was even a chance it might be an opposed landing. However, US Special Forces would be there to greet us. I wasn't terribly sure I liked the bit about the opposed landing, but I supposed these chaps knew what they were doing. However, I did notice that everyone was rather tense.

At 3 am, I was woken from a dreamless sleep. We had fifteen minutes to move. I gathered my things in the dark; no lights were allowed. We climbed into two Toyota Land Cruisers, and waited. After a few minutes, I heard the engines of a C-130, but could see nothing in the dark. Then a red light appeared which marked the ramp at the rear of the aircraft. Seconds later, the two Toyota Land Cruisers reversed inside and were strapped down, the ramp was coming up and we were taxiing. The flight took an hour and a half, during which I was invited up to the flight deck and given some welcome coffee. The view was magnificent; we were flying in brilliant moonlight above a thin band of cloud with the mountains of the Hindu Kush rising majestically through it.

As we started to descend, I returned to the Land Cruiser. I had a childlike faith in my companions, but what came next was still a surprise. Both vehicles had their engines running as the great ramp started to descend. At some signal, perhaps a green light, we accelerated, the tachometer needle surge into the red arc, and the tyres screeched against the aluminium floor of the aircraft. We hurtled down the ramp into complete darkness, and there was a minute pause before we hit the ground – perhaps 'collided with' the ground would more accurate – less than a metre below, and came to a halt in a cloud of dust. The silence, now the aircraft was gone, was extraordinary. We seemed to have survived driving out of an aircraft while it was still airborne.

Suddenly the door was wrenched open and a bearded man hopped in beside me. My heart missed a beat, and the longest two seconds of my life stretched to eternity, until he greeted me warmly in a Texan drawl; he was with US Special Forces and there to meet us. Soon we were off to the US Special Forces' base half an hour's drive away. During the drive, he briefed us on the situation, but this was largely a tribute to the Afghan warlord and politician Ismail Khan. I knew little about him, but this description of his munificence and martial skills, his humanitarian gestures and statesmanship, was perhaps a slight departure from fact.

The base was a guesthouse, modern and expensively fitted out, on a small mound with the desert stretching flat around it for miles. The rest of the Special Forces team were equally starry-eyed about their host. "He keeps us here for our own protection," said one. I'm sure he does, I thought, and wondered if this was a case of Stockholm syndrome.

A meeting had been arranged with the Emir for midday, giving us plenty of time to extract as much information as we could from our hosts. My questions about the civilian population were wasted as they had eyes only for military matters. On the way to the meeting, we paused at the Gawhar Shad mosque, one of Central Asia's most precious historic buildings, an architectural marvel surrounded by a pile of rubble.

In Herat we arrived at an impressive stone building and were taken upstairs to a large room prepared for a banquet. Everything told me that things were not well here. Hours passed, and neither our fellow guests nor our host appeared. My anxiety increased. The principle of support and influence was very simple – we provided the support and hopefully obtained the influence – but what if General Khan already had his preferred support? I could hear tanks moving below us. Were they Iranian, I wondered.

Finally, the great man burst into the room with a small entourage. Ismail Khan was small with a white bushy beard and clearly bad-tempered. There were three of them and six of us in this large room, where a banquet had been prepared for at least thirty. The conversation was in Dari, but I did not need to speak the language to see that it was not a success. Despite the charm of our leader, this meeting was clearly going nowhere, and I was certainly not going to be involved in it. The Emir, after some wild gesticulating, suddenly got to his feet and was gone. There was silence, and the room buzzed with negativity. The sooner we were gone the better.

Yet the journey was not completely wasted. Herat looked more prosperous than I had expected; with the Iranian border nearby, everyday items were easily found. I had heard from the Americans that there was a vast refugee camp to the west of the town. So while the others were arranging our return journey to Kabul, I spent an hour in the camp. Despite its enormous size, things were well-organised and I could happily exclude the humanitarian catastrophe predicted by the UN.

The Americans told us that the airport was abandoned and that we could use it. Built by the Russians fifteen years earlier, it had since been battered by the Afghan winters, and now merely looked mournful. In the last moments of daylight, I heard the engines of our C-130 approaching from the south-east. As soon as it touched the ground we raced out onto the runway, the ramp was down, we drove inside and the Land Cruisers were tied down, and we were up and away into the night.

The trip to Herat was not the success we all wanted, yet for me it had been useful. None of the humanitarian agencies had ventured outside Kabul and I had already been to Bamyan and Herat. From what I had seen there was no impending humanitarian emergency, but I was a lone voice in trying to shift priorities. Over the years, I had seen the importance of activities that demonstrated the benefits of peace, especially in the critical 100 days after a conflict ends. We had succeeded in Bosnia after the Dayton Peace Agreement, when the military ran a post-conflict programme with ruthless determination and a large budget. But Bosnia was tiny and accessible, and the war had ended with a peace agreement. Afghanistan was huge and inaccessible, and the war was only sporadically coming to an end, or rather the enemy was just disappearing back into the civilian population or over the border into Pakistan. DFID's desire to do everything through multinational agencies, and the absence of cash, made it inevitable that we would squander the opportunity we now had. Both these shortcomings would mean delay and take us well outside the critical 100 days needed to win the peace.

Four million people were living in Kabul; it was winter and they were hugely dependent on electrical power for cooking and heating. I frequently saw under-dressed Afghans warming themselves outside in front of one-bar electric heaters. The condition of the low-voltage distribution network was dire and the generation of electricity would be equally challenging. I went to see the director of the electricity company located near the airport. He was a friendly man in a brown suit; his office, tucked away in a corner of a dusty compound, told me as much as I needed to know – it was chaotic, dilapidated and desperate for a coat of paint. But he was delighted by my visit and, if I provided transport, he would take me to the hydro dam fifty kilometres east of the city.

At the British Embassy, I discussed this plan with colleagues. The consensus was that it was not a safe area. Even the electricity director had some reservations, but claimed it would be fine if we were back by midday, which seemed a rather strange stipulation.

We left the next day at dawn, picking up the electricity director on the way, and within an hour we were on a deserted road which plunged for many miles through a vast gorge, with not a vehicle or a person to be seen. The crags above reminded me in an unsettling way of the landscape described by Dr Brydon, who after the retreat from Kabul in the winter of 1842 rode his exhausted horse back to the garrison in Jalalabad, during Britain's calamitous withdrawal from the country that year.

The dam was an impressive affair built perhaps in the 1960s or 70s. The Afghans working on site were delighted to see us and led us off on an extensive tour. It was as extraordinary as any treatment of mechanical engineering seemed to be in Afghanistan, a mixture of wilful neglect and cunning improvisation. In the absence of spare parts, since the Russians had left twelve years before, all sorts of clever shortcuts and ingenious bodges had been devised. The turbine house was partially submerged in water and without a single pane of glass in its windows. They were even rewinding electric motors in a workshop. It all looked extremely precarious and downright dangerous. But four million people depended on the dozen or so men running this place. Then our guide took us inside the dam. Clambering down steel-runged ladders and squeezing through narrow galleries was claustrophobic and, given the dilapidated state of the entire structure, unsettling. Not a single electric lightbulb worked anywhere and the tour was conducted by torchlight. Back in the welcome sunlight, we thanked our hosts and were soon back on the road. I was pleased at my determination to see the hydro dam and happy with what I had managed to discover.

I remembered the warning about being out of this wild place by midday. It was now ten past twelve. But, under blue skies and warmed by the afternoon sun, our objective accomplished, I relaxed and began chatting to the electricity director about his life and family.

Back in the same ravine, the crags towered a thousand feet or more above us, and the road was full of massive potholes, forcing the driver to slow down to walking pace. Despite it being winter, the day was warm and both front windows were open. It all happened very quickly. As we approached some ruined buildings, a wild-looking individual brandishing an AK47 jumped out of a doorway, and in an instant the rifle barrel was against my head. With just one sweep he pulled out every radio wire, VHF and HF and, incredibly, the ignition key. We were all three made to get out of the vehicle, our hands above our heads. I did not dare turn around, but could hear men shouting in Pashto behind us. Then our assailants were gone in a cloud of dust, in our second vehicle.

I was standing quite alone in the middle of a road fifty kilometres from Kabul. Everyone else had vanished. Then one by one they rather sheepishly reappeared, my driver and the electricity director from behind a low wall, the others from behind a large rock. There was an awkward silence; perhaps we all felt as silly as each other, and thinking of the Ambassador and our respective organisations there was that moment remembered from childhood – what are we going to tell the parents?

Then suddenly a pickup with half a dozen Afghan men came round the corner at high speed. I stepped out and stopped it. My driver quickly explained what had happened, and within moments we were all bumping up the road on our way back to Kabul. The vehicle was horribly overloaded, its suspension bottoming on every rut. But the driver was delighted to have some paying passengers, and given the circumstances the fare was bound to be quite generous. I wondered if he was a cousin of those that had absconded with the stolen vehicle.

The Ambassador took it all remarkably well, and was just happy that nobody had been hurt. Outside on the veranda, the close support team were 'tooling up' for a mission to recover their vehicle. Huge quantities of ordinance were spread around on the floor and machine gun magazines were being charged. But the Ambassador forbade any such adventure, a censure that was greeted with dismay and displeasure.

Back at the DFID house, just as it was getting dark, my Afghan driver came up to me with the spare keys and a plan to recover our car. I was far from sure that this was a wise plan. Apart from anything else, there was a curfew and the vehicle was a long way from Kabul. Yet he was confident that all that was required was half a million Afghanis. This we had, so we filled a large backpack with bundles of dirty notes and he disappeared into the darkness. I woke the next morning to find the vehicle parked outside the house. I carefully entered the financial details in the receipt book: Recovery of DFID vehicle, 120 dollars.

The weeks had rushed by and I would soon be leaving Afghanistan. The fighting in the west of the country had almost come to an end and, judging by the new traffic jams, life was returning to Kabul. There was talk in the British Embassy of a visit to Abdul Rashid Dostum, the notorious Uzbek warlord, but there was also only one last C-130 flight out of Bagram to the UK via Oman before Christmas. I think we all felt the Dostum trip could wait and the flight down to Oman suddenly looked very attractive. At Bagram, although it was only a fortnight since I had last been there, I was impressed by the build-up of aircraft and equipment. It was getting dark and a cold wind blew across the airfield as I walked over to join the British military recce party who were also waiting for the aircraft. This group, led by Brigadier Barney White-Spunner, was there for a 'follow-on force' that was being planned.

As soon as the ramp at the rear of the aircraft was lowered, there was a Gadarene rush by all thirty of us to get on board. To my surprise, there were no procedures of any kind; we just piled in and sat on the nearest available seat. No one seemed interested who was in the back or even how many had managed to struggle across the concrete apron in the dark. After half an hour in the air, we cleared Afghan airspace and were able to take off our body armour.

Oman was a completely different world. Gone were the snow showers and biting wind; we were now in the desert under brilliant moonlight, the sky crammed with stars. The counterpoint between the two was extraordinary. In the British transit camp, left over from a large military exercise a year earlier, I went for an open-air shower and every drop of water seemed a luxury. Even the British Airways flight home the next day seemed a long-forgotten pleasure.

★★★

Back at home that night; I sat by the fire in the library until late, staring at the flames. I had learnt to avoid the 'return of the conquering hero' routine, however tempting it was to talk about my time away, and tried my hardest to show interest in the minutiae of domestic life, in a world where the death of a hamster loomed larger than the fate of nations. Nevertheless, as the stories did come out, my wife Sarah remarked, "Not many bags of rice delivered this time." It was an accurate and astute observation, and alerted me to the change in how I looked at humanitarian missions.

I had been engaged in activities that might bring peace to Afghanistan and, with it, economic prosperity. This was the real prize. Humanitarian programmes so often resulted from misguided or weak foreign policy, indecision, and now this new values-based foreign policy, which would be rejected on this stony ground and elsewhere. Peace could only be achieved at the political level, and if this happened the economic effects would soon be felt. Prevention of humanitarian emergencies was much more important than the cure. To be involved in this, as I had been in Afghanistan, was definitely the most useful thing I could have done. But would it make any difference? I had had my doubts even as I left. I approved of the military mission against the training camps, for it was in these camps that the attack on the Twin Towers had been plotted. They were without doubt and rightly a military target. We had arrived discreetly in civilian clothes and in small numbers, the camps had been destroyed and the Taliban removed from power. It should have been time to go home. This was Britain's fourth war in Afghanistan and everything in our history told us that would have been the right decision.

I also had my doubts about DFID policy, and the decision to do everything multilaterally. This seemed to dictate delay, and I knew what that would mean. It was now more than a year since the creation of DFID and already social development was the priority. I wondered how the Afghans, perhaps the most socially conservative society on earth, would accept DFID's development projects. Badly, as we were to find out. People generally, and the Afghans in particular, do not like foreigners lecturing them on such things as gender or education.

The new International Development Act became law in 2002. Since 1997, Clare Short, the Secretary of State, had made profound changes to British aid policy and this Act of Parliament made that brutally clear. The UK's foreign aid budget could now only be used for humanitarian aid and the eradication of poverty. To demonstrate that national interest was going to play no role whatsoever, DFID often set themselves apart from British Embassies, establishing themselves in separate buildings. The budget, a modest £3 billion under the previous Conservative government, would now be dramatically increased to 0.7 of Britain's GDP, and would reach £13 billion by 2017. The International Development Act and the budget were part of a complete cultural change at the massive new DFID office block in Palace Street, London. The office had already moved twice, from the dilapidated offices in Stag Place to Victoria Street. Both were later demolished, and a new office complete with atrium café was designed to show the new importance of international development. Gone were the traditional suits worn by civil servants; everyone was in jeans and T-shirts, and it seemed almost mandatory to walk around with coffee mug in hand.

The fire had died down to a few red embers and my whisky glass was empty. It was clear that my role in DFID's new world had come to an end. The next morning, I called the hospital and returned to my work in the Accident and Emergency Department.

20

The Sunni Uprising, Fallujah, Iraq 2004-2005

The following year, 2002, I was invited to join General Mike Jackson on what was described as a strategic review of the Balkans. I was one of two civilians joining Bill Rollo, then a Brigadier, and Mark Carleton-Smith, at that time a Lieutenant Colonel, for a week-long tour of Bosnia, Kosovo and Serbia.

It was a year since I had been in the Balkans and it was strange to be back there. So much seemed to have changed – once familiar places like the airport at Sarajevo seemed almost unrecognisable – yet somehow nothing had changed. My interpreter Vesna was right when she told me ten years earlier how long it would take for things to return to normal. Even the troops we visited were settling down for the long term.

It was an engaging, fascinating and exhausting week. We went first to Bosnia's second largest city, Banja Luka, and the capital, Sarajevo, before heading to Pristina, the capital of Kosovo. Our last stop was to be Belgrade in Serbia. Each time we landed a helicopter was waiting, its rotors turning, to take us from military headquarters to military headquarters. We received briefings at each one, followed by discussions, and every evening were invited to dinners until very late. We were back on the aircraft early each morning and as soon as we were airborne, Mike Jackson wanted our thoughts. There would be a lively debate. Certainly, there was no resting on the oars.

The Balkans were a backwater now, and a large number of troops kept an uneasy peace. Kosovo had 5,000 police as well as a massive military presence, yet even this failed to prevent the place becoming a hive of criminal activity. In Bosnia, the Dayton Peace Agreement had forced the different entities to work together. However, the lasting impression was that they made life as difficult as possible for each other in the process.

Serious defence diplomacy was planned for our final day in Belgrade. Three years after the war in Kosovo the country remained isolated and unloved, and the population were resentful of their pariah status, yet defiant. The time to improve relationships was long overdue and this was a real opportunity to kiss and make up. Under the able leadership of the British Ambassador, Charles Crawford, we had a round of meetings with the Serb Military Commanders. Each meeting started cautiously and ended with real warmth, as Mike Jackson was clearly liked by the Serb generals and used his charm to good effect. Our last visit was to see Alexander, Crown Prince of Yugoslavia, at his house on the top of a hill overlooking the Danube. We were given a drinks reception and, recognising his unstable political status, the conversation never drifted from safe subjects. Before leaving, we lined up for a photograph with the Prince and his young son.

The next morning, as the aircraft climbed out of Belgrade, I gazed in amazement at the Danube bridges, all destroyed by NATO bombing three years before and still in ruins. Anyone trying to cross the river – a matter of a few hundred metres – would need to make a fifty-kilometre detour. Britain was trying to improve the relationship with a defeated country, yet below us was a visible cause of seething resentment. If we were serious about healing conflict and being magnanimous in victory, how could we have failed to help rebuild this country? I reflected on the direction that British development projects had taken. Infrastructure repairs were firmly out, and social development was firmly centre stage. Projects such as repairing the bridges would have been passed to the World Bank, and in time, perhaps years later, something might have happened.

On 2 September 2002, we returned to Britain and drove to Bulford Manor, Mike Jackson's official residence. "Gilbert, stay and have some tea," he said. "I have a brief presentation in a few minutes, which may interest you." As the teacups and saucers clinked, two staff officers came in, set up a screen and began a PowerPoint presentation. It started with the imminent UK firefighters' strike and showed how the Armed Forces were going to provide emergency cover using vintage 1950s Green Goddess fire engines. Then, to my complete astonishment, I heard the first cut of the preparations for the invasion of Iraq.

As I drove home, I thought to myself: clearly, they know things the rest of us don't. Yet at the time, I had a security clearance that allowed me to know many things that other people did not know. I began to think about statistical probability. Saddam Hussein claimed to be sixty-three, yet what was his real age? What were the chances of him changing the world as we knew it in the few years he had left? I had been to Iraq twice now, and liked the people, but when it came to organising and maintaining technical things, they were less than impressive. We had hugely overestimated their capability in the First Gulf War – were we about to do it again?

By January 2003, planning for the war in Iraq dominated Whitehall, but at DFID all was strangely quiet. On three occasions, I was approached by the MOD to help with their post-conflict planning. Each time I discussed this at DFID my suggestion was firmly declined. On the last occasion, I was told by a civil servant that the Secretary of State did not approve of the war and there was to be no planning. Having worked with the Ministry of Defence for twelve years since the First Gulf War, there was an expectation in military circles that I would be involved. It was becoming increasingly clear that this time I would not.

It was a low moment, and one of deep introspection. I was forty-eight; and I had been involved in conflict-related humanitarian work for twenty-three years. Where had I gone wrong? A friend tried to cheer me up. "You're too white, too male and too bald," he joked. "Yes, definitely too bald." I felt like a naval officer I knew, who had found his ship in dry dock during the Falklands War or another who had been posted to a training depot at the beginning of the First Gulf War.

Once again, I remembered Mukesh Kapila saying of the DFID back in 1997, "Gilbert, you will never understand the new principles behind this new department." He was wrong – I understood them only too well – yet he was also right. I did not agree with them, and perhaps that was just too obvious.

Whatever the reason, I was not going to be involved, so I took the opportunity to fly a light aircraft to Cape Town instead. Dealing with total electrical failure over the Ghanaian Highlands during a thunderstorm in a single-engine aircraft certainly took my mind off things. When the Second Gulf War started, I was in Namibia.

Events in Iraq, for me, unfolded on hotel television screens across Africa. I saw the first triumphant moments whilst still in Namibia and then, as I returned from South Africa, a sorry picture of post-conflict chaos emerged. One particularly memorable image was the queues of people at filling stations in Baghdad. The Coalition might have won the war, but winning the peace was already in doubt.

***

Then one day I found myself staring at my inbox in disbelief. Yes, it really was an email from DFID, asking if I could go to Iraq. Since they had not involved me for the invasion over a year before, I was quite surprised. It was now nineteen months since victory had been claimed, and the war was looking decidedly lost. The Second Battle of Fallujah was underway and every night television screens were broadcasting heavy fighting, something that had not even been seen in the first heady days following the invasion. The Sunnis, humiliated by the Coalition's process of 'de-Ba'athification', intended to rid the country of the Ba'ath Party's influence for their hegemony during the Saddam years. They were now in open revolt and Fallujah had become the centre of opposition. For the US Marines, the battle for Fallujah was some of their heaviest urban combat fighting since the Battle of Hué in Vietnam, in 1968.

Four American contractors working for the private military company Blackwater had been ambushed and killed in Fallujah in March 2004, which led to the First Battle of Fallujah, a US-led operation to take back control of the city. This limited operation was halted midway for political reasons, and ended with the city being handed back to local Iraqi forces. This proved unsatisfactory. By September, the jihadist leader Abu al-Zarqawi was thought to have as many as 5,000 insurgents in the city. Expecting an attack, they stockpiled weapons and prepared to defend Fallujah. Events had tried the patience of the US military and the answer, they thought, was a major assault.

Fallujah was home to around 250,000 people, but before the Second Battle of Fallujah began on 7 November as many as 200,000 of them fled. British involvement was limited, but the 1st Battalion, The Black Watch, were responsible for surrounding the city to prevent any insurgents escaping. In total, nearly 14,000 troops were involved, and although the most intense fighting took place in the first week, sporadic fighting continued until Christmas. Coalition casualties were high; more than 100 lost their lives and over 600 were wounded. As many as 1,500 insurgents were killed, and 70% of the city lay in ruins.

At the DFID briefing, it did not take long to discover why I had been chosen. Iraq was toxic to DFID and, for civil servants, a place to avoid. Security outside Baghdad's Green Zone was precarious and the insurgents now held the airport road. And propping up the ailing interim Iraqi government looked unlikely to be rewarding. But why the panic to get me there as soon as possible? DFID wanted me to ensure that the 200,000 people displaced by the fighting had access to water, food, shelter and medical facilities. Here was an occupied country with a more or less functioning government with unheard-of sums of money to throw at any problem – it seemed fairly straightforward. Yet, was it?

Reading through files at DFID's office in London, I saw 'Brief for the Prime Minister'. According to this file, 216,000 Iraqis had been displaced, which was getting very special attention from Number 10. There was a question about a possible breach of international humanitarian law, and a ripple of anxiety could be detected in reports sent from the British Embassy in Baghdad. My job, it seemed, was to make sure there were no violations of international law.

The plan was to fly to Kuwait, then on to Baghdad. But there were problems getting helicopters from the airport into the city, and road transport was inadvisable. On two consecutive nights, as I was about to leave Gloucestershire for Heathrow, I was rung and told not to travel. Relations between DFID and the Ministry of Defence had soured over preparations for the Iraq war in 2003, so a DFID seat on a helicopter would hardly be a priority. On the third day, I asked DFID if I could organise the helicopter travel myself. It was an awkward conversation, as interfering with the chain of command is seldom welcome. Yet the defeated civil servant in London seemed almost pleased to have a solution to the problem. In Baghdad, I was supposed to join Lieutenant General John Kiszely, whom I had known since we were young officers in Germany. I rang his wife, Arabella, to get his telephone number in Iraq. "I'll get them to ring you back in an hour," she said. And within an hour, John's ADC, rang to say a helicopter would be waiting for me at Baghdad airport the following morning. Finally, I was off.

It was a strange journey. I was dropped off at Heathrow Airport in the cold November rain and upgraded to first class on Gulf Airways. Hardly more than five hours later, I was at the transit terminal on the military side of Kuwait airport. In a Portakabin, I slumped into a leatherette armchair for two hours' sleep before being corralled outside to the waiting C-130. About thirty of us struggled in the heat to the aircraft carrying our bags, body armour and helmets. I was glad it was winter here; 25 degrees was better than 40.

The aircraft was going first to Baghdad before returning to Basra, where most of the British troops were based. I was one of half a dozen civilians on board, and I was asked up to the flight deck to chat with the pilots. Looking down at the vast landscape below us, I realised we were in trouble. This was a country with 26 million inhabitants. The politicians had never discussed the cost of this enterprise, and it had been assumed that once the country was liberated our engagement would soon be over. Now we were armpit-deep in a counter-insurgency war of unknown duration, and it was going to be very expensive.

At Baghdad airport, I was allocated a place in a Puma helicopter. We flew over the rooftops at 100 knots, the door gunner watching every movement below from the open side door. The vast city of nearly 8 million spread out beneath us, and the skyline was dotted with observation balloons carrying cameras. We were an easy target for anybody in a block of flats with an AK47, but I consoled myself that the aircrew knew better than me.

The helipad in the Green Zone could be rated the noisiest place on earth. Helicopters landed and took off continuously night and day, and the noise was even bad inside the armoured Toyota Land Cruiser that had come to collect me. I was now in the hands of a private military contractor responsible for my road transport. I had never felt entirely comfortable about 'close protection', as this service is known. The only person responsible for my life, I thought, was me, and there was something about delegating this task to a group of mercenaries that irked me. They were ex-soldiers, hugely overpaid and cocksure with it. Worse, they had no manners towards either the clients or the population at large, for whom they showed complete contempt. After several days in Baghdad, I began to think that with every journey we made about a hundred enemies an hour. They drove me, exchanging few pleasantries, to my accommodation at the Ocean Cliffs, which I assumed from its rather beguiling name would be a hotel until we swept into an underground car park full of Corimec containerised accommodation. I had to admit it did meet the key criteria; it was safe, and turned out to be quite comfortable. An Iraqi Christian, one of the most persecuted minorities in the country, had been given the contract to supply breakfast, which was always delicious.

Traffic in the Green Zone was surprisingly busy. I was told that it was literally fatal to get too close to American military convoys as they frequently fired on any vehicle considered a threat. We had to wait at one intersection, as the US Ambassador was on the move accompanied by a convoy of at least twenty black vehicles with helicopters buzzing like wasps overhead.

The real surprise was how ugly and depressing the city was. Nothing had been done about the damage from the First Gulf War, and blast walls were ubiquitous, making the city I had visited in 1991 unrecognisable. The checkpoints every kilometre were manned by young US servicemen and women who could have been posted to the moon for all their understanding of their surroundings. Hearing my accent, occasionally they asked where I was from, but it was quite clear that for many of them the whereabouts of England was a mystery.

Baghdad felt like nowhere else that I had ever been; there was something wrong about it, a pervasive badness. Those who had been in Saigon in its dying days of US rule claimed it had the same characteristics. Chancers and contractors raking in absurd returns now populated the city, as well as the usual misfits and maniacs that are drawn to such places like moths to a lamp. A shop near Saddam's palace, now the US Embassy, sold all manner of macho gear, and specialised in shoulder and leg holsters for pistols, a gold mine for those with a pathological personality disorder.

Driving through security on the way to the British Embassy was quite a contrast to elsewhere as the security contractors were ex-Gurkhas, whose politeness and professionalism are legendary. The British Embassy was a low white modern building with an ancient field gun ceremoniously guarding the front door. DFID's Head of Mission, Lindy Cameron, was younger than I expected, but immediately impressive, welcoming and friendly. She and Tony Laurance, a senior civil servant at the Department of Health in the UK who had been sent to Baghdad to strengthen the intellectual firepower at the embassy, had been handling the Fallujah problem almost alone; clearly things had not been easy for them.

My first reaction was that we needed to simplify the plan if we were to achieve anything. I needed to go to Fallujah as a matter of priority, but it was not going to be that easy. Although only half an hour's helicopter ride away, like most things in Iraq involving the US it needed booking seventy-two hours in advance. I would have to wait. However, I had been asked to a meeting the next day at the Iraqi Ministry of Industry and Minerals, who had rather curiously been given responsibility for Fallujah. The meeting was in the Red Zone, which meant little to me, but I was about to find out that this would be a very new experience.

The next morning two armoured 4x4 vehicles were waiting for Tony and me at the embassy. We were given body armour and an earnest briefing, then driven to the outside world through the Assassins' Gate, one of four primary checkpoints for entry into the Green Zone. This high security 10 square kilometre area in central Baghdad was used by the Coalition and civilian authorities. Most Iraqis were excluded. Entrances to the Green Zone were massive affairs, with both Iraqi and US military layers of security and battlefield tanks parked up as additional deterrents. Once into the Red Zone, the rest of Iraq, we were off at high speed. Here the security was so bad that being trapped in the traffic might easily lead to kidnap, abduction or lynching by the crowd. It was immediately clear that I could expect very little protection from either the vehicle or my machine gun-wielding protectors in the front.

We moved fast, flashing our lights, and with liberal use of the horn; other road users were literally driven off the road. We drove down the dual carriageway in the wrong direction if it suited us, and made shortcuts along narrow residential streets sending pedestrians diving for their lives, many of them children. We were definitely making a hundred enemies an hour. It would be all too easy for our enemies to kill us; they would just need to box us in, pour a bucket of petrol over the car and throw a match. I could not see why they had not tried this already. I am not normally easily alarmed, but it just did not seem prudent to behave in this way. If this was the only way to survive in Iraq after our generous liberation, I doubted much now was going to be possible. Even more worrying was the attitude and arrogance of some of the private military contractors, which by association now included me.

In the First Gulf War, I had travelled in local taxis incognito. Yet with idiotic instructions about security being dispatched from London, there was no chance of doing that now. It was not even the security that bothered me; it was the danger of being killed in a car accident, still the most frequent cause of death or injury on mission. These armoured 4x4s weighed several tons and were just not capable of being driven safely in this way.

On arrival at the Ministry of Industry and Minerals, we climbed out of the vehicles in a dusty yard behind two metal gates. Instructions were bossily shouted at us by our protectors: "Right – you've got no more than 90 minutes in this place before we leave. And you'll be coming with us whether you like it or not. Don't think they haven't noticed we're here, it'll only be an hour or so before they start mortaring the place – couldn't hit a barn door, but all the same best avoided." The Ministry, which towered above its neighbours, almost inviting mortars, was a dreary building that clearly had not seen any maintenance since the First Gulf War in 1991. It occurred to me that this simple observation could be extrapolated to the entire country, and its infrastructure.

There was no minister in the building; we were told he was unwell. In fact, he never appeared over the next two months. Clearly, Fallujah was not good for his health. The Iraqi Permanent Secretary, however, was warm and friendly. He was stressed by the task of looking after the inhabitants of Fallujah and greeted us as saviours. At least twenty people sat around the table playing with their mobile phones or intermittently shouting into them. There was no agenda. It was very unclear what this meeting, which we had risked our lives to attend, might achieve.

The ninety minutes were soon gone. Our return journey was as eventful as our arrival; it even involved driving over the top of a roundabout rather than tediously going round it. At least no children were killed, but our behaviour surely did not fail to increase the number of people who now wished to kill us.

As we walked over to the canteen with some of the embassy staff, I noticed a building site at the back of the embassy grounds. "What's being built there?" I asked. "That'll be the new swimming pool." This place was getting stranger by the day – it was impossible to reach the airport by road, but we were building a new swimming pool. "How nice," I muttered.

My seventy-two hours were nearly up, and I was scheduled to visit Fallujah the next morning. I arrived at the helipad in good time for my first ride in a Black Hawk helicopter, an impressive machine compared to Britain's ageing Pumas that had been in service for thirty-five years. On arrival, I climbed into a military truck for a guided tour of part of the city, now deemed safe enough. It was not an ideal viewing platform as there was armour on the truck and seeing anything involved standing above the armoured plates. Given the sporadic shots still being fired in our direction, it was less than ideal.

There was much talk of the city being totally destroyed, but this proved to be very misleading and crucial to the humanitarian response. In reality, 70% of the city was very badly damaged. I estimated that 30% of the population – about 75,000 – were still in their homes. After the tour, I was given a briefing, and met the United States Marine Corps Commander, Lieutenant General John Sattler. He really did not like the idea of me. "Civilians?" he said brusquely, referring to the remaining inhabitants of Fallujah. "There are only terrorists in this city." Even asking about the welfare of these civilians was not going to be popular. I was surprised at the emotion with which he spoke, but considering the number of Marines that had been killed and wounded, I should not have been. At the end of the briefing, he stood up and, striking a clenched fist into the palm of his other hand, said, "Thank you, gentlemen. I have to take the fight to the enemy." No British General could have made such a comment without being ridiculed.

The following day, General Kiszely asked me to dinner. I knew if I asked for official transport from the British Embassy, there would be some mention of the seventy-two hours' notice. So I thought I might ask in the Prime Minister's office. "There are plenty of cars," I was told, and was shown a vast board overloaded with car keys. "How do I know which car to take?" I asked, "Oh, just take a set of keys and use the key fob to flash the car lights in the car park." I saw at least fifty parked cars, all finely coated in sand. I found my car, it had clearly not gone anywhere for a while.

I knew roughly where I was going and after fifteen minutes turned off the main road into a narrow street. It was now dark and a sign announced menacingly, 'Authorised vehicles only. Lethal force will be used.' As though sticking my spurs into the flank of a horse, I gave my borrowed car a metaphorical kick and hurtled down the narrow street. Half a mile further on, I arrived at my destination, one of the presidential lodges next to Saddam's palace, mercifully still alive. On the way home I was more cautious, in this city being shot by your own side was a present and hideous danger.

I returned the car the next day and asked about the other cars in the car park. "Yes, it's rather sad, isn't it?" said the Iraqi official. "Sad?" I asked. "Didn't you know? They're all dead – the Iraqi civil servants who used them, that is." Each day comments or chance observations like this gave chilling evidence that the occupation was drifting in the wrong direction. Individually they did not amount to much, but the individual pixels were beginning to produce a picture. This was not a war that was being won. On my next terrifying trip into the Red Zone, in an armoured Toyota, I mentioned that I had driven a soft-skinned vehicle from the Prime Minister's office at night. "You what?" my driver exclaimed. "Have a care, mate; we've only been hit by the Americans seven times so far." I decided to give borrowing cars from the Prime Minister's office a miss in future.

Progress was slow. The task of getting anything to the displaced in and around Fallujah was tortuous. It was not only the dysfunctional work of the Ministry of Industry and Minerals; the US Marines were just not interested, and now they wanted a ring of steel around the city with biometric screening of all who went in and out. I calculated a minimum of 500 metric tons a day were moved back and forth to allow the city to breathe on top of the 4,500 tons of food required each month. Progress was going to be glacially slow. John Kiszely, as Deputy Commander, more than anybody applied pressure in all the right places, but our allies could not see the merit in what we were trying to do. Our attempts to do what was right for the displaced, to comply with international humanitarian law, and perhaps prevent driving displaced Sunnis into the arms of the insurrection, were all important objectives, but not appreciated by everyone.

One morning as I came out from some fretful meeting, there was an almighty explosion near the Assassins' Gate checkpoint. A truck bomb had exploded, and although I was on the safe side of a 14-storey building, the blast lifted me off my feet. I ran to the corner to see vast billowing clouds of smoke only a few hundred yards away. To my amazement, I watched the panic-stricken Iraqi security forces shoot into the smoke, killing the remaining survivors.

On Friday, I went to work as usual, despite it technically being the weekend. I passed a US-manned security barrier on foot as a useful shortcut to get to the Prime Minister's office. However, on the way back the same American soldier consulted a clipboard and announced my name was not on it. Now, I had to walk a mile and a half, a long and dangerous journey, wearing my suit and body armour. It was not the first occasion I had doubts about working with our ally. If it was bad for me, what was it like for the Iraqis?

Working at the embassy with Tony was always entertaining. He would look at my latest missives for London and quietly, in his charming mandarin way, delete my superlatives or dryly say, "Gilbert, you can't write that." "And why would that be, Tony?" A gentle pause. "Because it isn't true." I admired his years in Whitehall and the training that made our civil service so impressive. I am sure he found my disregard for anything that stood in our way quite fun as long as I was responsible for it, including the guerrilla warfare when thwarted.

I was well-supported by the embassy, who made every effort to help me get the job done. However, one day I was accosted rather aggressively in the chancery by one of the embassy staff, asking who I was and what I was doing. Before I could explain, the Ambassador, who was passing, paused and said, "That…" I could see he was wondering how to describe me, "… is Gilbert… please leave him alone," and walked on.

★★★

Progress on anything to do with Fallujah was painfully slow. The internal meetings, the frightful trips into the Red Zone, and the unhelpfulness of the US Marine Corps continued until Christmas. Meanwhile, the overall security continued to deteriorate. I wondered why the insurgents did not copy the Tet Offensive, the largest military campaign of surprise attacks in the Vietnam War, when the Viet Cong mounted a major coordinated attack in January 1969 against targets in South Vietnam. A suicidal assault on the Green Zone followed by indiscriminate killing of civilians would have demonstrated to the whole world that we had lost the war. When I first arrived, there was a taboo in the embassy about admitting that things might not be going terribly well. Once I commented that something we had just done had staved off defeat for another day. I got agonised looks from the others, but it broke the ice and thereafter I felt we could actually stop pretending that everything was going quite so well. We could be a little more realistic and, more importantly, do something about it.

In late December, I was driven out to the helipad where an ancient British Puma helicopter was waiting. To my dismay, several mechanics were crawling all over it. This was not unusual, since these veteran helicopters were thirty-five years old and looked every hour of it. We sat waiting in the armoured Toyota for six hours. Somehow, I managed to get my connecting flight and finally walked into the kitchen at home. It was Christmas Eve.

"He's always away, you know," was the phrase I heard most often. But I was away for much shorter periods than many of my contemporaries in the army; I just went to many more places. On these trips, I was mostly alone and every day uncertainty created a constant subliminal anxiety, which didn't leave me for days when I returned home. I craved silence. The jolt of arriving at the house, of fitting instantly back into the round of social life, was challenging. I felt as though I had reappeared from Narnia through the fur coats at the back of the wardrobe. There always seemed to be a catalogue of domestic dramas, to which I found it difficult to give the necessary attention or concern. I may have been at home, but half of me was still on mission.

I returned to Baghdad in January to complete my work in Fallujah. I had managed to get all the Coalition partners to agree on what needed to be done. The displaced were destitute and their host families struggling to survive. The delivery of food aid was critical, and it was now just a case of doing it. In our rush to put the Iraqis in charge, we underestimated how difficult it would be for them to achieve what we expected. Sectarian murder was common, as was absenteeism, and the extreme caution being shown by the US Marine Corps towards anything the Iraqis did made for tortuous progress. However, bit by bit, things were achieved.

One morning I received a telephone call from Brigadier James Ellery, who had been the adjutant during my time in the army in Germany. Our paths had crossed several times on military operations, the last being in Kosovo six years earlier. James was now working for Aegis, a leading security and risk management company that employed tens of thousands of people in Iraq, and had enormous contracts there. "Gil, dinner tonight at the Al-Rasheed".

I arrived at the massive eighteen-storey hotel in the Green Zone at 8.15 pm and James was waiting for me on the marble steps of the grand lobby. It was always a delight to see him. He had left the army after a posting as a Brigadier with the UN in Sierra Leone and clearly loved his new life. We strode into the restaurant to find that a rocket had taken out most of one wall. The headwaiter came to greet us. "Your usual table, Brigadier?" James read the wine list while I gazed through an enormous gap in the wall the size of a double-decker bus. "The usual claret, Brigadier?" James nodded. It was a very convivial dinner. We were the only diners.

Almost every day I visited Saddam's palace, now the military headquarters and the US Embassy. It was a bizarre idea to liberate the country and then move into the palace; many Iraqis would see this as one tyranny replacing another. The place swarmed with servicemen, servicewomen and civilians. Getting in and out of it was a frantic affair, and I learnt quickly to take nothing more than a notebook in order to expedite the security screening. It was a vast hideous marble edifice built in the worst possible taste, and the Americans had converted it into their military headquarters using chipboard partitions. The contrast between the materials was so bizarre it added to the general unreality of the place. Eating seemed to take priority in every military establishment in Iraq; vast canteens groaned with almost anything that you could ever wish to eat, flown in from every continent.

On one occasion, I went to the palace for a meeting with General John Kiszely and his entourage. We had just started our meeting when a US servicewoman announced that the room had been double-booked and told us to go elsewhere. The General looked as amazed as the rest of us, but was too polite literally to pull rank on this petty official, who was quite insistent, not realising for a moment that she was talking to the Deputy Commander of all Allied Forces in Iraq. So much for the special relationship.

The following day I was to fly down to Al-Najaf, about one hundred kilometres south of Baghdad, to look at some Quick Impact Projects, apparently inspired by my programme in Bosnia a decade earlier. Once again, I was at the helipad soon after dawn. The sky was ice blue and there had been the thinnest layer of ice on the car windscreens as I left Ocean Cliffs. I could not fail to be impressed by the Black Hawk helicopters; I admired their sheer size and power, and the absence of vibrations that I was so familiar with when travelling in our Lynx and Sea King helicopters. The door gunner took up his position at the open side door, and only then did I realise I was rather underdressed for the ride. With the air only just above freezing and the door open, the next sixty minutes were distinctly chilly. We flew at no more than 500 feet all the way, the palm trees and desert flashing beneath us, the landscape almost featureless except for the ubiquitous plastic bags and mounds of rubbish, one of my least agreeable memories of Iraq.

In Al-Najaf, an American Colonel took me on a tour of his projects. They were similar to what we had done in Bosnia, and appeared to be a great success, judging by the fact that we left our vehicles and walked from project to project amongst a friendly crowd. I had spent the last two months in Iraq, and except in the Green Zone, where nothing was normal, this was the first time I was able to walk anywhere. I wished what was happening here could be repeated elsewhere in central and northern Iraq, but somehow I knew it wouldn't. The first 100 days were when we had a chance to win the peace, and nearly 800 days had now passed. Against a tidal wave of missed opportunities, misplaced assumptions and catastrophic decision-making, this tiny glimmer of hope stood little chance.

I had until January to make sure that humanitarian assistance was finally being delivered to Fallujah. Much of it was going to be delivered to host families and, since getting out on the ground proved almost impossible, it was a remarkably unrewarding experience. Regular field trips are always inspiring, times when plans can be adjusted and new solutions found for problems. It was now the last week in January 2005 and, frustratingly, I was soon to return home.

It was difficult to be optimistic, as absolutely nothing was going right. We had arrived twenty months earlier with a set of assumptions that one by one had proved fallacious. We were trying to run a country of 26 million people, and it was quite obvious that those in charge had absolutely no idea what to do next. I could see now why those civil servants back in London wanted to give Iraq a miss.

21

South of the Litani River, Israel's War with Lebanon 2006

The RAF helicopter skimmed over the waves as we left the British Sovereign Base Dhekelia in Cyprus. After ten days waiting in a beach hotel in Larnaka I was finally on my way to Beirut. We were flying below 500 feet to avoid Cypriot airspace, the result of some longstanding dispute with the Cypriot government, and the white horses below indicated a brisk south-easterly wind.

Israel's invasion of southern Lebanon several weeks before was intended to be a limited operation to destroy caches of Hezbollah weapons south of the Litani River. The build-up of Hezbollah's ordnance had been an open secret for some years and Israel's patience had finally been exhausted. Yet the invasion and indiscriminate bombing of infrastructure across Lebanon had been a disaster for Israel. Hezbollah boys on motorbikes with hand-held anti-tank weapons had been successful against Israeli tanks. The damage to motorway bridges, power lines and domestic housing had run into billions of dollars, causing international outrage and condemnation even within Israel itself. International attempts to bring about a ceasefire had been elusive. However, Israel's deliberate bombing of a UN observation post, killing four UN soldiers, changed everything. There was enough international pressure on Israel for a ceasefire, but despite this, Israeli troops inside southern Lebanon were in no mood to withdraw quickly. Now that there was a ceasefire, I had been told to get myself to Beirut.

With nearly a million people displaced in Lebanon by the fighting, it had been unclear how long the war was going to continue. Israeli jets were attacking all vehicles moving on the roads, which had prevented us from travelling to Lebanon.

So I had patiently waited in Cyprus with my fellow UNDAC members Ted Pearn and Carolina de Bourbon-Parma. We had been asked to set up a coordination centre in some unused rooms behind the swimming pool bar of a tourist hotel – the owner had been helpful to the UN on some previous occasion, hence the choice. We spent ten days creating databases and dealing with builders and electricians, many of them cockneys who, after a holiday on the island, had found the balmy Mediterranean climate to their liking and opted to emigrate. The counterpoint between the war, only 120 miles away, and the tourist hotel where we passed the bar full of holidaymakers in their swimwear to get to our office, was extreme.

Occasionally, we made the ninety-minute journey to the UN office at Nicosia airport. The airport remained exactly how it had been abandoned in 1974. Even a British Trident airliner was still at the 'holding point' waiting to take off, as it had been over forty years earlier following the Turkish invasion of Cyprus. Now windowless, its tyres long since deflated, it sat forlornly on its wheel rims, its paint faded in the Mediterranean sun. Weeds grew over the abandoned runways. The aerodrome terminal, completed in 1968, was now a spectacular ruin, having hardly ever seen the thousands of hoped-for passengers. Another destination for us was the British High Commission, which stood defiantly in the UN Buffer Zone, pristine and beautifully maintained amongst the ruins of buildings destroyed in the fighting of this ancient yet unresolved conflict.

From this restless and unrewarding work, I had suddenly been dispatched to Beirut. I was designated as Civil Military Adviser to the General commanding the United Nations Interim Force in Lebanon. The United Nations Interim Force in Lebanon (UNIFIL) was based south of the Litani River at Al-Naqoura. I was initially to report to the UN office in Beirut. There was one slight snag – there was no obvious way of getting to Beirut, as no civil flights were landing anywhere in Lebanon.

After multiple telephone calls, I found that an RAF helicopter was leaving for Beirut the next day from Dhekelia, and managed to secure a place on it. It was just a quick dash down the coast to the British Sovereign Base, which I had last visited as a Sandhurst officer cadet on our final military exercise in 1973. The Base was strangely familiar after thirty-three years; I even recognised the shower block where the Gurkhas had caused outrage by slaughtering a goat for their farewell party. A Griffin helicopter was waiting on the helipad. I waved to my two colleagues and was off, sensing their disappointment that we could not all go together.

The coast and skyline of Beirut finally appeared, with smoke rising from the recent bombing. As we flew into the port, I could see that the streets were empty. Not a car, not a person was anywhere to be seen save the British Embassy Range Rover waiting to meet me on a deserted quay.

Israeli jets had been strafing vehicles on the roads for some days and the entire country was shut down. It felt strange to drive through what appeared to be a deserted city. My first stop was at the embassy, to explain briefly what I was doing in the country, and then on to the Mövenpick Hotel, now the UN office. The fighting had displaced nearly a million people and the UN agencies were responding to what they perceived as massive need. There were multiple meetings to discuss access to ports, convoys and stocks of non-food items, and frenetic activity reigned throughout the building. I was to leave on one of the first convoys heading south that afternoon. I could hardly believe my luck, as days might have passed before I was in a position to do anything useful.

Two hours later, I set off with a small group in a couple of UN 4x4s with a convoy of trucks. Now there was a ceasefire, so too did the million displaced. This was a mid-income country and to be displaced meant getting in a car and driving to stay with relatives at the other end of it, a process that was equally reversible. Everybody was on the move, the roads choked with vehicles, and progress was painfully slow. Israeli jets had bombed the motorway bridges and at each one massive traffic jams formed. It was hot in the August sun and I was astonished to see boys in yellow Hezbollah T-shirts handing out bottles of cold drinking water. It was a masterful piece of image making and media management.

As we travelled, we saw substantial damage to infrastructure, reported in the media as running into billions of dollars. Yet it was not just the infrastructure; residential housing had been damaged too and, as we travelled south, it got progressively worse. We stopped at the city of Saida as it was getting dark and stayed, rather curiously, in a convent where the solitary nun in charge was most welcoming. I managed to buy a bottle of Lebanese wine nearby, as I was determined to celebrate my birthday. I was fifty-two.

The next day, travelling south, we were once more alone on the road. Israeli troops were still in the country and the Lebanese were terrified of air attack. At the UN office in the city of Tyre, I met Rob Holden whom I had worked with on many previous occasions at DFID. He was in Lebanon during the fighting and had a torrid time of it. The convoy had now reached its destination, and from here I would travel alone. I watched as sacks of wheat flour were unloaded from the trucks and reflected that this was a response suitable for a crisis in tropical Africa, rather than one on the shores of the Mediterranean. Welfare payments were needed here, not wheat flour and blankets.

Rob gave me a briefing, and I was soon on my way in a pickup truck to Al-Naqoura. We climbed a winding road until we reached a ridge with a spectacular view of the Mediterranean glinting under the August sun. The French fleet was several miles offshore, evidence of international pressure to stop the conflict. As he drove, my driver talked about his experiences of the recent fighting. Occasionally we saw rocket strikes on the road and cars burnt out in recent air attacks. The dry landscape was dotted with ugly concrete houses and small fields amongst a sea of stones and boulders. On the small hillocks, troops of Israeli tanks could be seen defiantly flying their flags. There was no evidence of the withdrawal much mentioned in the media.

After forty minutes we arrived at Al-Naqoura; the small town and its infamous Mingy Street were dwarfed by the large UNIFIL camp. Heat waves were rising up from the tarmac; not a person stirred, not a vehicle moved. On arrival, I met the French Army Major I was to work with for the next month. He was smartly dressed and looked hyper-fit. Although enthusiastic about my arrival, he was exasperated by his posting. His enthusiasm was a complete contrast to the rest of the camp, which had sunk into a state of lassitude and catatonia decades earlier.

The small French-led multinational force had endeavoured to keep the peace, but its success had been muted. Wars had come and gone like the tide, and at one time, the border had moved, leaving the camp in Israeli-controlled territory. At the start of the conflict, the civilian administrators and contractors had run away, leaving the camp paralysed. It was now a place with an abundance of chuff charts – prominent calendars on which each completed day of a mission is crossed off – a place where nothing could be done and, as was soon obvious, nothing *was* done. My accommodation was a small room in a low concrete building almost like a monastic cell. The ablution block behind it had one cubicle with a sign that said *Reservé – diarrhée et vomissements*. It was not an auspicious start. The waves were breaking on the rocks below, yet the sea was fenced off with rolls of razor wire. It was as if the entire camp had taken a sleeping draught. Nothing moved, nothing happened here. The place shimmered in the heat.

The General was a short, brusque, busy man, frustrated by the situation. The political pressure was now on his shoulders and even he was unable to supply his troops. I explained I had been sent to see how I could support the civilian population in the surrounding towns and villages damaged by the fighting. He looked at me with blank incomprehension, although I had been appointed by the UN as his adviser, I could see that I was going to struggle. But as I got up to leave, he asked, rather surprisingly, if there was anything he could do. I asked for a helicopter reconnaissance and this was arranged for the next day.

The helicopter was a veteran Bell 205 Huey. I asked Rob Holden to join me from the Tyre office, and our trip was revealing. There had been reports of severe and widespread destruction throughout southern Lebanon, but though we saw pockets of intensive destruction, the majority of the settlements remained unscathed. Our aerial reconnaissance was extremely useful; in just one hour, we gained information it would have taken days to gather on the ground. I now knew where to go to do my assessments, and started almost daily visits to villages and small towns battered by the recent fighting. I travelled in a white UN pickup, mostly alone with a local civilian UNIFIL driver, and sometimes with my French colleague. During the conflict, the IDF had targeted the low voltage electricity network, and without electricity, there was a major problem of water supply, not only for human consumption but also for agriculture. I was able to persuade the local electricity workers to repair the lines, but they often complained of being shot at or intimidated by IDF troops still in the area. On such occasions, I had to negotiate with the IDF tank troops in their defensive positions on the hilltops. With the UN flag flying on the vehicle, we would approach cautiously to within a few hundred metres. I would then proceed on foot, a machine gun on one of the tanks covering my every move. Negotiations took place with an Israeli soldier pointing a rifle at my head.

If the Israelis were intransigent, it was not much better trying to get UNIFIL to do something useful. Even the simple task of protecting the electricity workers seemed too onerous for them. There were a number of large generators in the camp, but it took nearly two weeks to get one of them to a nearby town. UNIFIL also had an armoured bulldozer; heaven-sent for removing debris containing unexploded ordnance, but helping the civilian population did not seem to be part of the mission. And if anything was undertaken, it was painfully slow with every obstacle put in its way. The days passed listlessly, and I felt mounting frustration; the General was never available, the civilian contractors responsible for making the force viable had not returned, and nobody seemed to know when they might reappear.

My driver lived in a nearby village and had worked for UNIFIL most of his life. He spoke good English and chatted away throughout our trips, giving me advice when I needed it and just as often when I did not. He complained ceaselessly that a shell had hit his house, making it uninhabitable. We often passed the house, and it looked untouched. I ignored him.

My aim while at UNIFIL was to get the UN troops to support the civilian population as we had done in Bosnia. The problems were very similar. Like Bosnia, this was a mid-income country, also the troops were blue helmet – that is, not party to the conflict – and were superbly equipped to do the work. However, I had not appreciated how Iraq had changed people's perceptions. All Armed Forces were now tarnished by that conflict, and even senior UN officials in New York were incredulous that I wanted to use UNIFIL troops to help with post-conflict recovery. I was equally surprised by the mindless responses I received. By the time I began to make progress with New York, the moment had passed and the failure to act had been exploited by quite another organisation, Hezbollah. Even if I had been able to mobilise UNIFIL there would have been the problem of funding Quick Impact Projects. The reason this worked in Bosnia was that each contributing nation funded the projects undertaken by its own troops. The risk of fraud or mismanagement remained with their national governments. In Kosovo, I had attempted to fund QIPS with NATO money, which proved hugely bureaucratic. With UN troops, it seemed an impossibility as the whole system was designed to prevent fraud, and ultimately prevented everything. It was agony to see UNIFIL resources available and yet unavailable.

When I finally did get permission to move a generator from the UNIFIL Headquarters at Al-Naqoura to supply a vitally-needed water pump, I found that the civilian administration responsible for the fuel was absent, so my plan stalled once again. Al-Naqoura really was Handbrake House, cautious, timid, self-serving, sclerotic and idle. Apart from the French, the only breath of life in the place was supplied by the contingent from the Republic of Ireland. Without them, the place would have sunk into a catatonic trance. They were as supportive of me as the system allowed and knew, if something could be done, how it could be achieved. Many of the staff officers had been with UNIFIL on multiple tours. They did heroic work negotiating with the Israeli Defence Force, getting withdrawal of IDF underway and de-escalating any incidents along the border. Failure in any of these could have easily caused a breakdown of the ceasefire.

Hezbollah had stepped into the vacuum left by UNIFIL and proved masters of media management. I had already seen the boys in yellow Hezbollah T-shirts handing out bottled water. Now, families whose houses had been destroyed were given an immediate 10,000-dollar allowance for temporary accommodation, and further funds – I assumed from Iran – were offered for rebuilding. Hezbollah were also running medical clinics and distributing humanitarian relief. They were very good at it, and understood perfectly that military action was only part of their campaign; having the backing of the civilian population was the real goal. They were also very polite, which I mentioned to my driver, who responded gruffly, "They've had their instructions." It may have been true, but charm, though a false virtue, is much more powerful than aggression.

Much of the time in camp was spent reporting to the UN in Beirut, Geneva and New York. I had been travelling alone south of the Litani River and my assessment reports had helped to direct humanitarian assistance to where it was needed. Despite the frustration, I felt I had at least done something useful.

Then the French Foreign Legion arrived at Al-Naqoura, and it was as though the place had been given an injection of steroids. The civilian administrators were returning at last and, in small steps, the camp began to function again. The French officers were intelligent, thoughtful and good company. Their manner and discipline indicated serious force projection. They spoke to me in English and I spoke to them in French, which improved everyone's language skills.

The last ten days with UNIFIL were spent dealing with the hundreds of cluster bombs the IDF had dropped in the final days of the conflict.

The device, a single bomb that releases hundreds of individual bomblets when approaching the ground, is an appalling weapon. It was designed for use against infantry in open ground, with devastating effects. Yet here they had been dropped in areas of high civilian density. Worse, sixteen percent of the bomblets fail to explode and these innocent-looking devices, the size of a Coke can, with jolly tapes at the rear, are fascinating to children. Highly unstable, they explode when touched. They fell in orchards and fields, preventing people going about their normal work, and lying in ruined buildings they hugely delayed any rebuilding work. Much to their credit, the Chinese UNIFIL contingent did everything they could to clear unexploded ordnance.

One evening towards the end of my time with UNIFIL, I was returning to the base; impatient to get back as the canteen at the camp would soon be closing. As we approached the village where he lived just outside the base, my garrulous driver started once again on the story of his house, rather like the complaints of the old woman in Voltaire's *Candide*. It was now or never. I asked him to pull over and show me the damage. His home, a neat concrete bungalow, unexceptional among its neighbours, showed no external evidence of damage. We went inside and to my amazement the room was coal black. The walls, which had been white, had been subject to intense heat and everything was covered in thick black soot. Carefully, he led me to a bedroom at the back where there was a large hole in the wall the size of a car. The bed was at an odd angle; and there lying like a baby, coddled in a blanket, was a 155mm shell, totally intact. "Blimey," I muttered, almost in a whisper, as if any encouragement might set the thing off. Very gingerly, we backed out of the room. I felt a wave of contrition for all my unkind remarks and irritation over the previous weeks, and my failure to take the problem seriously. I called the Chinese UXO (Unexploded Ordnance) team, who came out straight away and dealt with it without mishap.

My weeks in Al-Naqoura had been extraordinary. The conflict had been a disaster for the IDF. Hezbollah had wrong-footed their heavily armed opponents by riding motorcycles at high speed with hand-held anti-tank weapons, and had been very effective. They had also dominated the media campaign, always finding young people to give interviews in good English. The serious damage to housing and infrastructure by Israeli air attacks was, on the whole, localised, but in places it had been very intensive and Israel had been widely criticised. However, it was in these locations that the media images were focused, giving an impression of Armageddon. Some of them were of towns that I had visited, where I knew the damage was restricted to only a few streets. The media interpretation of the war was now as important as fighting it.

My attempts to mobilise neutral peacekeepers to help civilians proved an abject failure. I was surprised by the mindless and prejudicial communications from New York, and sad that UNIFIL had failed to rise to the task. They might have surprised themselves, and done much for the UN's reputation. It was an idea that had done so much good in Bosnia, and had been marginal in Kosovo, yet it had failed in Iraq and was finally discredited in Afghanistan. Lastly, this conflict changed the way humanitarian agencies responded in mid-income countries. It was a process that had begun in the Balkans a decade earlier, and was familiar to those who had worked there. Yet many of those working for agencies in Lebanon, who had gained their experience in Africa, still had the mindset of tents, sacks of wheat flour, blankets and cooking pots. What was needed here was speed of delivery and welfare cash payments, which had the merit of stimulating the local economy. It was a surprise after all to find that Hezbollah was leading the way.

22

Hope Fades, Afghanistan 2006

Five years had passed since I was last in Afghanistan and it was difficult to believe it was the same country. The Taliban had drifted back into the general population, scuttling back to Helmand or re-emerging from among their kinsmen on the other side of the Pakistan border. Kabul was once more a bustling city – judging by the traffic jams – and business was brisk. This gave the illusion that all was well, but this was a narco-economy; there was every reason to be cautious.

I was in Kabul on a UNDAC mission to help the Afghan government prepare for the frequent natural disasters that occurred not just every year, but sometimes twice a year. Earthquakes were frequent, and the Afghans also had to cope with flash floods and landslides caused by melting spring snow. The population had grown rapidly and, with more people living on marginal land, the risk of disaster was ever-present.

Being one of the poorest countries in the world, Afghanistan's unstable natural environment was as uncertain as its political future. UN missions were offered to help the Afghans mitigate the effects of disasters. Our team leader was Ted Pearn, whose courtesy and capacity for massive understatement are legendary. After retiring as HM Chief Inspector of Fire Services, he led teams for decades to every type of natural disaster. This time seven of us would stay in Afghanistan for three weeks. We could travel wherever we wanted, and visit any government department we wanted to involve in preparing for natural disasters. Although we had a report to produce, I would take the opportunity to assess nearly the whole government structure. Did the government control anything fifty kilometres from Kabul? Was it even effective in Kabul? I was going to find out.

We stayed at the new Safi Landmark Hotel, quite a change from my accommodation only a few years before. Security was now benign, we could travel with few restrictions, and the UN club where we went after work even sold beer.

Early on, we paid a diplomatic courtesy call to the Vice President, Karim Khalili, the warlord I had met in Bamyan in 2001. He did not recognise me, which was rather a relief, but he seemed generally interested in what we had come to do. Ted, an impressive diplomat, bounced the metaphorical ball of diplomacy back and forth; occasionally the ball had a spin on it and he would tap it back to the Vice President with a twinkle in his eye. In the time-honoured UN way, we had to produce what turned out to be a 60-page report in two weeks. As well as visiting agencies and government departments in Kabul, we also had two field trips to the cities of Mazar-i-Sharif and Jalalabad. Ted divided the task and we had at least seventy meetings covering every facet of life in Afghanistan. Whether this was going to do any good, it was a fabulous opportunity to see how the country worked, or did not, as soon became obvious. After three days, it was clear that the government writ did not after all extend more than fifty kilometres from Kabul. Some government departments, often with a payroll of several hundred people, existed in name only, having been handed to warlords as a reward after victory in 2001, like sinecures in the medieval church.

I was given the task of visiting one ministry. I found the traffic difficult to get used to after the empty streets of five years before. New 4x4s were everywhere, the narco-economy fuelling a consumer boom for a tiny proportion of the population. The ministry was built in the 1960s, and perforated breeze blocks had been used in an unsuccessful attempt at lightening the grim, shabby painted concrete façade. The sign hung at an angle, the tiled steps were broken, and the gloomy interior was painted a curious shade of green. But after the hubbub outside, it was surprisingly quiet.

In a large, dirty room there were two desks. A civil servant in traditional Afghan dress slept peacefully at one; at the other his colleague was picking his toes. Behind him a filthy cabinet bulged with papers, some of which had cascaded onto the floor. Two fluorescent tubes hung forlornly above us, covered in dust. The meeting told me nothing more than I could see. The others at the UN office told similar stories. Within a week, we realised that the glue holding this administration together was fragile. We would have to exercise caution; reforming the government was not our job, making existing structures capable of some response to natural disasters was.

I heard that Brigadier Ed Butler with 16 Air Assault Brigade was now in Helmand, and rumours were reaching Kabul about the population there being displaced by renewed fighting. They were only rumours, but they added to the false euphoria of life in Kabul. Moreover, the narco-economy was not meaningful economic growth; it was consumption paid for by heroin. Now I knew that the central government did not really govern anything, the combination of all these factors was unsettling.

During the second week, our team split and I flew to Mazar-i-Sharif with Tatiana Garakani, a Canadian whose parents had fled Iran during the revolution, and Trevor Glass, a South African. The others went to Jalalabad. At Kabul International Airport I remembered, five years earlier, standing on this same runway with the Coalition military engineers beside a crater, pondering what to do about an unexploded bomb. Back then, destroyed Afghan civilian airliners were still parked on the apron, tails and bits of wings missing, fuselages torn by the bombardment. I could still see two, now at their final resting place near the perimeter fence.

As we approached Mazar from the south, the harsh mountains of the Hindu Kush softened into rolling foothills, with the mighty River Oxus to the north. I saw a compound full of new 4x4 vehicles destined for the narco-capital of the former warlord General Atta Noor, now the Provincial Governor. Mazar was quiet and calm. The tension I felt in Kabul was absent here, and there was little animosity towards us since the northerners here had won the war with Coalition help. Rivalry between the Uzbek General Dostum and the Tajik General Atta was well known, but it did not involve us. We could move around freely. Our meetings with the UN agencies and various government departments were unmemorable except that none gave me confidence that much would happen in the event of a catastrophe. I had been in Afghanistan for two earthquakes, and remembered all too well that nothing had happened.

Mid-morning, we were scheduled to meet General Atta; we had been given a whole hour with him. A well-known warlord, Atta had a ferocious reputation and some of the allegations about him were disconcerting. We were driven by the UN to what appeared to be a sumptuous new narco-palace, almost glittering in the sun, and after extensive security checks we were allowed in. There seemed to be a great deal of black and gold; taste was a secondary consideration in this monument to power. A boy in dark glasses escorted us, much to our surprise, to a bedroom, where we waited – Tatiana, Trevor and I – for half an hour, perhaps longer. The wait was part of the whole protocol of meeting an important person. Finally, we were ushered into the presence of the big man. He was surprisingly tall, with large hands, a sharp intelligent face and remarkable presence, almost pushing a bow wave in front of him as he entered the room. Tatiana, using her headscarf as a veil, was our interpreter. As I explained our business, I felt he was pleased to have the delegation, but only if he could get something out of it. At the end of our discussion, he asked me a penetrating question about the relationship between central and provincial government, which came with such spin it was almost impossible to answer without getting myself into trouble. Playing safe, I said I would have to discuss it with the Vice President in Kabul. His eyes flashed, and he suddenly and alarmingly sprang to his feet and announced, "Here, I am the President!" The interview was over.

We flew back to Kabul the next day. A few minutes before landing, alerted by our pilot, we looked out to see a US Air Force F15 on each wing. For a moment we felt rather important, but then in unison the jets turned away and climbed towards Bagram air base, two tiny specks against the vast mountains.

The pressure was on to complete our report in the few remaining days, a fretful and never terribly rewarding task, since it involved endless compromise. Was it going to be any use? I had my doubts, as governance in Afghanistan was all about using central funds to distribute political patronage, a system that held the place together. It was not a country in any meaningful sense, rather a place populated by the spill-over from its neighbours: Uzbeks, Tajiks, Pashtuns; and recreational violence was a way of life. Our report showed how, using existing structures, something could be done in the event of a natural disaster. However, there was a small difficulty that 'could' might not mean 'would'. To be prepared meant stockpiling relief supplies, but such items could readily be turned into cash that just might be too tempting. The only good thing was that the contacts made on these trips were often invaluable.

For me, the trip had quite another merit. I had spent two weeks looking at most aspects of governance in Afghanistan and had grave reservations about what the UK and the US governments were trying to do. The US were advocating that a strong, democratic central state was a barrier to global terrorism. This was nonsense, in every way one looked at it. There was talk of ungoverned spaces harbouring terrorists – yet more nonsense. There was no fertile soil for democracy here either. There was just not any governance and what governance there was reached all of fifty kilometres from Kabul. Yet within the next few years, the US government would spend one billion dollars a month attempting to establish a modern democratic state. Of this massive amount, only 4% would be spent on improving the lives of Afghans.

There was very little information about what was going on in Helmand, but what little there was added to the sense of unease. The military mission back in 2001 had been the removal of the Al-Qaeda training camps. Since then, justification for maintaining military forces in the country had been to counter the narcotics trade. Now it seemed that the barrier to global terrorism was to be a strong democratic central state.

Before we left, we had one last appointment, a presentation by the Kabul Fire Service. The main fire station compound was a collection of decrepit buildings with broken windows, the odd gutter hanging off, and a couple of acres of oil-stained tarmac. Yet there was a collection of brand-new shiny gadgets, a new fire engine, pumps and vehicles of all makes – the gifts of generous donors. I immediately wondered where the spare parts would be found for these marvels of Western engineering once the paint had faded in the Central Asian sun. The Afghans might have been better off with ex-Soviet hardware that had been tried and tested in their country. Here, anything that couldn't be mended with a four-pound hammer was not going to last.

We gathered in a yard the size of a small parade ground. At a signal, a fire engine leapt from its garage. Afghans dashed in all directions, and one was very nearly run over. My heart nearly missed a beat, but worse was to follow – the high ladder was deployed upwards into a tangle of overhead telephone and electricity cables. In the enthusiasm to show off, chaos began to envelop this piece of theatre. I could hardly watch anything beyond the high ladder as it finally engaged with the electricity wires. Men now appeared with bolt cutters and, seeing this was going to end in tragedy, Ted intervened to thank our hosts, declaring that we had been greatly impressed by their consummate skill and there was no need to continue. Honour was thus saved and life preserved.

23

A Collective Loss of Common Sense, Afghanistan 2010

There was a cold November wind from the north-west, and RAF Brize Norton looked particularly hideous in the rain. To get to my seat in the Boeing C-17 I had to pass a rack of stretchers; one of them was bloodstained, a salutary reminder of the human cost of this military adventure in Afghanistan. I was euphoric to be on the flight, as it had taken months of determination. A casual mention by the Chief of the Defence Staff, General Richards, that I might find ways of improving the lives of ordinary Afghans had resulted in an invitation to Afghanistan by General Nick Parker, Deputy Commander of the International Security Assistance Force (ISAF).

Finding a suitable moment for me to go had proved surprisingly difficult. However, by the time it was decided, Nick Parker had finished his 12-month tour of Afghanistan and James Bucknall had taken over as Deputy Commander. The 'surprising difficulty' had come from the British Embassy in Kabul. I had suffered weeks of prevarication, designed to delay or prevent my arrival, and it was not until I actually did arrive that I realised how much energy had gone into making sure I never got there.

Twenty-four hours before the flight, a sixth sense told me that body armour would be required. An RAF sergeant told me in no uncertain terms that without it I would not get on the plane. I tried the RAF stores, who said it was impossible to issue a civilian with body armour. Undaunted, I rang my old regiment at Windsor and the adjutant, delighted to be helpful, invited me to breakfast. I left an hour later with a set. So here I was, boarding a military aircraft, sponsored as an adviser to the Ministry of Defence, but under no formal contract from DFID, my usual employer. The MOD assumed that I was working for DFID, but DFID were equally adamant that my terms of reference were only of interest to the MOD and were determined that I should be paid by them. This ping-pong between Departments of State had been going on for three months and, faced with either working pro bono or not going at all, I chose the former.

Much was not going right in Afghanistan. A hint of this was revealed at a meeting set up for me by DFID's Secretary of State Andrew Mitchell two weeks before I left. The day before the meeting, a junior civil servant rang, asking what I needed to know about DFID's country programme. I was rather surprised, and fired off at least twenty questions; some of the answers were in the public domain, such as Afghanistan's GDP, its income from taxation, and its population, but many were not. At the meeting the next day, this junior civil servant was unable to answer any of the questions and there was no effort to be helpful or friendly. I had experienced prevarication, but this was close to obstruction. What were they all so alarmed that I might see?

On the flight, I sat next to a Lieutenant Colonel who told me his job in Kabul was 'situational awareness'. "That sounds interesting," I said. "You'll obviously be travelling all over the country." "No," he replied awkwardly, "I won't leave the base for the whole six months."

We stopped at RAF Akrotiri in Cyprus to refuel and, since flights into Kandahar were only allowed at night, had plenty of time to drink coffee in the warm Mediterranean sun. The sudden descent into Kandahar was, like those into Sarajevo years before, a moment for introspection. Landing aircraft were easy targets for anybody with a hand-held missile, I imagined, which was enough to cause a moment of anxiety, but we landed safely. I was met by a contractor who, with his former Sergeant Major, ran the Foreign Office compound. Although it was nearly 2 am, the place hummed with activity, with aircraft taking off and landing and helicopters coming and going. Our accommodation was half a dozen Corimecs surrounded by blast walls, each comfortably set up as a hotel room. I was fast asleep within moments.

At breakfast in the military canteen, I reflected on the very different army of the 1970s, when 'compo' rations contained memorable tins of steak and kidney pudding and spam, known as baby's head and truncheon meat.

Things were different now – copious eating seemed to be a pastime in military life, something I had already witnessed in Iraq. It was also reflected in the size of the servicemen and women.

I had a few hours to wait before catching an aircraft to Kabul and was taken for a tour of the base. I was mesmerised by the size of the place and shuddered at the cost. Everywhere contractors were expanding and improving the facilities. Only a few days before, some mortars had landed inside the perimeter, and radars were now being placed on containers built into towers so they could 'see out' over the defences. I thought of the economic cost of asymmetric warfare – an Afghan with one donkey and a mortar could wander across the desert, fire off half a dozen mortar bombs and destroy several aircraft costing millions. This had actually happened. I looked wistfully at the little FCO compound with its two full-time staff working twenty-four hours a day and imagined what the contractors charged. Even I was astonished when I found out.

I was surprised at the changes in Kabul since my last visit four years earlier. There was now a military terminal at the airport, and blast walls everywhere. The British Contingent Headquarters was an untidy-looking building bristling with antennae and satellite dishes, with a cluster of Corimecs at the back. Lieutenant Colonel Richard King and Wing Commander Wendy Rothery seemed delighted I had finally arrived. Richard warned me of the fight they had to get me to Kabul against an implacably hostile embassy and an even more hostile DFID. Without Wendy's tireless endeavours, I never would have got to Afghanistan at all.

ISAF Headquarters was a strange place, being both workplace and home to 1,700 staff officers incarcerated here for a six-month tour of duty. Only a tiny percentage of these men and women would ever leave the base, except for a few days' R&R, during their whole tour. It was claustrophobic, completely divorced from the real world. The mantra 'Solid progress, more to be done' was an article of belief in the headquarters and disseminated to capitals. Field reports and ground truth caused anxiety and alarm, the messengers of both being viewed as dissenters. Chuff charts were prominent, and if a commander made it to the end of their tour without mishap, they got a medal and a promotion.

The British Contingent Headquarters was different. Everyone had spotted that the emperor had no clothes, but a good-humoured 'Get on and do your job' mentality had taken over. They saw my mission as a means of getting their message back via a slightly different channel, and I realised I had to tread carefully. I was allocated a small windowless room in the back of the building and Richard King took me through what he thought might be a useful programme. He had been General Nick Parker's military attaché and I was hugely impressed by the amount of work he had already done to help me. I could travel anywhere and see anyone, and everything was possible. However, before I started work I needed to put on a jacket and tie and visit the Ambassador.

It struck me as very odd that I needed to be escorted inside the embassy, especially with my security clearance, and since I was in the company of a British Lieutenant Colonel in uniform. I was ushered into the Ambassador's office. Sir William Patey sat glaring at me, and waved me to a seat. There was a pause and I explained the purpose of my visit, giving him my carefully worded terms of reference on how we might advance the interest of the civilian population in Afghanistan. It was not a very controversial brief. I had been invited by the Deputy Commander of ISAF and was well known for my work supporting civilians in conflict over three decades. I had also obeyed the protocol of visiting the Ambassador before starting work on his patch to explain what I intended to do and get his advice.

I was taken aback to be mocked for thinking that I might make any contribution at all. "Do you really think you know better than the advisers already employed here?" he almost snarled. Then came his Exocet: "Who's paying you?" I was surprised by this line of attack, and said, "No one." He clearly did not believe me. But I remained courteous and said I would like to brief him before leaving the country. "Don't bother," he said, "I'm sure it will be in your report." Inwardly I smiled and thought: yes, but the report isn't for you. I left feeling rather battered, but it was hardly better downstairs when I met the DFID Head of Office, Pauline Hayes. Charm made no dent in her armour; she remained passive, uncomfortable and even intimidated by my presence. Despite my chat about electricity generation and distribution, transformers and water pumps, she looked alarmed. This was a different world to her daily work of social development and issues of gender. Richard and I made our way back to ISAF Headquarters. I was in a rather sombre mood; naked aggression and rudeness from the Ambassador and unresponsive silence from DFID were not a great start.

However, it did not take long to realise there were real divisions between the British Embassy and the British Contingent Headquarters, and even between the forty-eight contributing nations of ISAF. It was an unhappy muddle. To succeed, the entire operation in Afghanistan needed a simple unified command and a common purpose. As each day passed, I had less and less faith that the Coalition could achieve anything. 'A house divided against itself cannot stand' was the sum of my first day's thoughts.

The next morning my spirits were revived by the glorious winter sunshine. My first appointment was with General James Bucknall. After my experience the day before, it was a delight to be given such a warm welcome. James was both pleased that I had managed to get to Kabul and interested in what I was planning to do. We discussed 'civil effect' at national level and in Helmand Province, and how it could be maximised over the next twenty-four months. There was also a transitional civil programme to consider, which would support the planned military drawdown from the country, but this was not seen as a pressing issue. Civil effect is defined as the impact of civilian projects and activities that can be supportive of military objectives and take place within the military timeframe. All Commanders who had served in the Balkans realised the importance of a prosperous and contented civilian population. It was vital that the Afghans' quality of life was improved, and this had to be woven into the military plan. As I left James's office, the pressure was on. I had to find something that could reach millions, be easy to implement, be owned by the Afghan government, and be completed within two years.

Richard and I moved from meeting to meeting, the World Bank, US Agency for International Development (USAID), the Danish Embassy and a galaxy of ISAF units. We were shown myriad organigrams; most were a spider's web of complexity. There were PowerPoint displays of such ingenuity that I was more fascinated by the operator's skill than by the content. The more I saw, the less I felt that anybody really understood what was going on in Afghanistan. Obsession with force protection meant that most never left the camp. Even if they wanted to, the bureaucracy of achieving it was weary-making. Transport had to be booked in advance, always two vehicles. Once, we were sitting in the back of an armoured vehicle waiting to be taken to a meeting already wearing our body armour, helmets and safety glasses, the vehicle commander said we were not going anywhere until we put on our gloves. It was all very exhausting, and made me increasingly rebellious.

I was hugely grateful to Richard for organising the programme. Had it been left until my arrival, I would have needed an extra week and achieved substantially less. As it was, I was able to travel and meet a wide group of people throughout the country. Aside from ISAF, we met with Afghan government departments, utilities, humanitarian agencies, embassies, the UN, the EU, even the Asian Development Bank. I got tired of hearing the ISAF mantra 'Solid progress, more to be done' from those who never left their offices. Those who did gave quite a different view. Another story was unfolding and it was not a happy one.

At the end of the first week, we decided we had neither the time nor the energy to go through the rigmarole of booking transport – after all, I was not under contract to anybody and could do what I liked. Many meetings were nearby, so we decided to walk. It was a liberating experience; Kabul looked and felt quite different when not seen through bulletproof glass. As we walked along broken pavements covered in leaves, Richard said, "I'm right behind you, sir, armed with a pencil." Indeed he was.

The Provincial Reconstruction Teams were providing most of the civil effect, but they were struggling. Their projects were mostly perceived as conditional bribes, and access to the rural population was dangerous and difficult. In very poor countries, Quick Impact Projects are neither quick nor do they have much impact. The teams also run into conflict with the development agencies, who find ample and often good reasons to criticise them.

Afghanistan's urban population was about 10 million of the 25 million people living in the country. They had been used to decent water and reliable electricity supplies, but decades of war and the absence of spare parts had made these increasingly precarious. These people could be reached easily and safely by increasing the supply of electricity and clean drinking water. It was the ideal project. The advantage of supporting utilities was that Afghan companies supplied them. If we could source, ship and store spare parts and release them in a carefully monitored way, supplies could be increased by 20%. Even better, the Afghan government, who would own the project, could take the credit. This would be achievable in twenty-four months.

Of the opinion formers in Kabul, USAID were enthusiastic, as were the Danish Embassy. I had a productive meeting with Mark Sedwill, NATO's Senior Civilian Representative in Afghanistan, who said my idea was something that had interested the Afghan President's Chief Adviser, Ashraf

Ghani. I went to see Staffan de Mistura, the UN Special Representative to the Secretary General, who I had met in 1999 in Albania. He had a reputation as a consummate diplomat and his charm was legendary. We chatted about the problems facing Afghanistan over a pot of china tea on his veranda. He gave me useful advice and I was grateful for his support and encouragement.

By the end of the first week, I felt I had made some progress. Most of the important organisations were supportive, but not the DFID office back at the embassy. Their interest was social development. Unfortunately, the timespan for change in Afghanistan was generational, and they were unlikely to achieve anything radical in the next twenty-four months except possibly alienating the Afghan population with their socially progressive ideas.

My plan for electricity and clean water was met with silent and overt hostility. The DFID office was approximately fifty strong, yet only three of these were deployed in Helmand Province. Their 'hardship arrangements' allowed a return flight to the UK every six weeks, compared with one R&R trip every six months for service personnel. This, and the fact that alcohol was allowed in the embassy while ISAF was dry, made for a less-than-ideal relationship. These arrangements for DFID and their security allegedly cost £350,000 per person on top of their salaries. They needed to do something fairly useful to justify this.

The UK, like most of the ISAF member states, had a broad range of programmes not necessarily closely connected to their military effort. The main objectives were less about delivering material benefits to the Afghans, and more about building institutions for a modern state. The timeline was going to be measured in decades, and was unlikely to touch the lives of many in the short term.

I found it all vaguely depressing. I wondered if those fifty people that never left the compound could possibly do their jobs in London. Faced with a real problem, the answer seemed to be to throw huge amounts of people and money at it; a DFID handout showed a programme budget of £291 million for the current year. It was difficult to discover how much the whole adventure in Afghanistan was costing, but probably in the region of £8 billion annually. The same handout informed me the UK was in Afghanistan to prevent Afghanistan being used by Al-Qaeda to attack the UK and our allies. That had certainly been the case nine years earlier, but now there was a miasmic collation of different objectives, with forty-eight participating nations more or less involved and very few of them actually engaged in the fighting down in Helmand Province. It was time to go there and have a look.

Richard and I flew down to Camp Bastion. Flying with the RAF required Zen-like patience. Afghanistan is the size of France and the flight would take an hour and a half in a C-130. I had been travelling in these aircraft, with their noise, canvas seats, absence of windows and the curious air-conditioning system that froze your backside and boiled your head, since I was nineteen. I was now fifty-six. Snails seal themselves up in a state of aestivation when the environment is not to their liking. I had long adopted a similar survival mechanism.

Camp Bastion was far bigger than I imagined, about the size of Reading. The extension of the second runway had recently been completed, part of a 141 million dollar expansion project. It was a city in the desert, home to almost 30,000 servicemen and women and contractors, and the hub from where the war was being fought. We would spend the day here before flying to Lashkargah. At each of a series of meetings arranged at Camp Leatherneck adjacent to the base, I was given a PowerPoint presentation. There was nothing wrong with the presentations, but there was not much right about them either. The Provincial Reconstruction Teams were valiantly trying a variety of projects to wean the local people off an economy based on growing opium poppies and cultivate wheat or pomegranates instead. I had managed projects like this, but always post-conflict when the objective had been to demonstrate the benefits of peace. I asked frequently about the difference in yield from a hectare of opium poppies and a hectare of wheat. To my complete amazement no one knew, and I only got an answer on my last day in Afghanistan. The crop substitution plan would mean a 75% decrease in income for farmers.

There were additional problems in cultivating wheat. The crop had to be taken by road for milling or sale, which gave the police the opportunity to rob farmers on their way to market and again on their return. Producing opium was easy by comparison. It would probably involve a nocturnal visit from characters in black turbans with an advance payment for the grower, and the crop being collected in a similar way. Some of the high arid plateaus were unfriendly and unreliable places for wheat cultivation, yet the rocky soils were ideal for opium poppies.

"We have nothing to do with counter-narcotics; that's been handed over to the Afghans," one officer said. "We merely give the Governor several million dollars to organise the eradication of poppy fields." I had a good idea how the eradication might work in practice, whose crops would be chosen for destruction and why. As for the fate of those who did not show suitable gratitude to the Governor, or defied him – I shuddered.

That evening we went to dinner at Camp Leatherneck with the US Commander. It was surf and turf night and lobsters and steak had been flown in for the evening in such quantities that many servicemen and women seemed to be eating their own weight in crustaceans, almost invisible behind walls of discarded shells. Seeing such mountains of food in such a poor country was unsettling and surprisingly unappetising.

We set off the next morning for a 6.45 am flight to Lashkargah in a Merlin helicopter. These new three-engine machines were magnificent, but technically complicated and, at £50 million each, too expensive for our strained defence budget. I wondered, given the scarcity of helicopters in Afghanistan, if we would have been better off buying something slightly cheaper but twice as many.

The atmosphere in Lashkargah was quite different; there was a brutal efficiency about the place, and a palpable tension. I was accommodated in a low stone-built house known as the English House. It was previously called the Russian House, which was hardly reassuring.

I had two days to see as much and talk to as many people as I could. We started with operations, which was impressive, well-led and achieving the military objectives they had been given. It was when we came to the rule of law, policy and programmes or counter-narcotics that I suspected there was a vast gap between the talk and reality. The small DFID team of three were concentrating on a few sensible projects, but with so little contact with local people that it was difficult to see how they had any chance of lasting success. One project started by the Americans in the 1950s was the Helmand irrigation scheme, which brought real prosperity to the province but had long since fallen into disrepair. If more energy had been directed to restoring it, this might have been reversed, but nine years into this conflict, I was only told that yet another feasibility study was in progress.

I had now been in the country for ten days and there was one thing that was reflected in so many ways: the Afghans, proudly independent, wanted us all gone. Some perhaps not until they had extracted as much money from us as possible. But in our generosity and real concern to improve the lives of some of the poorest people on earth, we just could not see that.

It was rudely brought home to me when we left the base to go to Muktyala Fort, for a briefing on military operations in the vicinity. I walked out to the vehicle park to find my vehicle, a Mastiff, a monstrous armoured 17-ton truck. The carcass of a similar vehicle lay against the perimeter wall. It had been hit by an IED, which had wrenched off the front axle, wheel and hub assembly. Given its fate, I listened attentively to the safety brief. I had to make sure I was wearing a seatbelt – surviving a roadside bomb attack in this vehicle was possible, but being thrown around inside and having one's skull pierced by a jagged piece of metal would be unwelcome. Great shackles that could have dragged the Titanic up from the bed of the Atlantic hung behind the rear axle. The sergeant pointed to two handles either side of the steps into the machine. "Those," he said, "are to help you climb in with your body armour. Don't touch them, they bend." Not much of this huge beast looked as if it was bendable.

All the other vehicle engines were now running and we were ready to move. The metal gates out of the base were thrown open and we emerged into the town. In the bowels of the vehicle, I could only see a glimpse of the sky through the machine gunner's turret. Suddenly, there was a deafening din as stones thrown by a grateful populace hit the vehicle, amplified as if they were hitting a tin can. Some came in through the turret. A particularly large one hit the gunner; with blood streaming down his face he spun the turret round and cocked the gun. I had to assume after a few minutes that we had left the town as the cacophony of stones ended. We trundled along ponderously, claustrophobically and uncomfortably, for another half an hour.

The Fort stood on a slight mound above the plain, and bristled with activity. The professional competence and tactical success of our troops were beyond question. Yet the anger and alienation of the civilian population, that I had witnessed only an hour or so earlier, reminded me there were '100 days to win the peace'. It was now nearly 100 months since those euphoric days back in 2001, when we had chased the Taliban from Kabul.

My second day at Lashkargah was memorable for a discussion about counter-narcotics. I was probably more frank than I should have been about this policy. It was clearly a major driver in the conflict and foolish on many levels. A senior civil servant at DFID had dryly commented, about our UK drug problem, "Domestic problem, domestic solution." The idea that we should travel across the world to one of the poorest countries, and engage in a war to take away their best hope of a livelihood, was extraordinary, especially as narcotics are grown under licence in the EU. A number of soldiers who extolled to me the virtues of crop substitution were rather surprised when I asked if they were farmers. I listened to a presentation on the rule of law, which I thought rather fatuous, since the rule of the law, as they understood it, did not exist beyond the perimeter of the base. Another presentation, both competent and informative, reflected the importance of getting a positive message out to a doubtful population back in the UK.

Lashkargah looked brutally poor, with ugly two-storey blockwork buildings and rubbish everywhere, but surprisingly it did seem to have some life in it. Uniformed police officers were even standing at a crossroads on traffic duty. This made no sense in a counter-insurgency war where all agents of the state would have been legitimate targets. This raised questions about the real dynamics of this war. How much of it really was a counter-insurgency? How many Taliban were narco-warriors? How many were freedom fighters?

Richard faced a problem to do with our return to Kabul. I could travel direct from Kabul in the British Embassy Beechcraft King Air; he, however, could not, as it had no defence suite (the system of flares and chaff – aluminium foil released to distract anti-aircraft missiles). Amazingly, he had to get a derogation from no less than the Deputy Commander of ISAF so that we could travel back together.

At the airport, we learned there would be a delay of some hours. Travelling in conflict zones, expectations are wonderfully lowered to the point that arriving on the same day is counted a good journey. Time like this is never wasted, and I chatted to our close protection team and other passengers from the base. It was such fragments of conversation that would eventually help me to understand what was really happening in this unfortunate country.

Once airborne I squeezed between the pilots' seats on the flight deck. Suddenly, a huge black object appeared in front of us, and instinctively we all ducked as it passed down the port wing. "Blimey," said one pilot, "that must have been a drone driven by some dozy twat in California." "Yes" said the other "probably just finishing the night shift and thinking about getting the children to school." Evidently, this was not an infrequent event.

By the time we landed in Kabul, I was an hour and a half late for my meeting at the British Embassy with the Head of the Asian Development Bank. The military transport that Richard had booked had come and gone. Seeing there was a spare seat in the embassy car, I explained the situation. The driver lethargically picked up his clipboard. "Your name's not on the list," he muttered contemptuously. We waited another hour for the return of the military transport.

During the three days before my return home, my office in the British Contingent Headquarters became a hub of activity as everyone whose previous attempts to be heard had failed tried to bypass the chain of command. Each delegation told me something more alarming than the last – about corruption in the police force, or the customs arrangements, which were run as a franchise operation by a handful of Afghan families and were responsible for the bulk of Afghanistan's national income. Finally, there was the Combined Joint Inter-Agency Task Force – Shafafiyat, the key anti-corruption task force. After an hour of this, any optimism I felt after seeing all the hard work, military success, boundless goodwill and even hope for this country was quite crushed.

What was I to make of these extraordinary three weeks? What was it that I was not supposed to see? It was both nothing and everything. This enormous enterprise lacked common sense, yet one billion dollars a month was being spent by the American military alone. The objectives had shifted three times. A laudable operation to remove the terrorists' camps had been wholly successful. It had then developed into a foolish campaign to eradicate poppy production, and on to a hapless programme of nation building that had no possibility of delivering results in the timeframe allocated. With forty-eight countries involved, there were too many cooks in the kitchen, and trying to maintain a unified command and common purpose was always going to be a challenge. Yet more than anything else, nobody in this fiercely independent country wanted us here, and when they did tolerate us, it was I suspected driven by financial gain.

At our final meeting, the Deputy Commander James Bucknall told me it was refreshing to have existing concepts and thinking challenged from a different angle. Most importantly, what I had suggested chimed with Ashraf Ghani's and the Afghan government's ideas. This was heartening, but he did warn me of the labyrinthine process required to convert any idea into action on the ground. I had seen first-hand the labyrinthine process, and did not have the confidence of either the embassy or DFID or even DFID's Secretary of State. I knew from Bosnia that for things to happen they needed to be driven forward and managed by a single individual, not the 'infrastructure development cluster' in which our Secretary of State, Andrew Mitchell, had such confidence.

I had come to help the Afghan civilian population, hoping in the process to shorten the war. But it was too late – what I was suggesting should all have happened ten years earlier. As I boarded the plane at Kandahar airport, I noticed that the tower of sea containers built to house the radar was gone, replaced by an elegant concrete tower – this was a good time to be a contractor.

Flying home, I reflected on the imbalance of the civil and military funding. Afghanistan would soon have, between the police and the army, around 300,000 men under arms. Yet it was one of the poorest countries on earth – how would this ever be funded? We had come to plant democracy and human rights in this rocky soil, but there did not seem much enthusiasm for either. Afghanistan had become too expensive, and the public in the UK had not been convinced by the idea in the first place and were tired of it. Now David Cameron had set our date for going home. Another of Clausewitz's principles of war – surprise – had been sacrificed to domestic politics. Asked what Afghanistan would look like in ten years' time, one leading UK politician replied, "Like one of its neighbours. It just depends which one." I was not convinced that anything I had seen would make any difference.

24

The World on the Move, Libya 2011

T E Lawrence allegedly said he liked the desert because it was clean. He would not have liked this one. The 500-kilometre drive from Tunis to the Libyan border was often just a depressing sea of plastic bags, and outside every settlement there were collections of domestic rubbish.

Civil war had broken out in Libya the previous week, and migrant workers, nearly a third of the population, had been denied food. With Arab shopkeepers refusing to sell them any, they had little choice but to leave the country as quickly as possible. West Africans and Bangladeshis made up the majority and, with the Tunisian border so close to the Libyan capital, Tripoli, large numbers of migrants were arriving at the desert crossing point of Ras al-Jadir.

My small UN team of five had been mobilised quickly and we were lucky to have a Tunisian, Ramzi Dhafer, as a team member. Ramzi had been a member of the UNDAC team for many years and was well-known to all of us. Working for the Tunisian Civil Defence, he had been able to book accommodation and provide vehicles on arrival. At customs our satellite telephone was impounded, a reflection of the underlying authoritarian instinct despite the recent revolution. Then we were on our way to the Libyan border. The country was unsettled and more dangerous than it appeared; two months earlier in January, the President, Ben Ali, had gone into exile and only a few days before we arrived the Prime Minister had resigned. The atmosphere was nervous, and people were cautious. Local knowledge is the best security and I was pleased

Ramzi was with us for our 500-kilometre journey across revolutionary Tunisia.

The journey took a whole day, even with little traffic. Near Tunis, arable fields benefited from the coastal rainfall, but once the road moved inland, the countryside seemed less favoured. Ramzi had arranged for his colleagues to kill a sheep and prepare a surprise barbecue en route, and in

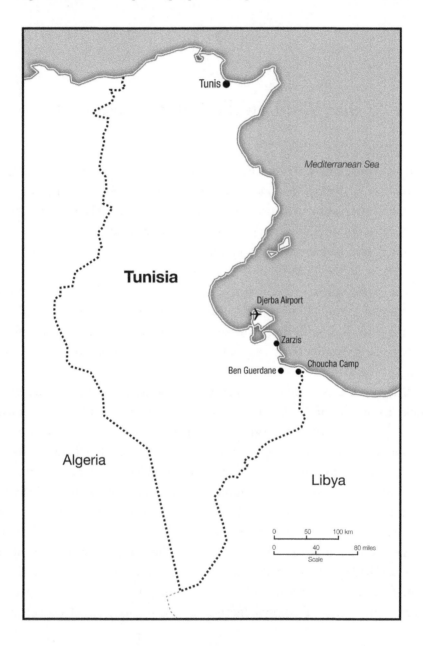

a brief hour, we saw the best of North African hospitality. I could hardly believe so few people could devour an entire sheep in such a short time, and felt I could go a week without further eating.

In Zarsis, normally a holiday destination, we pulled up at a vast tourist hotel, palatial by any standards; it was a relief to find a bed rather than a sleeping bag on a cold concrete floor. Rather surprisingly, the hotel still had a few tourists who, despite the political instability, seemed blissfully ignorant of the troubles unfolding inside Tunisia and only fifty kilometres away in Libya. We were each given an all-inclusive hotel bracelet to wear, as if the beach bar was the only objective of our stay.

I had hardly been there ten minutes when I heard that the British Ambassador, accompanied by Andrew Mitchell, the British Secretary of State for DFID, wanted me to join them for dinner. I was the last to arrive at the nearby hotel restaurant, and already thirty people were there. Vast plates of food were brought, and half a sheep gurgled inside me – a second banquet in one day was an endeavour rather than a pleasure. I was flattered to be invited, but I was asked a multitude of questions about a situation I had yet to see. I only wished that this encounter could have happened twenty-four hours later, when I could have used it to extract exactly what was needed from the British government.

The next day, we drove ninety-minutes to the border, passing through featureless desert with camels roaming free. In the town of Ben Guerdane, a few kilometres from the border, there was a military checkpoint in the town centre. The population looked hostile, the wind blew sand across the road, the air was full of grit, the sky grey, and the place emitted a brooding malevolence. At the UNHCR camp, blue tents were scattered almost at random along the roadside, and at one end, the Tunisian Army had made a small headquarters of military tents corralled inside a ring of military vehicles. Walking down the road from the border came crowds of young men, mainly of West African origin, clutching suitcases, and there were several thousand people – again all young men – near the road. It was a chaotic and potentially dangerous situation. For nearly an hour, we wandered around the camp – if one could call it a camp – looking for somebody in charge, until a Tunisian Army officer referred us to UNHCR. When we asked for their office, we were told that they did not have one. At the back of the site, we found a splendidly robust Englishwoman from Tunis with a band of volunteers providing

1,000 cooked meals a day. Three days later, she was providing 3,000, and the number was growing all the time.

Eventually I found the UNHCR Head of Mission, a Jordanian whose charm and relaxed manner belied the alarming situation that was developing around us. I explained that we had come from Geneva to help with the coordination; he nodded as if I had announced I had come to take the dog for a walk. "Where should we set up?" I asked. He looked rather surprised. "Set up? Oh, anywhere you like." We grabbed a UN family refugee tent, found a suitable piece of ground and were operational within the hour. I set off for the border; parking some distance away as the road was full of migrants on the move. On the Libyan side, the customs and immigration buildings appeared abandoned; on the Tunisian side officials had been overwhelmed by the numbers trying to cross. Thousands of migrants were milling about amongst discarded blankets, items of clothing, discarded shoes and other personal effects scattered on the road. I asked my driver to interpret for me and one tired-looking customs official told me that the previous day around 17,000 people had crossed into Tunisia. While we were talking, a few battered Mercedes cars arrived from Libya. The drivers wore dark glasses and looked menacing. "Who are they?" I asked cautiously. I could see from the body language that the question was unwelcome, and the subject was changed.

When I got back to the camp, the team had answers to most of the things I needed to know. I was concerned about the water supply, given that we were in the Sahara desert. Fortunately, a water main ran beside the road, which was being used by the camp. Amazingly, there was no UNHCR presence in the camp at night to distribute tents or allocate tent pitches, hence the chaotic layout. Food had been largely provided as a gift from the Tunisians, and the Tunisian and Moroccan armies were providing medical cover. Most telling was that the humanitarian coordination meetings were held every evening at the holiday resort at Zarsis, an hour and a half away. The expected permanent NGO or UN agency presence in the camp was wholly absent. I soon discovered that most of the NGOs at Zarsis were waiting to redeploy to Libya and had little interest in working in Tunisia.

I was unpleasantly surprised by a UNHCR meeting on our second evening. It was as if no progress had been made in thirty years. Although around one hundred people were present, every single one was from an international humanitarian NGO or UN agency; there was no one from the Tunisian government, and the meeting was conducted exclusively in English. There was no agenda or structure; people spoke when they felt like it, and clearly empty vessels made the most noise. It was everything I had spent the last thirty years trying to overcome. We were here to coordinate the international response for the Tunisian government, but all I saw was an appalling waste of time, an insult to the very government we had come to help. It was the last one I attended.

My parent organisation OCHA, had already scented there might be difficulties and called from Geneva asking me to use my best diplomatic skills to address the problem. OCHA had the mandate for coordination, but UNHCR had over many years de facto done the job. UNHCR was a huge, well-funded organisation and OCHA a mere minnow by comparison. If I were to succeed as coordinator, the key would be getting a coordination mechanism set up in the camp.

Trying to run the operation from a refugee family tent was clearly impossible and I asked the World Health Organization to loan us a Rubb Hall, a large fluorescent orange inflatable tent. I had requested that the British NGO, MapAction, join us on this mission. Their ability to map every aspect of what I was trying to do and put it on the web gave me the management tool I needed. Despite the loss of one sat-phone, and working with limited bandwidth, MapAction were already producing some high-quality material. We had also been joined by a young team of Scandinavian 'techies', who soon improved our communications. They proved very versatile, and I gave them additional assessment tasks, something they had never done before, but proved to be rather better at than most. Linguistically, the mission was challenging. The main team language was French, but the Scandinavians only spoke English and the Tunisians preferred we spoke Arabic.

Ramzi and I went to look for the Tunisian Army Commander and the Head of Civil Protection. We soon found them, unhappy to the point of incandescent fury. We sustained a torrent of invective, complete with angry body language and dramatic gestures. Afterwards Ramzi explained that the Tunisians felt insulted by the international humanitarian agencies. "Is this not their country? How have all these foreigners arrived and begun working without discussing matters with them first?" And on it went. Ramzi wisely had asked if they would address the first coordination meeting later that day. We had luckily caught the situation just in time, but much diplomatic work would be needed.

There were now 15,000 people in the camp, with more arriving every day. The site was drowning in rubbish, the desert around it was a vast latrine, and the wind blew clouds of grit into our tent and computers. Lewis Carroll's poem, *"The Walrus and the Carpenter"*, came bizarrely to mind.

"If seven maids with seven mops
Swept it for half a year.
Do you suppose," the Walrus said,
"That they could get it clear?"
"I doubt it," said the Carpenter,
And shed a bitter tear.

On our third day, I heard from Geneva that Valerie Amos, Head of OCHA, was to visit the camp. VIP field visits are a mixed blessing. Everything would have to stop, and all energy would be devoted to the visit. However, this was usually worthwhile, as the results were often hugely beneficial and real influence would be brought to bear in capitals.

The Head of OCHA arrived in time for our first coordination meeting. The Tunisian Army Colonel chaired the meeting, obviously satisfied at recovering his authority. Valerie Amos was impressive, asking many thoughtful questions, and was genuinely interested in all the team members. After the meeting, she was taken on a tour of the camp and interviewed by Sam Kiley, who was now working for Sky News. In the midst of the television interview, a riot broke out – the Bangladeshis were complaining about the Tunisian food, all of which had been donated by local people.

Forty-eight hours after our arrival I had a proper management structure in place. The team was now ten strong and we were joined by two more from the European Union. I was offered a support package by Geneva. Within two days the Italian government, who provided it, had erected a tented compound for us to move into, with office space, meeting tents and everything we needed to manage the operation professionally. The daily coordination brief was a crisp one-hour meeting attracting between fifty and sixty people: humanitarian agencies, diplomats, politicians, journalists and donors. It allowed the Tunisian government to feel firmly in command and to hold to account the operational agencies working in the camp.

The unsung heroes were the International Organization for Migration (IOM), whose job it was to move as many migrants out of the camp as they could. In three weeks, the camp held over 130,000 people in transit. The tide of humanity pouring out of Libya would have placed an intolerable burden otherwise on Tunisia, itself recovering from its own revolution only three months earlier. The plan was to repatriate everyone in the camp to their country of origin. IOM had the job of organising buses from the camp and chartering flights from Djerba Airport sixty kilometres away, a task they carried out with consummate efficiency. Being winter, there was spare airline capacity to move people to sixty-two different countries.

UNHCR, relieved of their coordination role, were able to concentrate on improving the camp. Used to providing camps for refugees who stayed for months if not years, some UNHCR staff found it difficult to see this as a transit camp, where a ten-day stay was long enough. There were new needs that I had never had to think about before, such as charging points for mobile phones. Generally, the migrants were good-humoured and above all healthy. Wages in Libya had been around 100 US dollars a month higher than in Tunisia, and these were fit, well-nourished young men, mostly under twenty-five. However, the uncertainty of their future and animosities between certain national groups created opportunities for trouble, especially between the Nigerians and Somalis. A football pitch was cleared and excess testosterone was dissipated in soccer matches. Trouble, though, was never far below the surface now that around 25,000 people were in the camp. On one occasion, bands of young men gathered outside our compound, chanting demands in an aggressive and frightening manner. Years later, I discovered that an ISIS cell had been established in the camp, intent on radicalising these vulnerable young men.

Tunisia had confiscated passports at the border to prevent the refugees drifting into the general population. These passports had subsequently been handed to IOM and getting them back from IOM was itself a piece of theatre. Each day a vast crowd would gather to hear names read out for transport to the airport the following day. The lucky person then ran to register for the flight home as if they had won the lottery, cheered by the crowd, their faces beaming with delight. It was a simple yet hugely effective system.

I went back to the border from time to time to talk to immigration officials. Numbers fluctuated from day to day, averaging around 5,000, but on occasions two or three times as many. Nevertheless, as the days passed the camp and transit arrangements improved and the number of migrants arriving from Libya began to fall. It had been a battle in the early days to balance those leaving with those arriving, but European countries seemed only too willing to pay tranches of 5 million dollars for the flights. Again, I saw battered Mercedes cars with Libyan number plates crossing the border. I asked my Tunisian driver what was going on. "Oh," he said, "they're our people." I looked surprised, given the Libyan number plates. "Many of them are our relatives," he said. "They trade in petrol." Smuggling would have been a more appropriate term I thought. The border here was meaningless. Instead of dividing nations, it separated one people. It also showed, as I had seen in Bosnia that war and revolution are not complete barriers to trade.

The migrant emergency had demonstrated all the really useful changes in humanitarian work over the past thirty years. The speed of deployment had been impressive, the use of IT and the internet helped manage the emergency, and finally there was the deployment of the support module, the tents and additional equipment I needed for the team. To have a large multinational team who worked so successfully together despite never having met, backed by Scandinavian IT support, had been remarkable. The greatest achievement was to provide support for the Tunisian Army and Civil Defence, who in three weeks put 130,000 migrants on aircraft back to their countries of origin, without a murmur of criticism in the international media. This migrant emergency was the first glimpse of what was to come. The number of migrants working in Libya had staggered me; although mainly from West Africa and Bangladesh, they had come from sixty-two countries. I had seen something that was going to cause political turmoil in Europe over the coming years, but failed to see its significance. The problem was not limited to Libya. The whole world was on the move.

25

Crucible of Chaos, Iraq 2016

From my room on the seventh floor of the Al Racheed Hotel, I gaze over the rooftops of Baghdad. It is sunset, the sky is hazy, the mood uncertain, and now the call to prayer is sounding from a hundred minarets. It is almost exactly twenty-five years since I first came to Iraq, and I have returned to what is left of it – a crucible of chaos. Wars and continued violence have sundered it geographically, culturally and institutionally. The north-east, the autonomous Kurdish Region, is almost another country. Sunni-Shia violence has left the country ungovernable.

ISIS has taken Mosul, Iraq's second city, home to 1 million people. The entire infrastructure of the country, lacking maintenance since sanctions were imposed in 1991, is crumbling. Those glorious moments in Kurdistan during the First Gulf War were full of hope, but no country in living memory has seen such a prolonged descent into violence and chaos.

Of all the disasters, misfortunes and woes to sweep this land, the Mosul Dam was now centre stage. The project – begun in 1986 for Saddam Hussein to control the Tigris River – was misguided from the start. Built on water-soluble gypsum and karstic limestone, it requires a complicated system of grouting, injecting concrete into the foundations of the dam wall, to maintain its stability. Sanctions starved it of funds after 1991, and there was no maintenance after the war in 2003. The instability of the dam was now alarming.

The reservoir holds 11.1 cubic kilometres of water, and the simple expedient of reducing the water level was made problematic by a broken guard gate. Each guard gate releases 885 cubic metres of water per second, and one gate used in isolation risks undermining the wall of the dam. Alternatively, releasing water through the turbines would supply ISIS – who hold Mosul – with electricity, something the government in Baghdad was loath to do. Briefly, ISIS had controlled the dam and all maintenance work had stopped, but happily, the Kurdish Peshmerga had now retaken control.

The US Army Corps of Engineers had commissioned a report, which had raised the alarm in capitals. Spring meltwaters from Turkey were raising the water level dangerously, representing a threat to the entire country. Something had to be done; what, nobody knew. Despite protestation that all was well, even the government in Baghdad had been alarmed by the sinkholes that had emerged in the tail of the dam wall. Their first reaction was to fill them with rubble, but wiser heads recognised help was needed. When an UNDAC team was offered, it was reluctantly accepted.

I was selected by Geneva to join four others to travel to Baghdad. We were to be led by UN staff member Rajan Gengaje and be joined by Venetia Bellers, a UK team member. She had worked for DFID in London and was known to be very experienced. Our other member, Wael Yacoub, an Egyptian UN official from the office in Cairo, meant we had one Arabic speaker. However, I wondered whether his being Sunni would matter in a Baghdad now dominated by religious warfare.

A trip to a conflict zone is never uneventful, and is nearly always unusual. Twenty-four hour airport life is now a global reality and the itinerary sent to me by Geneva was a complex arrangement of connecting flights that all seemed to leave between midnight and dawn. However, a delay in acquiring visas gave me time to research the Mosul Dam. The more I found out, the more alarming the problems appeared.

A week passed. I suspected that, given the complexity of Iraqi and UN politics, other reasons might be in play. Nevertheless, finally we were off. I would be in transit at Istanbul Airport for four hours, possibly the most dangerous part of the entire mission. At 6 am, Baghdad airport was empty. The few passengers were almost all connected to some international organisation and were met by security companies. My driver, a taciturn individual, looked peeved to be meeting such an early flight. I was driven into Baghdad along the famous airport road that I was unable to use back in 2004. I could see why – even now it had a distinctly unsettling feel. At the first checkpoint we were joined by a second UN armoured Toyota, and travelled on in convoy. "K9," said the driver pointing to a large sign naming the security contractor – a limp reference to the canines that had sniffed at our luggage and the interior of the vehicle at the checkpoint.

Along the route, sprinklers were in action to revive a series of worn-out lawns and broken concrete fountains once intended to echo the fabled Nineveh and Babylon. Yet all I saw was a profligate misuse of water. In the Green Zone, security was no longer left solely to the Iraqis, but had been delegated to a private military company, who demonstrated a professional competence previously absent.

I was dropped off at the Al Racheed Hotel, there was no evidence of the damage from the rocket attack twelve years earlier. Though its grandeur had faded, I was relieved to be somewhere so comfortable.

The big change was the near-absence of traffic in the Green Zone. Blast walls, twenty-foot long concrete T-pieces, were ubiquitous and brought a uniform ugliness to the city. At several checkpoints Iraqi soldiers laconically waved us through. At the UN compound, security was more robust, and our briefcases were scanned, an activity replicated everywhere we moved for the next three weeks. The UN compound, a ten-minute drive from the hotel, was cramped and depressing, with every available space utilised as offices and accommodation.

We, as a team, were expected to meet the Head of OCHA at midday. On the way to the OCHA office we passed a sandbagged bomb shelter. We were shown to a windowless room on the first floor – this really was architecture for a country in perpetual conflict – then went down to the canteen to meet the Head of OCHA. Giovanni Bosco, a small, light-boned, energetic man, with a strong Italian accent, explained that the delay in getting us to Baghdad had been his decision, due to security in the Green Zone. We looked at each other; a wholly different reason had been given to us while we waited a week to be deployed. The conversation didn't stray from the superficial for the first twenty minutes, until he decided to brief us more formally. This I found inappropriate in such a public place, and was rather more relaxed when we finally went upstairs to his office.

From my many UNDAC missions I knew how critical these early meetings could be. I listened attentively, and gradually it became clear that international pressure, mainly from the United States, had pushed the UN to do something about the dam. OCHA had decided that the problems of obtaining visas and bringing humanitarian goods through customs meant responding to any new calamity in Iraq would be almost impossible. The task of facilitating the arrival of humanitarian agencies and goods was given to us. It was a case of doing something, but essentially doing nothing very much.

Although the dam was a threat to the country, Giovanni had the newly-liberated towns on the Euphrates River to think about. Of course, there was also the problem of Mosul, where 1.2 million people might flee the city if government forces tried to retake it. He implied that the problems posed by the dam were so big it was best not to think about them. On no account were we to make any contingency plans. OCHA had no capacity to do this, he said, and then announced he was leaving Baghdad the following day for a three-week holiday.

We had been given mixed messages. I did not feel Giovanni was remotely interested in our mission, which had clearly been pushed on him by New York and Geneva. Something had to be done, and the standard UN response was process. I thought about the customs waivers and fast track visa applications available on arrival. These should be relatively straightforward, but here in Iraq nothing was. Every individual entering the country was considered a spy or a terrorist, and domestic administration was a cradle of political intrigue. For some things we wanted to do, the law would have to be changed, and that I knew was impossible.

Despite Rajan, our team leader, not arriving for another twenty-four hours, we started work. Venetia focused on the visa and customs waivers, Wael organised our programme for the next week, and I tried to understand the many problems posed by the dam. It was difficult to sort fact from rumour. Few people in the humanitarian agencies knew anything about the dam, other than that it was unstable and might collapse. "What would your organisation do in the event the dam burst?" I asked. "Oh, we'd evacuate," they replied. "And where would you go?" "Erbil," was the standard response. Saving themselves seemed to be the only priority. Erbil, however, was 366 kilometres to the north. But given the fighting in the country and all the flooding, how would they get there? This was a question that had not been given much serious thought. "Wouldn't the local population in Baghdad need your assistance?" I asked. This was met with an awkward silence and the subject was changed. They had a separate, more pressing assistance programme along the River Euphrates to think about.

I quickly discovered no one particularly cared. The view was that there was a low probability of the dam collapsing, and if it did, the catastrophe would be so great that nothing could be done. It was better just to ignore the problem. Twenty-four hours into this mission, I was ashamed how self-serving the humanitarian agencies had become. The atmosphere at the UN compound was one of claustrophobia, the security situation was so bad that no one left the Green Zone, and many never even left the compound. They all worked in a large open-plan building, with low partitions between each agency; no more than two square metres was given to each workstation. It looked like a hen house.

On the wall of our office hung a United Nations Assistance Mission for Iraq (UNAMI) map showing the potential area of flooding if the dam burst. Somebody in the compound must have produced this, so I went to find the UNAMI Geographic Information System (GIS) office, at the end of the corridor. I was greeted by the friendly ex-US Marine Corps serviceman in charge of mapping for UNAMI. He was delighted that I had called in and explained that, despite weeks of work, he had failed to get anybody interested in the many maps he had produced. He was a treasure trove of information on the dam, and I went back to the office knowing that these computerised models were the secret to doing something useful over the next three weeks. However, the set of maps I had seen were not politically useful. The reservoir water levels shown were either unrealistically high or too low, and would be easily dismissed by the Iraqi government. I needed levels that were realistic, and if we were to ask the government to lower the water, we needed ones that were politically acceptable. If we could model the potential flooding, at say, three levels of water in the reservoir, I could calculate how many people would be in danger. With this information, we could encourage the government and humanitarian agencies to mitigate the risk.

With Rajan, an experienced full-time UN official, as our team leader we could supply the all-important process for UN documents and give our report the gravitas it required. Rajan was happy for me to continue my approach, an ambitious plan that challenged the low expectations of the UN in Baghdad and Geneva. It was soon obvious that the driver behind our deployment had been a fellow UNDAC member, René Nijenhuis, a tall Dutchman in his early forties who had arrived from Geneva a few days earlier. After extolling the merits of a UNDAC team to Giovanni, he had left for Erbil. He arrived back the following day. Within minutes, his limited objectives were at variance with my views on the broader ideas of mitigating risk. Already, the facts were terrifying. If the dam was breached, a 19-metre wave would pass through Mosul, killing 250,000 people, more than the Indian Ocean tsunami. Seventy-two hours later a six-metre wave would pass through Baghdad, home to 7.8 million people. The disruption of clean water supplies would be calamitous and lead to appalling mortality.

As I argued my case quietly and dispassionately, I watched the body language of the others. At first, they were uncomfortable, then uncertain, but I felt I was making ground. René was stubbornly opposed to any broadening of the mission, and after nearly two hours, we just had to disagree. The dam represented an existential threat to the entire country and what René and Giovanni were proposing was mere window dressing, doing something without actually doing anything. René left for Geneva the next day and Giovanni disappeared on leave. We were on our own.

I saw computer modelling as the only way to focus concern on the dam. My friendly US colleague at the UNAMI GIS office was no longer there; his daughter had a life-threatening illness back in the USA and he had been rushed home.

I contacted Geneva and explained what I wanted to do. Within hours I received an email from the European Research Centre in Brussels, who were assembling a team to run computer simulations on any scenarios I gave them. It was an exciting breakthrough so early in the mission.

I had now to look carefully at the reservoir water levels. The UNAMI maps had used very high levels. I thought the key would be to find levels that might be acceptable both from a political and a practical point of view, and then persuade the Iraqi government to adopt a sensible water level. If the level was too high, the danger of the dam collapsing would be unacceptable. If it was too low, irrigation from the Tigris River would be impossible and cause political problems. There was the added problem that low water flow would increase pollution and, down in Basra, salinisation of the city's drinking water. There had to be a level that took hundreds of thousands of people out of danger while still providing enough water for the country.

Wael had organised a useful programme of meetings. One of our first was with the UN Security Officer, deep in the bowels of the UN building in yet another windowless room, where we were given a gloomy scenario of life in Iraq. Three to five bombs went off every day in Baghdad alone, killing as many as eighty people. Busy markets were the favoured locations for suicide bombers. The liberation of the Sunni towns along the Euphrates had not been much of a liberation for the unfortunate people who lived there, whose homes had been reduced to piles of rubble. It was a further opportunity for persecution by the Shi'a militias. Our meeting also revealed the underlying tension within the UN system throughout the country.

Our next meeting was at the brand-new US Embassy as guests of USAID, where we met the US Military Commander. Pristine and organised, with multiple eating halls and accommodation blocks, this vast campus even had its own power station. The Americans took the problem of the dam very seriously, knowing that, should it fail, they would be the only ones able to pick up the pieces. They liked the way we were approaching the problem, and USAID happily agreed to fund any risk mitigation measures we identified. Things at last were going in the right direction.

The following day I went to see DFID at the British Embassy. Since DFID in London had been keen to deploy two British UNDAC members, I assumed the pressure for this had come from the embassy in Baghdad. It was a false assumption, as I might have guessed from the difficulty in getting an appointment. The British Embassy was a shadow of its former self. Although it was Sunday, no one seemed to inhabit the place, quite a change from 2004, when it was busy seven days a week.

The DFID representative led me to an office, which was locked. "Let's go and sit by the pool," he said. This was the pool that was being built at the height of the insurgency in 2004. To me, the locked office and the casual attitude demonstrated that the dam and my visit were low priority here. I asked what he knew about the dam. It was soon obvious – absolutely nothing. Where would the floodwaters go? How many people might be affected? He didn't know. The conversation was pointless.

He took me to see the Defence Attaché who had curiously only one ambition – to return to the UK for a few days to renew his visa. "So difficult to do it here, you know," he said. I found all this incredulous, given the millions the UK was still giving to Iraq. It was just a matter of telling the Iraqi government quite firmly to sort it out.

The UN driver had warned me that as it was Sunday I might expect a delay before being picked up. So I asked my hosts if the embassy driver could drop me back at the UN compound. "Oh no," they said. "We don't think the insurance would allow it." I felt like walking back to the UN compound, but there was a reasonable chance my body might be returned minus my head and I decided against it. On our way back to the gate, I mentioned how lucky the embassy was to have Jordanians running the security and how charming they were. There was a pause. "Oh, are they Jordanians?"

The next day we had our first meeting with the Iraqi government in the former Prime Minister's office. Over twelve years, blast walls had changed the once-familiar landscape and I almost failed to recognise the building. The meeting was awkward, and the Iraqis used the expression 'so-called propaganda' when I referred to the US engineering report. They were unwilling to admit – especially to a foreigner – that there was anything to worry about. Yet I detected a genuine concern, and the idea of modelling a possible breach of the dam was readily accepted. It was another faltering step forward.

Gradually, the Emergency Research Centre in Brussels began to send us useful material. They modelled types of breaches in the dam wall and the various reservoir levels I had indicated. The potential number of people who would be affected was extraordinary. The humanitarian agencies were bemused. Their ability to run their existing programmes was already in question and the problem of the dam was met, on the whole, with silence. A notable exception was UNICEF, who took the view that prevention – reducing the water level in the reservoir – was the only answer.

At the beginning of the second week, we were joined by Dr Ian Norton from the World Health Organization. Gifted, enthusiastic and positive, he greatly restored our morale. By breaking the problem down into its constituent parts, we had shown it was possible to mitigate the risk of this potential calamity. Part of the mitigation was a communications plan to reach the population of Mosul. UNDP planned to drop leaflets over the city, but Iraq was a world of rumour and propaganda and I was sceptical of this 1940s-style idea. I received an email from Emma Winberg, who was working as a consultant to UNDP. She was coming to Baghdad to help with their communication strategy. I had known Emma for some years and knew if anybody could discover a sensible way of communicating to the population of Mosul, she could. She planned to use Facebook and text, but the problem was the absence of any electricity supply to the city. The Iraqi government had been reluctant to release water from the Mosul Dam, as it would supply ISIS with electricity. They had held Mosul since June. However, by doing this it would also allow us to communicate with the people in the city. Dropping the water level in the reservoir would also lower the risk of a breach in the dam, and the number of people in danger would be substantially reduced.

We had been in Baghdad nearly two weeks and would soon fly to Erbil, the capital of Iraqi Kurdistan, for the second half of our mission. The autonomous Kurdish region was effectively another country. We spent our last days in Baghdad revisiting many of the organisations we had seen soon after our arrival. Many were astonished by what we had achieved. Flood maps were available for three different water levels in the reservoir, showing how over 1 million people could be taken out of danger simply by releasing more water. The maps also helped humanitarian organisations plan how they might deliver assistance. Although there was no more talk of evacuation, the mood among the agencies was subdued, and devoid of hope. I had not lost my youthful enthusiasm for this work. However, here it was like stirring glue. Was it because the whole humanitarian 'industry' had become so self-serving, living off the fat of government grants? Or was the situation particularly dismal here in Iraq?

The Coalition had attacked one of the most successful, sophisticated secular states in the Middle East, and this was the result – civil war on three fronts, institutional collapse, destitution for a large portion of the population and infrastructure collapsing after twenty-five years of sanctions. It was enough to depress anyone. Whatever the shortcomings of the humanitarian organisations, it would be difficult to be optimistic here. However, I did feel that attitudes towards humanitarian work had changed over the years. The absence of proper management, something I had identified in Cambodia, had never been properly addressed. The sector had tried hard with training and raising standards with the Sphere Project, which was launched in 1997 to develop standards in core areas of humanitarian assistance, but many of those I met here would not have held down jobs in the commercial sector back in their own countries. I just felt that many of them simply didn't care very much about those they had come to help. Over the years, as funding from government donors had increased, working for an NGO had become a life-style choice rather than a vocation. Now, security made it impossible to get out amongst the people. Given that they stayed huddled behind blast walls in the UN compound, I wondered just how much the humanitarian agencies changed anything. After nearly forty years of this work, I found it dispiriting that it had come to this.

We had a final meeting with the Iraqi government to discuss the Emergency Research Centre's report. We presented our report to a stony-faced Iraqi minister. A long silence followed. "Ah," he said finally. "You have not considered our ability to transfer water from the Tigris into the Euphrates at the town of Samarra." I knew there was a barrage on the river there and a canal, but even wrong-footed as I was, I thought this preposterous. I suggested I could get this scenario modelled and report back to the government. I got in touch with Brussels. "Give us six hours," they said. In six hours, I received a humorous email. The canal, they said, would have to take more water than the Ganges to achieve what the Iraqi government suggested, and in any case, the volume of water would sweep the barrage away. I communicated our latest findings as diplomatically as I could, which finally seemed to break the government's resistance to dropping the water in the reservoir. The next day they announced they would open the turbines and drop the water by four metres.

Venetia was putting her final touches to the visa and customs waivers. She had discovered early on that what at first had looked straightforward was in fact depressingly complicated. After multiple meetings and tough negotiations, she had at last made solid progress. However, we all had our doubts about what would happen in the face of such a calamitous event. Governance hardly existed in Iraq as it was, and if half of Baghdad was flooded there would simply be no government at all.

Rajan left us for another assignment in South East Asia and Wael, Venetia and I set off to Erbil. The contrast between Baghdad and Erbil could not have been greater. Gone was the oppressive atmosphere. The airfield on the edge of the city was surrounded by green fields, relaxing to look at and refreshing after the harsh desert. Everything, even the uniforms worn by the immigration officers, looked brand new, and a gentle breeze seemed to breathe life into the place. We were driven in a soft-skinned vehicle to the UN compound a few kilometres away, a building yet again with the windowless architecture spawned by years of violence. Being Sunday, the place was deserted except for the Head of Mission who briefed us. The picture he gave of the autonomous Kurdish region was positive. Yet when it came to preparations for the mass movement of people out of

Mosul, he was less hopeful. The Kurds, he explained, had made his work very difficult. Sites for IDP camps had been agreed, then withdrawn, and new sites proposed in highly unsuitable places. The reality was that Sunni Arabs were viewed as a terrorist threat, and were not welcome here.

The Kurds had seen an extraordinary economic boom, and this new city had sprung out of the plain in just a few years. The collapse in the price of oil had been just one factor of many that had led to a slump. The idle cranes on the skyline above the city were evidence enough. But, despite this, the place still had a prosperous energy. The Kurds' view of Mosul city and its dam was not exactly indifference, but opportunity. If the dam did breach, they would certainly have the problem of hundreds of thousands of displaced Arab Iraqis heading in their direction, all potential terrorists as far as they were concerned. But the floodwaters would pass safely to the south, while the collapse of ISIS in Mosul might give them an opportunity to extend the Kurdish territory into Syria.

The work of our team here was going to be much easier than in Baghdad. The Kurdish government had a reputation for being easy to work with and already there were systems in place for customs waivers and visas for humanitarian agencies. The more pressing issue was: where would everyone fleeing Mosul go? Where would they be accommodated? And in the worst-case scenario, were the Kurds' medical facilities adequate to manage such an event?

The UN team in Erbil worked independently of the teams in Baghdad and I could see why all the agency staff wanted to be in this pleasant friendly place. We were free to wander about, go to restaurants and live normal lives. The splendidly-named Hotel Classy was in the Christian district of Erbil, and had a bar well-stocked with beer. Our team was now under time pressure. The customs and visa waivers could be straightforward, but there were meetings to be arranged and they always took time. We needed to assess the capacity of agencies to deal with several hundred thousand internally displaced people from Mosul and look at the medical facilities in Dohūk, the nearest Kurdish city to Mosul. Then, once this was done, we had to put together our report. We had just five days.

It was twenty-five years since I was last in Dohūk and I was mentally prepared for the changes. We set off early from Hotel Classy, and were soon out of Erbil. Grassy plains stretched for miles dotted with patches of cultivated land. We passed settlements of blockwork houses, disordered, untidy, busy places. I was surprised that the UN, or even DFID who hardly allowed their officials to leave the consulate, had not forbidden this trip, as it passed close to the front line with ISIS. However, we were travelling with OCHA's Head of Office and it was a journey he knew well. As always, local knowledge is the best security.

The plan was to visit the main hospital in Dohūk and meet the hospital director, to assess the capability of the health system to cope with a mass evacuation from Mosul. Contingency plans were being made by the UN anyway to cope with the impending final assault on Mosul, and our concerns about the dam fitted neatly into these.

As we began the climb into the Kurdish mountains our driver, a child of six at the time of the Kurdish Uprising in 1991, mentioned his family's flight into the mountains. "We suffered," he said. "I was too big for my father to carry me as he was already carrying my sister. I was almost too small to walk without my older brother pulling me along the mountain tracks." Nearly everyone we met told stories of those extraordinary days of March 1991. It was easy to understand how the Kurdish people had been forged into a crypto-nation by these traumatic events.

Finally, the city came into view. In 1991, I had approached the city from the north, and for a moment I was disorientated, less by the geography than by the modern city we now entered. I was mentally prepared for such a change, but still I was surprised. The hospital director's office projected a sense of competence and quiet efficiency. We chatted over coffee, and in flawless English he told us of his adventures in the mountains as a teenager after the 1991 uprising. He confirmed he had the capability to handle the influx of medical cases from conflict or if the dam burst. Yet at the end, he said, "As I'm sure you're aware, some additional funding and perhaps the assistance of specialist staff would help." From the UN's point of view, funding and the short-term support of, say, a surgical team, would be very easy to provide.

Despite these reassurances, we needed to see the hospital, a vast place built by Saddam in the 1980s. I was impressed that it was run on such a meagre budget. The organisational competence was impressive, quite different from elsewhere in Iraq. The director telephoned a small hospital close to the front line that we could visit on our way home to give us a better idea of the level of healthcare away from the city. As we left, I could see the car park of the old hospital where I had sent the nurses during the First Gulf War. The past really is another country.

We stopped at the little hospital on the way home as planned. Again, there was the confidence and ability to run a decent modern hospital with surprisingly little resource. These people were tough and resilient, with every intention of defending their autonomous Kurdistan.

The next day was our last round of meetings. It was the usual kaleidoscope of faces, places and organisations, but one stuck out as very different – the visit to DFID. The British Consulate was located in a large modern tower block hotel. Unlike Hotel Classy, the place swarmed with security. There was a bar area on a upper floor where I was taken by the Defence Attaché. Other tables were occupied, and since we were discussing the Kurdish Peshmerga's ability to manage a large exodus from Mosul, I found the lack of privacy astonishing. I also discovered that the freedom that DFID officials had to travel and meet local people was severely constrained by security concerns. They spent most of their time at the hotel. I could see that British officials might be a target, how special intelligence might dictate caution, but the sentiment was all wrong. This was defensive, cautious, unambitious and in the end worthless. If we wanted to succeed, we needed to take risks, be on our front foot, and be on the offensive. Unless we were prepared to get out amongst the people and engage with them, we should not have bothered to come at all.

One by one my team left, a timetable dictated by flight availability rather than convenience. I was the last to leave. I gazed at the high-rise buildings of this impressive modern city and watched the Kurds conducting security at a checkpoint. They were sharp, organised, modern, all dressed in smart uniforms. I looked towards the new airport and daydreamed for a few seconds. Suddenly, it was 1991 again and I was back in the mountains only a few kilometres from here, where it had all begun. I was handing over the first five Land Rovers, discussing which fledgling ministries the Kurds should establish. I remembered the look the Brigadier's POLAD gave me when I discussed setting up an administration for Kurdistan with the Peshmerga. From a little acorn, a mighty oak had grown.

Epilogue

I am home in Gloucestershire. It is winter now; the wind is in the north, and icy gusts blow across the park bringing the occasional snow flurry with them. At four o' clock the day is already being drained of light. I make my way back towards the house, its austere Regency Greek Revival architecture as severe and uncompromising as the weather, past the Trafalgar oak planted to celebrate Nelson's victory in 1805. On my right is the curiously named cuckoo pen, where a string of bombs was dropped hastily by a German bomber in World War II; now it is nothing more exciting than a wood yard.

I have always felt that being able to come back here, from the sea of human tragedy to a normal life, is a great strength. Many people in the aid organisations and NGOs I worked with over the years were itinerant, ungrounded and rootless, working from mission to mission. Yet for those living in modern Europe, sheltered from risk, exposure to calamitous events is not necessarily a bad thing. There is always the chance that, rather than growing cynical and battle-hardened, we will become less spoilt, more grateful for simple pleasures, more compassionate.

Since my early days in Cambodia and Uganda, a mighty industry has grown up to deal with calamities. The last three decades have been marked by feeble foreign policy in the West, which couldn't decide how to deal with the complications created at the end of the Cold War. The European Union boasted that it could handle the disintegration of Yugoslavia – an idle boast, as it turned out – and years of political vacillation over the Balkans caused the first mass movement of refugees and IDPs in Europe since World War II. We didn't know it then, but more was to come.

With the wars in Iraq and Afghanistan, the concept of neutrality expired. European humanitarian agencies could no longer intervene without the threat of abduction and almost certain execution of their staff. Perhaps a Christian vocation drove many in the 1970s and 1980s to work in humanitarian organisations. But as these organisations proliferated over the last twenty years it became a job like any other, with training and professional standards, yet increasingly cautious. Litigation and duties of care have to be considered, and the appetite for risk has diminished.

Talk of 'humanitarian space' suddenly seems naive. The liberal democratic values and socially progressive ideas that underpin Western humanitarian organisations now clash head-on with social conservatism. Islamic societies often have a negative view of Western humanitarian organisations, seeing them as a threat to their values and way of life, or at worst as agents of a hostile power. In recent years, humanitarians have found themselves working behind the blast walls, rather than engaging with the population – something I could never have imagined back in 1979. Humanitarian intervention in conflict by Westerners has become so difficult the work has been delegated to local staff, while the parent organisations devote their time to advocacy. Compassion, urgency, robustness of spirit – all have been lost.

By contrast, the response to natural disasters has been increasingly impressive. Fewer countries now need international assistance, and those that do get a more appropriate and professional response. The harnessing of technology, satellite imagery, IT systems, training and global organisation have all helped, and countries most at risk are assisted to prepare for the hurricanes, earthquakes or floods they experience so frequently.

As I look back, I regret the loss of opportunity to travel alone when the concept of neutrality still held, to have had the goodwill of all sides to a conflict, and hopefully to have achieved some lasting good. Crossing front lines, brokering peace agreements, negotiating with warlords, even running power stations in conflict zones – these were activities of a different age.

It is almost dark now. I walk up the gravel drive to the house. My marriage has ended, my children have grown up and gone. A single light burns in a ground floor window; the rest of the great brooding mass of the building is dark. And I remember General Richards introducing me to his staff in the Ministry of Defence: "This is Gilbert Greenall; he is our combat civilian."

Index

Acheson, Sir Donald, WHO in Bosnia 66

ActionAid, in Somalia 94, 97–8

Addis Ababa, Ethiopia 94

Afghanistan **139**, 198, 202–3, 207, 257
- airdrop operation 140–2
- assessment (2010) 246–58
- earthquakes (1998) 138–48
- Freedom Bridge 201–2
- fuel for helicopters 145–6, 147
- government structure 242–3, 244–5
- narco-economy 241, 242
- Northern Alliance 138, 139–40, 198, 200
- opium poppy cultivation 253–4, 255–6, 257
- preparation for natural disasters (2006) 241–5
- Provincial Reconstruction Teams 251, 253
- Quick Impact Projects 205, 207–8, 251
- support and influence (2001) 198–216
- Taliban 138, 139, 198, 200, 256
- tensions between agencies 248–50

Ahmeti, Ali 186, 192–3

AICF, in Uganda 16

Al-Najaf, Iraq 230–1

Al-Naqoura, Lebanon 235, 237–8

Albania 149–57
- bureaucracy 155–6
- construction of camps 155
- Emergency Management Group 151, 154–5
- NGO Forums 152
- refugees from Kosovo in 149–57, 158

Albanian National Liberation Army 186, 192–3

Alexander, Crown Prince of Yugoslavia 218

Amin, Idi, Ugandan President 10, 12, 13, 14

Amos, Valerie, OCHA 264

Amra, UNHCR 55–6

Amu Darya (Oxus) river 140, 141

Angola 81–92, **83**
- ceasefire agreement 86, 90
- changing aircraft tyre in 88–9
- civil war 81–2
- immunisation programme 85–6, 87, 90, 91, 92

Antigua 103, 106
- hurricane 105–7

reception centres 105, 107

Aranyaprathet, Thailand 1, 5–6

armed forces
and humanitarian aid 24, 31, 44–6, 47–9, 123
see also British Army; Ministry of Defence; Royal Marines

Arua hospital, Uganda 26–7, 28–9

Ascot, Lawrence 26–7

ASF (Aviation Sans Frontières) 17

Ashe, Robert, Christian Outreach 5–6, 7

Asian Development Bank, Afghanistan 251, 257

Atta Noor, General, Afghanistan 243–4

Australia, and East Timor 168, 177

Back, Steve, *Daily Mail* 85

Baghdad, Iraq 48, 222–4, 229, 267, 269

Bagram Air Base 202, 208, 214

Bakhtaran, Iran 37

Balkans 52–5, **54**
ethnic cleansing 60, 73, 189
humanitarian crisis 56–7
strategic review (2002) 217–19
see also Albania; Bosnia; Kosovo

Bamyan, Afghanistan 205–7, 208

Bangkok 4–5

Banja Luka, Bosnia 76, 116–17, 217

Barre, Siad, President of Somalia 93

Baucau, East Timor 171, 172–5, 177

BBC, and *ITN* 90, 91

Bearpark, Andy, ODA 53–5, 126
and Angola 81–2, 84–5, 92
and Bosnia 69–70, 111–12, 117–18
and Irian Jaya 123
and Montserrat 102–3
and Somalia 93

and WHO 66

Beijing, China 132–3

Beirut, Lebanon 232, 234

Belgrade, Serbia 64, 217, 218

Bellers, Venetia, UNDAC 268, 270, 276–7

Berbera, Somalia 94, 99–100

Besse, Christopher 66

Bethlehem 182–3

Bildt, Carl, High Representative, Bosnia and Herzegovina 118–19

Bird, Lester, Prime Minister of Antigua 107

Black Watch, Fallujah 220

Blair, Tony, Prime Minister 185, 186

Borama Conference, Somalia 93, 94, 96–7

Borei, Bertram, ECMM 62

Bosco, Giovanni, OCHA 269–70, 271–2

Bosnia **54**, 55–67, 74–6
economic progress 118, 120
elections 118–19
humanitarian infrastructure plan 65–7
and Mostar road 68–9, 70–2
post-war reconstruction 111–22
power supplies 57, 60, 66–7, 115, 116
Quick Impact Projects 114, 115–18, 121
Stabilisation Plan 114–15
travel difficulties 59–60, 67, 72–3, 112, 113

Bourbon-Parma, Carolina de, UNDAC 233

Brade, Karen 66

Brandt Report, on international development 4

Brčko corridor, Republika Srpska 62–4

British Army

in Afghanistan 199–200
in Albania 154
in Bosnia 62–3
in Macedonia 186–7
British Caribbean Development Division 109
British Geological Survey, and Montserrat 104–5, 108–9
British Red Cross, and Kurdish refugees 33, 37
Brown, James 174
Bucknall, General James 246, 250, 257
Burao, Somalia 98–9
Butler, Brigadier Ed 243

Cambodia 1–2, 7–8
Cameron, David, Prime Minister 258
Cameron, Lindy, DFID 223
Camp Bastion, Afghanistan 253
Campbell, David 29
CARE International, in Iraq 45
Carleton-Smith, Lt Col Mark 217
Chalker, Lynda, Minister for Overseas Development 55
and Angola 82
visit to Bosnia 69–72
Chamberlain, Ernie, UNDAC 169
Cheltenham General Hospital, author at 53, 81
Cheshire Regiment, in Bosnia 72–3
China 134, 135
floods 132–7
Christian Outreach 5
Churcher, Bob, FCO 169
Cisternino, Fr Mario 25
'civil effect', Afghanistan 250
cluster bombs, Lebanon 238–9

coal mines, Bosnia 67, 79
Coffee, Neil, ODA 44
Concern charity, Karamoja 22
Cook, Colonel Mark 62
Cook, Robin, Foreign Secretary 166, 185
Cordy-Simpson, Brigadier Roddy 75
Cosgrave, Major General Peter 170, 172
Crawford, Charles, Ambassador in Belgrade 218
Croatia 55, 149
Croatian War of Independence (1991) 53
Cyprus 233–4

Darling, Major Patrick 119
Davis, Neil, Australian cameraman 5, 9
Dawlat Kol, Afghanistan 143
Dayton Peace Agreement (1995) 111, 149, 218
deforestation
China 136
illegal logging in Irian Jaya 127, 128
Denmark, and Afghanistan 250, 251
development programmes, management of 84
DFID (Department for International Development) 124, 197, 215–16
and Afghanistan 200–1, 203, 247, 249, 252, 258
and Iraq (2004–2005) 220–1
in Iraq (2016) 273–4, 279
and Macedonia 193, 197
multilateral policy 215
operational methods 204–5
and UN 207
Dili, East Timor 167, 169–72, 177
Djibouti 95–6
Dodge, Cole, UNICEF 13

Dohūk, Iraq 40, 42, 43, 44, 277–9

Dostum, Abdul Rashid, Afghanistan 214, 243

Douglas-Hamilton, Iain 19

Durres, Albania, seaport 155–6

Dushanbe, Tajikistan 139–40, 141, 148

earthquakes
    Afghanistan 138–48
    Montserrat 102–10

East Jerusalem 181

East Timor (1999) 167–77, **168**
    independence 168
    Indonesian soldiers in 172, 173

ECMM (European Community Monitoring Mission), Balkans 53, 60, 61–2

ECTF (European Community Task Force), Bosnia 76, 78–80

Egal, Mohamed, President-Elect of Somalia 97

Ellery, Brigadier James 229–30

Elmquist, Michael, UNDAC 169

Emergency Aid Department 84–5

Emergency Management Group, Albania 151, 154–5

emergency programmes, management of 84–5, 92

Entebbe, Uganda 10–11, 18

Erbil, Iraq 270, 275, 276–7

ethnic cleansing, Balkans 60, 73, 189

EU
    and Balkans 53, 280
    Customs Assistance Mission to Albania 156
    and Macedonia 191, 195
    relations with UN in Bosnia 78–80

    relations with UN in Iraq 48, 49–50
    UK presidency 76

European Emergency Research Centre 272, 274, 275

Evans, Stephen, FCO 47, 51, 203

Expanded Programme of Immunisation (EPI), Angola 85–6, 87, 90, 91, 92

FALINTIL, East Timor guerrillas 168, 176

Fallujah, Iraq 224, 225–6, 228, 231

Fallujah, Second Battle of 220–1

famine
    Irian Jaya 127, 128
    Somalia 99
    Uganda 10–26, 29

Fayzabad, Afghanistan 142–4, 145, 146–7

Fazzina, Carlo, Hebron 183

food aid
    Angola 83–4
    Iraq 221, 229

food security, development programme in Karamoja 21

France
    diplomats in Iraq 48, 49–50
    and Somalia 96

Fraser, Angus, WFP 143–4

French Army, helicopters in Karamoja 24

French Foreign Legion, Lebanon 238

Fry, Rob, RM 42, 46

Garakani, Tatiana, UNDAC 243, 244

Gaza 178, **179**, 181, 184

Gengaje, Rajan, UN 268, 270, 271, 276

Gentiloni, Fabrizio, UN 132

Germont, Thierry, ICRC 76–7

Ghani, Ashraf 251–2, 257

Giovanni, Janine di 207
Glass, Trevor, UNDAC 243, 244
Gornji Vakuf, Bosnia 112–13
Greenall, Gilbert (author)
    MBA 2–3
    medical career 23, 32, 53, 81
Greenall, Johnny, and Gabrielle 27–8
Greenalls, Warrington 2
Griffiths, Martin, Deputy SRSG in
    Kosovo 161
Gulf War (1990-91) 32
    Northern Iraq 40–51
Gurkhas, in East Timor 171–2, 174, 176
Guthrie, General Charles 158, 159

Halabja, Iraq 48, 49
Hanning, Hugh 158, 159
Harbin, Heilongjiang province, China
    133–6
Hargeisa, Somalia 95, 97, 100–1
Hartley, Brian 21
Hayes, Pauline, DFID 249
Hayes, Roland 190–1
Hayr, Air Marshal Sir Kenneth 62
Hazebrouck, Richard van, UNDAC 160
Healing, Tim 66
health clinics, Iran 35–6
Hebron, West Bank 180, 182, 183
helicopters
    in Afghanistan 143–4, 145–7
    Karamoja 24
Helmand, Afghanistan 245, 252, 254
Herat, Afghanistan 208–11
Hezbollah, in Lebanon 232, 237, 238,
    239–40
Hindu Kush 140, 141, 142
Hochschild, Fabrizio, UNDAC 149,
151, 152–3, 155–6
Holden, Rob, UN 235, 236
Houston, Doug, ODA 72, 73, 74
Hoxha, Enver, Albanian dictator 149, 150
Huambo, Angola 85, 90
Human Rights Watch, and Angola 82
humanitarian agencies
    changing character of 240, 271, 275–6
    relations with military 43, 44, 47–8
    and social conservatism 281
humanitarian infrastructure, concept of
    65–7
humanitarian relief
    as career 52
    constraints 280–1
    and emotion and empathy 58
    and foreign policy 214–15, 280
    natural disasters 241–5, 281
    need for political action 79, 101
    and risk aversion 194, 196
    role of military 24, 31, 44–6, 47–9, 123
    see also DFID; Overseas Development
        Agency
hydroelectric dams
    Mostar 71, 79
    near Kabul 211–13

IFOR (Implementation Force), Bosnia
    111–12
Inge, General Sir Peter 121
INSEAD business school, Paris 2–3
INTERFET (International Force East
    Timor) 170
International Development Act (1997)
    124, 125
International Development Act (2002)
    215

International Management Group 194

International Organization for Migration 264–5

International Red Cross 66, 76

    and Afghan earthquakes 140, 144, 146

    in Afghanistan 199

    Somalia 94, 100

Iran 34, 34

    Kurdish refugees (1991) 32–9, 45

Iranian Red Crescent 33, 34–5

Iraq **41**

    aid for Kurds in 36, 38–9, 40–51

    assessment of humanitarian needs 48–50

    British withdrawal 48–51

    displaced people in 221

    food aid 221, 229

    Kurdish refugees from 32–9

    Ministry of Industry and Minerals 224, 225, 227

    and Mosul Dam 267–77

    private military contractors 222, 224, 269

    Safe Haven 43–50, 52

    Second Gulf War 219–20

    'way stations' 43

Iraqi Kurdistan 267, 276–9

Irian Jaya **124**, 128, 129

    forest fires 126–31

    Mission Aviation Fellowship 127–9

Iriri, Uganda 15, 21

ISAF (International Security Assistance Force), Afghanistan 248, 250, 251

ISIS

    control of Mosul 267, 268, 275

    in Tunisia 265

Islamabad, Pakistan, UN in 138, 142, 148, 199

Ismail Khan, Mohammad, Herat 208, 209–10

Israel, war with Lebanon (2006) 232–40

Israeli Defence Force (IDF) 178, 184, 236

    use of cluster bombs 238–9

    view of UN 182, 185

IT support, requirement for 263, 265, 266

ITN, and *BBC* 90, 91

Izetbegović, Alija, Bosnia 80, 111

Jackson, Major General Mike 115, 217, 218

    IFOR 111–12, 114, 119

    in Kosovo 161, 166

Jakarta, Indonesia 127

Jenkins, Brigadier David 62

Jequier, Nicolas, OECD 3

Johansson, Eva, UNDAC 132

Joint Civil Commissions, Kosovo 162–3

Kabul, Afghanistan 200, 202–5, 211, 241, 242–3, 248–52

    British Contingent HQ 248–9

    British Embassy 246, 249–50, 258

    hydroelectric dam 211–13

Kampala, Uganda 12–13, 18–19, 25–6

Kandahar, Afghanistan 247

Kapila, Mukesh, DFID 126, 197, 219

Karadžić, Radovan 111

Karamoja, Uganda 13

    Catholic Mission 14, 15–16

    cattle raiding 13, 15, 20–1, 23, 30–1

    famine 10, 15–17, 20–6, 29

Keeling, Andy, RM 42

Kennedy, Kevin, UN 178

KFOR (British Kosovo Force) 162, 163, 165–6

Khalili, Karim, in Bamyan 205–6, 242

Khao-I-Dang, Thailand, refugee camp 9

khat, use in Djibouti 95, 96

Khmer Rouge, Cambodia 1, 2, 7–8

Khwaja Ghar airstrip, Afghanistan 140–1

Kiley, Sam, journalist 88, 150, 207, 264

King, Lt Col Richard 248, 249, 251, 253, 256

Kirkuk, Iraq 48

Kiseljak, Bosnia 75

Kiszely, Arabella 221

Kiszely, General John 120, 121
  Baghdad 221, 226, 227, 230

Kosovar Albanians, as refugees in Albania 149–57

Kosovo 158–66, 217–18
  Joint Civil Commissions 162–3, 164
  public utilities 161, 163
  Reintegration Boards 163, 164
  returning refugees 161, 163, 164–5
  Safe Havens 158
  Serbs in 162, 164

Kosovo, Battle of (1389) 149, 165

Kosovo Liberation Army 149, 162–3

Kouchner, Bernard, MSF 79–80

Kuito, Angola 82, 87
  EPI initiative 85, 87, 90, 91, 92

Kukes, Albania 153–4

Kumanovo Peace Plan, Kosovo (1999) 160

Kurdish refugees
  in Iran (1991) 32–9
  in Iraq 40–51

Kurdistan 33, 42, 45
  Northern Iraq 267, 276–9

Land, Tony, UNHCR 62–3, 64–5, 68–9

Las Anod, Somalia 97–8

Lashkargah, Afghanistan 253, 254, 255–6

Laurance, Tony, DoH 223, 224, 228

Lebanon 232–40

Lee, Mark, journalist 12, 19–20, 27

Leitner, Kerstin, UNDP 133

Levy, Lord 185

Lewis, David, Irian Jaya 127

Libya 259
  migrants in Tunisia 261–6

The Limits to Growth 4

Litani River, Lebanon 232

Llewellyn, Ed 195

Lloyd-Davies, Major Vanessa 62

London Conference on Bosnia (1992) 76, 78

Lospalos, East Timor 175–6

Luanda, Angola 82–3
  International Airport 86–7

Macedonia, Former Yugoslav Republic of 149, 158, 186–97
  Albanians in 187, 189, 191–2
  Framework Agreement 187–8, 196
  weapons collection 187, 191, 194, 195, 196

Maclean, Sir Fitzroy 63–4

McLoughlin, Dr Mary, SCF 33, 35–7, 38

McNamara, Kevin, UNHCR 165

Maglaj, Bosnia 73

Major, John, Prime Minister 76, 119–20, 123

Malloch-Brown, Mark 8–9

Manjača, Bosnia, Serbian prison camp 77

MapAction, Tunisia 263

Marler, Lee, UN Chief of International

Law 181, 184

Mayhew, Barney, in Bosnia 76, 77–8

Mazar-i-Sharif, Afghanistan 207, 242, 243–4

Médécins Sans Frontières
  Afghanistan 143, 144, 146
  Bosnia 79–80

medical supplies
  Bosnia 65–6
  in Uganda 28, 29

Mendiluce, José María, UNHCR 61, 78–9

military contractors, private 222, 224, 269

Milošević, Slobodan 111, 149, 159

Ministry of Defence
  and ODA 92, 114, 124–5
  relations with DFID 221

Mission Aviation Fellowship, Irian Jaya 127–9

Mistura, Staffan de, UN 252

Mitchell, Andrew, Secretary of State (DFID) 247, 258, 261

Mogadishu, Somalia 93

Montravel, Guillaume de, UNDAC 159–60, 161–2, 163–4, 165

Montserrat **103**, 105
  earthquakes and volcanic eruption (1995) 102–10

Mora Castro, Daniel, UNHCR 151, 157

Morillon, Major General Philippe, UNPROFOR 62, 75

Moroto, Uganda 15, 23, 25

Mostar, Bosnia 70–2
  hospital 70, 71
  hydroelectric dam 71, 79

Mostar road, Bosnia 68–9, 70–2

Mosul Dam, Iraq, risk of breach 267–77

computer modelling 272, 274–5

Mouchet, Jacques, UNHCR 156

Mountain, Ross, UN Humanitarian Coordinator 170, 172, 174

Mulder, Taco, ICRC 141

Muller, Rudolph, UNDAC 142

Munk, Niels, UNDAC 149

Murchison Falls National Park, Uganda 27

Mustard, Guy, ODA 39

Nabarro, David, ODA 38–9, 48–50
  and Bosnia 55–6, 58
  and Iraq 43, 44

Nabilatuk, Uganda 20, 22

Nairobi, Kenya 18

Najibulla, Mohammad 208

NATO
  in Albania 154, 155
  bombing of Serbia 149, 156, 158–9
  in Macedonia 190

Natolla, Grace, Oxfam 18–19

Naumann, Roger, Oxfam 10, 29

Nicholson, Michael, *ITN* **85**, 91

Nijenhuis, René 271–2

Northern Ireland Electricity Board and, power stations in Bosnia 67, 79

Norton, Dr Ian, WHO 274

Obote, Milton, President of Uganda 19

OCHA (UN Office for the Coordination of Humanitarian Affairs) 123, 130
  Afghanistan 139
  Albania 151–2
  Iraq 269–70
  Tunisia 263

ODA (Overseas Development

Administration) 38–9, 92, 124
and aid in Iraq 44, 45–6
and Bosnia 66
civil servants on Montserrat 106–7, 109
and Emergency Aid Department 84–5
and Somalia 95
Olshausen, General 161
Operation Allied Harbour, Albania 154
Operation Essential Harvest, Macedonia 187, 194, 197
Operation Safe Haven, Northern Iraq 43–50, 52
Oshima, Kenzo, OCHA 193, 197
Oxfam 10, 35
in Uganda 16–19, 20–1

Pakistan
Grand Trunk Road 140, 201
see also Islamabad; Peshawar
Pakistani Army, and Afghan earthquakes 146–8
Palestine 178–85, 179
breaches of international law 181, 184–5
medical emergency 178–9
Parker, General Nick 246
Patey, Sir William, Ambassador in Kabul 249
Patten, Chris, EU Commissioner 195
Pearn, Ted, UNDAC 233, 241, 242, 245
Peshawar, Pakistan 140–1, 201
Peshmerga, Kurdish troops 43, 46, 268
Phnom Penh, Cambodia 2
PKK (Kurdistan Workers' Party) 51
Plymouth, Montserrat 104, 105, 109–10

Pol Pot, Khmer Rouge 2
Popovic, Lt Col Bozidar 77
Potter, Dickie, Macedonia 188–9, 190, 194
Pounds, Lt Col Nick, RM 102–3, 104–8
power stations
Bosnia 66–7
East Timor 170, 171
Kosovo 163, 165
power supplies 65
Afghanistan 211–12, 251
Bosnia 57, 60, 66–7, 115, 116
Lebanon 236–7
Macedonia 191, 193, 194, 195
Pristina, Kosovo 160, 161–3, 217

Quick Impact Projects
for Afghanistan 205, 207–8, 251
Bosnia 114, 115–18, 121
funding for 237
for Iraq 230–1

Rabbani, Burhanuddin, Afghan President 139, 147
Dhafer, Ramzi, UNDAC 259–61, 263
refugees
Cambodian 1, 2, 6–7, 8–9
crisis of 280
IDPs in Angola 82
IDPs in Balkans 55, 56–7
Kosovar Albanians 149–57, 161
Kurds 32–9, 40–51
Libyans in Tunisia 261–6
Reith, Lieutenant General John 154
Richards, Brigadier David 171–2, 174, 177, 246
Richardson, Dr Ricky 32
Rifkind, Malcolm 101

risk aversion, UN 194, 196

Ritchie, Andrew, Bosnia 113

Rivero, Juliette de, OCHA 130

Rollo, Brigadier Bill 217

Ross, Annabel 41

Ross, General Robin 41, 158, 159, 163

Rothery, Wing Commander Wendy 248

Route Gull, Bosnia, bridge repairs 117–18, 121

Rowland, Jim, Uganda 16

Royal Engineers, in Bosnia 115

Royal Marines 47
    Commando Logistics Regiment 102–3, 105, 106, 107, 108
    in Northern Iraq 38, 41–2, 43, 48, 50

Rustaq, Afghanistan 140, 141

Saddam Hussein, and Kurds 32, 33, 49

Safe Havens
    Iraq 43–50
    Kosovo 158

Said Sadiq, Iraq 48, 49

Sarajevo, Bosnia 55–7, 64–5, 75–6, 119, 217

Sattler, Lt Gen John, US Marines 226

Savage, Frank, Governor of Montserrat 103–4

Savimbi, Jonas, UNITA 82

SCF (Save the Children Fund)
    in Somalia 94, 97
    in Uganda 16–17

Schumacher, E.F., *Small is Beautiful* 4

Second Gulf War (2003) 219–20, 222

Sedwill, Mark, NATO 251

Serbia, NATO bombing 149, 156, 158–9

Serbs 53, 149
    prison camps in Bosnia 76–8

Sersink, Northern Iraq 41, 43

Sharon, Ariel 178

Shepherd-Barron, James 79

Short, Clare, Secretary of State (DFID) 123, 215

Simpson, John, BBC 85, 91

Šipovo, Bosnia 114

Skavdal, Terje, UNDAC 132, 133, 134, 136

Skopje, Macedonia 159, 160, 187

Smith, Admiral Leighton 116

social development, as DFID priority 215

Somali Red Crescent 98, 99–100

Somalia 93–101, **94**
    Borama Conference 93, 94, 96–7
    drought and famine 99
    lawlessness 93, 98–9, 100, 101

Somaliland, recognition of 93, 99–100, 101

Sparrow, Bryan, British Ambassador in Croatia 55, 58, 69

Sphere Project 275

Split, Croatia 58, 63

Srebrenica, Bosnia 158

Stewart, Lt Col Bob, in Bosnia 64, 72–4

Stirrup, Air Chief Marshal Jock 199, 200

Stoddard, Major 171, 174

Strippoli, Francesco, WFP 13

Suharto, President of Indonesia 168

Sulaymaniyah, Iraq 48, 50

Swain, John, *Sunday Times* 172–3

Swartling, Peter, UNDAC 142, 144

Takhar Province, Afghanistan 140, 142

Talabani, Jalal, Kurdish politician 50

Tepeth tribe, Karamoja 25

Termez, Uzbekistan 201

Thailand **3**
  Cambodian refugees 1, 6–9
Thomann, Major General 161
Tirana, Albania 149–53
Tito, Marshal Josip 52–3
Travnik, Bosnia 60–1
Trent, Australian volunteer 17, 24
Trnopolje, Bosnia, Serbian prison camp
  77–8
Tuđman, Franjo 111
Tunisia 259–61, **260**
  Libyan migrant camp in 261–6
Turkey 50–1
  and Kurds 45, 46
Tuzla, Bosnia 74–5

Uganda **11**, 12
  famine 10–26
  flying in 17–18, 19–20, 29–30
  security 12, 14, 17, 20–1, 22–3, 28–9
UN 9
  and Afghanistan 138–48, 198
  in Bakhtaran, Iran 37
  in Bosnia 56, 61, 62–4, 68, 78–80
  and coordination problems 151–2, 156
  'Corridors of Peace' (healthcare
    for) 85, 87
  and Iraq 48–9, 277–8
  in Kosovo 165
  and Macedonia 189, 193–4
  Mission in East Timor 168
  relations with EU 78–80
  security protocols 187, 189
  see also OCHA; UNDAC
UN Joint Logistics Centre, Albania 154
UN Military and Civil Defence Unit,
  East Timor 168

UN Security Council, Resolution on
  Bosnia (1992) 75
UNAMI (Iraq) 271, 272
UNDAC (UN Disaster Assessment and
  Coordination) 123, 125–6, 130–1
  and Afghanistan 138–40, 142, 148
  and Albania 149–57
  and China 137
  Iraq 268, 271
  and Kosovo 159
  see also OCHA
UNDP
  China 133
  Iraq 274
  Uganda 13–14, 22
UNHCR
  Albania 150
  Bosnia 56–7, 62
  Kosovo 160–1
  Tunisia 261, 262–3, 265
  Uganda 16, 20, 22–3
UNICEF
  Angola 83–4, 85–6, 88–9, 91
  Iraq 274
  Uganda 13
UNIFIL (Lebanon) 233, 235, 236–7, 240
UNITA party, Angola 82
United Kingdom 102
  and ethical foreign policy 166, 185,
    186
  see also DFID; Ministry of Defence;
    ODA
United States
  and Afghanistan 198, 199, 245, 257
  and Somalia 93
UNMIK (Kosovo) 159, 160–1, 164
UNPROFOR (Croatia) 62–3, 64–5, 111

UNRWA, Palestine 180, 181
UNSCO (UN Special Coordinator for the Middle East Peace Process) 180, 184
Urmia, Iran 33, 34
US CENTCOM, Afghanistan 198, 199
US forces, Iraq 46, 220, 223, 226, 227–8
US Special Forces, Afghanistan 209–10
USAID
    Afghanistan 250, 251
    Iraq 273

Vance-Owen Plan (1992) 61, 149
Verona Fathers, Missions, Uganda 12–13, 15–16, 26–7, 28
Vesna, interpreter in Bosnia 58, 59–61, 74, 80
    and Mostar road 68–9, 70, 72
Vieira de Mello, Sérgio, SRSG in Kosovo 159
Viggers, Brigadier Freddie 120
Vitez, Bosnia 59, 60

Walker, Air Commodore David 199
Walker, General Mike, Bosnia 116, 120
Wall, Brigadier Peter 198, 200
Wamena, Irian Jaya 127–8, 130
Warrington, Major Tim 176
water pumps 115
water supplies
    Afghanistan 251
    Albania 153
    Bosnia 66, 115
    Macedonia 191, 193, 194, 195
    West Bank 180
Wecksten, Simo, UNDAC 142, 145, 146
West Bank 178, **179**, 180, 183

WFP, Uganda 13, 22
White-Spunner, Brigadier Barney 186, 188, 194, 214
Whitechurch, John 21
Williams, Lt Col Trefor 153
Winberg, Emma, UNDP 274–5
Witschi-Cestari, Alfredo, UN Coordinator 148
World Bank, Afghanistan 250
World Health Organization (WHO) 65–6, 180, 263
World Trade Center, 9/11 attacks (2001) 196, 198

Xave, Australian volunteer 17, 24–5

Yacoub, Wael, UNDAC 268, 270, 272–3
Yugoslav People's Army (JNA) 53

Zagreb, Croatia 57–8, 61, 62
Zakhu, Iraq 33, 40, 45
al-Zarqawi, Abu 220
Zenica, Bosnia 60